D0866236

Getting Even
With
Getting Old

Getting Even With Getting Old

Julia Braun Kessler

Nelson-Hall nh Chicago

Library of Congress Cataloging in Publication Data

Kessler, Julia Braun.
    Getting even with getting old.

    Bibliography: p.
    Includes index.
    1.   Aged—United States—Social conditions.
2.   Aged—United States—Political activity.   3.   Old
age.   I.   Title.
HQ1064.U5K474   305.2′6   80–11045
ISBN 0–88229–663–9 (cloth)
ISBN 0–88229–754–6 (paper)

Copyright © 1980 by Julia Braun Kessler

Manufactured in the United States of America

10   9   8   7   6   5   4   3   2   1

This book is for us all—
all of us lucky enough to be
getting older right now—
in these coming decades of
liberation and justice for
the aging in America.

Contents

Part 1

Where We Stand Today: How Did It Happen?

1.
Getting Even

Each day in a hundred ways we Americans fight a relentless war against our own old age—denying, refusing, and rejecting it, desperately trying to cream and bleach it away. It is time to stop. It is time to give up the folly of such vain battle and instead to join in a fight *for* old age and our right to enjoy it. We must assert our right to exercise power in our own behalf, to stand up and lay claim to what is rightfully ours: *full* citizenship for the *whole* of life, not just a part of it.

I am talking about the crying need for the liberation of the aging and aged of this country. Liberation, both political and personal, from a national disease as potent as racism or sexism, and certainly as prevalent. It is called *agism*. Its symptoms are everywhere. They are characterized by a pervasive, inbred conviction that to grow old is to be ugly, obsolete, and to be thrust out of the mainstream of American life. Arthur Miller's supremely American salesman, Willy Loman, sums up the attitude best when he observes bitterly that "life is a sloughing off." This is taken as gospel by millions of our countrymen, old and young. Is it any wonder that age is dreaded and associated with loneliness, incompetence, useless decrepitude, and abject poverty as well?

Today voices come from every quarter; minority groups are clamoring and fighting for their rights, demanding their share.

Until they raised their voices and formed militant groups, no one listened. What about those growing old in America today? They are an oppressed minority larger than the Black population; a minority that is silent, ignored, and virtually invisible. The most universal of all human groups is being rejected by its own people. The old are becoming foreigners in their own country. Where is the affirmative action for them?

Nowhere. Not yet, anyway. This book proposes to rouse Americans to that fact—to bring the matter out of the shadows and into the spotlight where the deeper issues behind the neglect and abuse of older people can be seen. Never again will genteel taboos govern the subject, dismissing it as "depressing" or ending a cocktail party conversation at the first mention of it. This work aims to provoke: to make people conscious, to awaken them to the situation. After they see and understand there will be no turning away. Nor will anyone wish to.

Despite all the recent attention from media people, and from psychoanalysts, social workers, and gerontologists, and despite the shelves of standardized, homogenized manuals (the handbooks featuring "uplift," and peptalks for the "golden years") —there simply has not been a solid formulation and clarification of the real issues. There has been no exposition of the revolutionary theme: Americans over fifty must, in order to liberate themselves, emerge as aggressive, tough, demanding, uncompromising human beings. Instead of waiting and assuming that benefits will naturally accrue to them from half a lifetime of service and work, they must take a firm stand of outspoken activism. To be heard, they must become militant in their own cause. I call this Affirmative Action for Aging Americans. No one else can do the job for them—nor would anyone dream of it, not in today's America.

The statistics suggest just how urgently such a movement is needed. Today 1 in 9 Americans is over sixty-five. The ratio in 1900 was 1 in 25, when life expectancy was a mere forty-seven years. Compare that to our present life expectancy of over seventy years. Right now there are 24 million of these over-sixty-five, and census figures predict that in fifty years the 1 in 9 proportion could go down to 1 in 7. There are even experts who project that by the year 2000, up to a third of Americans may be over fifty years old, and most of the group will be living in retirement. What this means is that from twenty to twenty-five years of life are left to be lived *after* "retirement"—a time span longer than the periods of childhood, adolescence, and early maturity! Consider this: the greater percentage of those over forty-five today are likely to survive into the twenty-first century.

Today 46 million people over fifty-five are actually being forced to retire from their pursuit of happiness, not merely their jobs; to retire from social responsibilities; to retire from the power to govern their own lives and determine their own fates. Obviously they cannot tolerate this situation much longer. Nor should they: change is in the air, change is coming.

There are today and have been in the past powerful political movements and pressure groups working for the old. The American Association of Retired Persons claims a membership list of 13 million, growing at the rate of sixty thousand subscribers per month. The National Council of Senior Citizens has over 3.5 million members. Both groups employ lobbyists and lawyers in Washington and at state capitals. There is also the comparatively new Gray Panther organization that is gaining national attention through its militancy. Politically minded older people are organizing themselves, banding together to beat down the indifference surrounding their cause. There have been solid accomplishments in Social Security, pension benefits, and low-cost housing. The trouble is that many, many older people are unaware, uninterested, and apathetic. It is simplistic to urge these people to enter politics and revolutionary activity. This will certainly be demonstrated in the review of the old age politics of the past and the nature of today's organizations.

Likening the aged to a minority subculture is no idle comparison. Theirs is a self-image possessing all the negative characteristics generally associated with such groups: self-hatred, timidity, fear. And like the typical beaten-down minority, older Americans accept and are dominated by the image which the majority culture imposes on them. They can only see themselves as they are seen, and so acquire through such distortions, simplifications, and exaggerations the damaged ego and the unsure handicapped look that we recognize as that of the average older American today. No amount of urging will bring these people out to man any sort of barricade.

This book's argument goes deeper than politics. It describes a personal revolution as well, one that demands change in thought and behavior. It will take such a transformation before Americans will make room for their old. But what has not yet been spelled out is that upcoming generations, the forty-, fifty-, and sixty-year-olds, are the very people who have lived through the minority rebellions, antiwar demonstrations, and turbulent upheavals of the 1960s. These people are wholly different from their earlier counterparts—a growing number of them see themselves as under siege, and feel that the very foundations of their lives are being destroyed. They are unwilling to be silently shunted off into oblivion. They are ready to listen and learn. They are ready to act, not only in their own, but in everybody's, behalf.

Here, for these generations, are the practical means for vital changes, for radically changing the image of the aging and providing fresh ground upon which to build reforms. Challenged is the accepted mythology of our culture—*the way it is and the way it must be*—the estrangement, disruption, and isolation. Examined are the policies and politics in the past and the present, with specific lessons for use in the future. Here too are the newest concepts for retaining soundness of body and mind, for maintaining sexual pleasure, for financial stability, and for legal rights—in short, for seizing control of our lives with every possible means. No final blueprint is offered. Instead, this book hopes to provide a clear understanding of the diverse needs of 46 million people for solutions to the one great challenge: aging. For some, this involves the right to continued professional pursuits after retirement age; for others, meaningful social action; for still others, a turning to the life of contemplation in a newfound freedom of mind and spirit. Above all, for all the old: choices, options, and opportunities!

Age was once synonymous with wisdom. Yet somehow, somewhere, we have lost that connection. Our generation must seek it, to recover and reinstate its value in our lives. If older people are ever again to be listened to and heard, they must make themselves vital and whole. Only the whole human being can speak wisely and well.

Old age is worthy of honor only
when it defends itself, when it
asserts its rights, is subservient
to no one, and to the last breath,
rules over its own domain.

Cicero, *De Senectute,* Book XI

2.
The Invisible American

There are places on earth today where people cherish a wrinkled face and even search eagerly for their first gray hairs. We may find that altogether astonishing. Yet for many, old age is life's true beginning, a time when the spirit emerges and the heart expands. Old people are glorified, even deified, as magicians, priests, seers, wise men, and wise women—not just in the past but today.

Why then, for what conceivable reason, should Americans so willingly accept the debilitating myths about aging? These fictions are disheartening. They engulf us as we move towards our maturity, making us depressed onlookers instead of participants in our own lives. Worse still, they have reduced us and virtually devastated us. Today, it is our old people, some 24 million or more, who are this country's most invisible Americans.

The aging sit penalized on the sidelines while the rest of us are mesmerized and intimidated by young people. Within recent memory we've watched vast numbers of them: students, flower children, communards, revolutionaries on the march, rebels on campuses, or in the streets, manning barricades, and demanding their "right" to be heard on everything from the traumatic Vietnam War and the coming of world famine, to saving the whales from extinction. In every major city of our nation, younger children are disappearing from our way of life, dropping from sight into a kind of secret society of their own, an underground life in which they are

completely detached from other generations, and mostly unattended and unloved by parents, grandparents, or other adults.
And we seem mere spectators, powerless to intervene.

It's time we start taking a good look around us, that we consider
what's best in the relationship of old and young, what's natural,
and what's possible outside our own experience. We desperately
need to break out of our up-with-youth-and-down-with-age attitudes before we can think intelligently about our future. We must
study other customs, share experiences, learn and adapt everything
we can from other people in order to improve the lot of our older
citizens. There are plenty of good models to choose from, beginning
with rural Ireland, a country that's sometimes referred to as an
"idyllic gerontocracy." There, the real business of living has always
been and still is firmly in the hands of older people. There the aged
are respected, while the antics of the young are benignly tolerated
by their indulgent elders. In fact, a man's a mere boy until he mar-
ries, and since this rarely happens until he's over forty, the picture
is one of the middle-aged "boys," brawling and boozing in the pub
with all the abandon of youth.

To Americans such a way of life is hardly comprehensible. We
can't imagine such dependent youth in such a repressive situation.
We shrug off the Irish scene as merely an amusing relic. Perhaps
we'd like to think they haven't caught up with us. Our skeptical
countrymen have never allowed people of other cultures to unsettle
or disturb their sense of security. We are generally quite confident
that ours is the "natural" course of development—that *we* are the
pioneers in enlightened behavior. And the assumption behind this
is that our technological society represents the future—everyone's
future.

All we need to do is glance at other places in our world to see
that this is simplistic nonsense. Other societies may be moderniz-
ing, but their changes are not necessarily going to make them more
like us. Instead, they're each developing from their own earlier
ways of living, and will most likely remain as alien to our customs
as ever. There is no one course of development that is inevitable
for all people. People can make a great many adjustments to
changes in their lives, and the adjustments will seem quite normal
to those who make them.

Anthropologists have taught us that even our simplest daily actions, the rounds we follow as part of life in our society, the standards we automatically suppose are common to all mankind, are merely ways in which we react to the demands of our own culture. Just that and nothing more. We can't conceive that such thoughts, manners, and ethical standards are not valid everywhere. Yet as soon as we think about any one of the characteristics considered common to all human beings, for example, modesty or good manners, we immediately encounter problems. Any traveler will tell you that there are many interpretations of modesty and good manners in different cultures.

Margaret Mead took us a step farther by explaining just how strong the effects of such cultural assumptions can be. They can determine how people feel, whether frustrated, pleased, or fulfilled. Even more than our biological drives, they can be responsible for how happy people can be in a particular place and time. This is because unquestioned beliefs encourage us to develop some of our natural drives while they suppress others. A great deal of *how* we live depends on *where* and *when* we live.

The noted anthropologist gave us a poignant example when she compared the sexual experiences of the women of Victorian England with those of our American contemporaries. A Victorian lady was not expected to enjoy sexual intercourse, and would hardly confess to it if she did. For her, a "proper" abhorrence of sex was considered perfectly normal. Consider her contemporary descendants in modern America: If our young females find such experiences unsatisfactory, they are likely to be alarmed. Their hearty sexuality is assumed, and if an individual finds herself sexually unresponsive, she is tormented by fears of frigidity or abnormality.[1]

Indeed, what's natural may prove to be mere mythology, a result of a particular adaptation to the problems of one place and time. If this is true of so many other aspects of life, it certainly must be true of our relationships to older people.

It's sheer folly to dismiss other cultures' solutions on the assumption that all mankind is steadily merging into one amorphous, mechanized mass. Never mind whether their ways seem backward or outmoded to us. We must suspend judgment and put aside our prejudices. What counts is that older people have found, and are still finding, ingenious ways of maintaining comfortable existences. They have continued to thrive in many lands around the globe and they have endured, however arbitrary the means. Since it is our aim to plan a strategy for survival, we can reject nothing in our search.

What we need is the larger view, a look at the whole, wide picture, both past and present. We can not afford to ignore history. And surely, whether we approve or not, the more we discover about the exotic, distant lives of our contemporaries, the better equipped we'll be to cope with the disaster facing us here and now. Then, fortified with such new awareness, how much more serious our approach will be to comprehending our own situation and to understanding how trends from our past are reshuffling and combining to create an undesirable future for our old. Above all we must ponder what we can do to avert such a fate.

It would seem that our biggest problems today stem from our country's obsession with progress. Daily we witness a continuing thrust towards greater social efficiency—in the name of modernization—whatever the cost in human terms. The swift changes in postwar America, and indeed in much of Western Europe, (i.e. the denial of our once-sacred beliefs of duty to parent, child, kin, clan, country) demonstrate not only the breakdown of our former way of life, but also the extension of that indiscriminate push toward the elimination of the less useful elements in society.

Given this tendency, it is the borderline person who must look to his own lot, not just the sick, the handicapped, and the elderly, but people in later middle age, too. The position of the aging is hardly secure today. Whatever the causes may be, we must begin our discussion by recognizing that our own present condition is neither inevitable nor irreversible. There are scores of precedents from the past to prove it and plenty of places in the world today where old peoples' circumstances are still a good deal better than our own. We can draw on these examples selectively and critically for the betterment of our own situation.

If the land of the Irish country folk has been a kind of paradise for the old, this is surely no accident. The aging experience there fits in with their whole style of life. And despite the many changes visible over recent years, and some noticeably louder grumbling on the part of the young, older people hold their place of honor and privilege. Though not always greatly loved or admired, they are esteemed within their families. They are even treated with deference by neighbors and strangers. The old man of the family continues during his lifetime to have almost absolute power over the welfare of his sons. This is tied to the possession and maintenance of the farm from generation to generation. His authority still goes unquestioned, and his sons are frequently not paid wages for their labor on the farm. That is at the discretion of the elder man, who, to this very day, may or may not present his sons with "spending money."

Things are really not so different as this is written from what the anthropologist Conrad Arensberg saw back in 1937.[2] The Irish system seems like a rivalry to the death between father and son, with the father in complete control. But it simply does not work that way in practice. Both young and old are the products of an intimate familial round, an arrangement based on their age and position in society. So a person grows up and develops his feelings and personality in terms of the place he occupies. He thinks with his age group, moving on to the next stage only when the others do. Early on, the young are instilled with the Christian injunction to honor their mother and their father. Within their Catholic world, they are taught by the clergy, who exercise control over much of their early thought and behavior. Religion thus becomes a powerful means of reinforcing reverence for the old. The Catholic church itself tends to be structured as a gerontocracy, where a priest labors long years as a curate before he oversees his own parish at age sixty or later.

Young men are encouraged to enjoy a bachelor life, to postpone dating and marriage, sometimes for as long as their mothers are alive. Yet they don't necessarily see this as deprivation. Marriage for them implies limitation and responsibility. It is to be avoided for as long as possible. Meanwhile, they have the company they need in the other bachelors and a refuge from loneliness in the local pub—all ways of prolonging their adolescence with sport, drinking, whoring and gambling. The adult male of country Ireland remains in a dependent position for almost half his life, and is keenly aware that in the eyes of his family he will always be a child. He seldom interests himself in community affairs, and even when the older men meet informally to discuss public issues, he listens in silence while they talk. It takes a bold young fellow to venture an opinion.

Irish late marriages may be merely a function of economics. Yet often marriages are postponed even when money is no issue. It is generally the mother who stands opposed to early marriage, and in some cases to marriage altogether. Mother and son are so close that sometimes their relationship is warmer than the one she has with her husband. She discourages her son from marrying. She wants no daughter-in-law brought into her household to sow discontent, and, quite unabashedly, she needs her son to take care of her in her old age.

In a sense this system serves the old by prolonging a careless life for the young. Judging from statistics, there's plenty of vitality still left in it.[3] It remains a fact that Irish people marry later than most others in the world and that a large percentage never marry at all. There are about four times as many single persons between the ages of thirty-five and forty in Ireland than in America. This means that in old age there are large numbers of bachelors and spinsters who live alone or with other relatives, many of whom are also unmarried. For those sixty-five to seventy-four years old, Irish figures (in 1961) showed that 27 percent had remained single, whereas in America that same age group had only 7 percent unmarried.

What the Irish show us is just one way. Adulation of the old can take many and various forms. Halfway across the world in Africa live black people whose high regard for their aged has traditionally placed older persons at the apex of tribal existence. More than a thousand different tribes of Bantu-speaking peoples live south of the Sahara, and despite variations in the ways in which they maintain themselves, whether through farming, grazing, fishing, or hunting, their traditions have elevated their old people to positions of central importance in their societies. They consider their elders to be their continuation, the medium through which the younger generation can ascend to the realm of the spirits. Thus, their old have been the natural spokesmen for the living to the dead. And this has proved a trump card for security in age.

In this way even the very eldest, who can no longer function well physically, have the precious assurances of regard. Soon to be with the divine ancestors, they are thought to act as representatives using their powers for the good of their descendants. And since they may also return to their children in the form of spirits, their power over life, health, victory, peace, and prosperity goes unquestioned.

Gray beards and white heads are equated with wisdom among the many Bantu-speaking societies. To be old is to be wise. Even the terms used for "grandfather" or "grandmother" imply superior knowledge. Among the Bantu, the holding and distribution of land rights has always been in the hands of the elderly. This is because land is seen traditionally as "ancestor territory." The job of the old, in fact, is to tell the spirits who will possess the land and control its use. A son might conceivably assume responsibility for the cultivation of the family plot if a parent becomes too enfeebled to continue, but it would merely be the obligation to work it, never to own it—not while the older man lives, for this would violate the very foundations of Bantu culture. It would offend the ancestors!

Even food supply has been controlled by the aging. The father, whether he be tribal chief or actually the paternal head of an extended family, has always distributed the food himself or delegated such distribution through his wife. Everyone is obliged to observe the seniority rules of age, rank, and sex.

The power of the system is such that in times of famine, various groups assembled themselves at the family shrine to share what little food they had with their ancestors. It was proffered in the hope that the forebears would be influential in ending the drought or making the fields produce. Above all, the belief persisted that, as fathers, the old were ever providers and feeders of their people.

There have been no limits to the involvement of the old in daily affairs. Their influence is solicited in the choice of mates; rarely do young people decide for themselves about a marriage. In the polygamous societies where very old men often take young wives, nobody considers this unusual. In fact, there's never even a suggestion that an interest in sex wanes with the coming of age. One anthropologist describes a ninety-year-old chief presenting his young wife and infant daughter to the tribes and no one even questioning his paternity.[4] On the contrary, continuing sexual interest is simply assumed. During festivals the eldest are among the most conspicuous dancers, always the first out, old women stepping into the center of the circle to graphically illustrate the movements of sex. The young stay quietly in the background, venturing forward only after the old women have danced.

So the Bantu are people whose entire lives are built on familial ties and kinship. The future and the past are linked, and every thought and deed is involved with the family and its ancestors. Old people are merely advancing towards their rightful place in the divine order: the older they get, the nearer they stand to that place. Age is a source of great security for them.

And though these African cultures, once so rooted in centuries of domination by elders, are now in jeopardy, their system continues to work even today. Of course, Africans have been besieged by foreigners since the nineteenth century, by people who urged alien ways upon them and even coerced them. With the advent of colonialism, their young, who once learned from their own aged kin, were taught by new teachers (a good many of them young themselves), and exposed to other standards and psychologies. Despite such onslaughts and the adjustments needed to meet them, seniority, with all its rules for maintaining authority, respect, and privilege for the old, remains the name of the game in this part of the world.[5]

From culture to culture we see variations of systems such as these. The marvelous fact is that, with the exception of a very few of the crudest of primitives, the old all over the world and throughout history have managed to maintain themselves at the very core of their societies. This is especially interesting because biologists make it perfectly plain that *physiologically* speaking there is no demonstrable instinct to protect and preserve them. The classic stereotype that shows the young mother leaping into the flames to save her baby doesn't apply with the infirm or disabled parent or grandparent. Even in the animal kingdom, male primates will instinctively jump to protect their females and their young, but they abandon the old apes to attackers without a struggle.

Of humankind, one could argue for the "higher virtues," the humane and the civilized as opposed to the barbaric and animal. But that would probably be too simple and idealistic. Old people have secured their positions, kept control, and solved problems over the centuries by far more practical methods.[6] Primarily, they've sought to preserve their lives for as long as possible. To do this they have searched out reprieves from hard physical labor, and in many places graduated into sedentary positions while holding onto the advisory and supervisory ones. Above all, they've stayed involved; societies have felt their influence and participation.

Food, vital for survival, is a great concern to those who can no longer get it themselves. Given the usual early loss of teeth, life becomes more uncertain yet. It is fascinating to learn that some form of food sharing has existed for as long as we know. Notably, it has almost always included the aged, though other disadvantaged groups did not fare as well. Papuan hunters of New Guinea, for instance, were required to distribute their game and could be punished for keeping secret a large catch. And to Samoan Islanders, it was inconceivable that the sick or aged person go hungry.

In most places hospitality was elaborate too. The old were fed, bedded, and kept as guests for long periods. They were even expected to receive frequent gifts from their hosts. The Aztecs and Incas provided for them through well-regulated systems of old age assistance. Among native American Indians, the sharing of food was common, involving great sociability. Old people among the Crow would move back and forth between lodges while food was distributed freely to them. When a man killed many buffalo, he would publicly announce that he had no intention of taking his arrows from the carcasses, which was a sign to the old that they were to have their share of the catch. Iron Bull, a great Sioux chieftain, was a renowned hunter who surrounded himself with the poorest of the old people of his tribe so that he could provide them with food. At the time of the Sun Dance ceremonies, the elderly would sit by the lodges, feasting and singing to their hearts' delight.

The pattern was much the same in many other parts of the world. Among primitive people, the old—man and woman alike—could count on provisions and support from a communal store.

In fact, when the physical environment was particularly barren, as in the Sahara or the frozen Arctic, such conditions enhanced their chances. People constantly threatened by hunger and privation found it absolutely necessary to devise regular methods of sharing in order to survive at all. Otherwise only the strongest could have been able to maintain themselves. Therefore, because the social group had to survive, the aged often prospered even in the coldest, most parched regions.

It has not only been the simple society that has shared food with its aged. Simone de Beauvoir reminds us that among the cultivated ancient Greeks, the word *gera* or *geron* meant "great age"; but it also means "the *privileges* and *rights of seniority*."[7] As for the ancient Hebrews, they saw no need to prescribe for their old at all. Deutronomy refers specifically to the stranger, the fatherless, and the widow, but significantly omits mention of the aged. Precisely because for the ancient Hebrews the patriarch was the giver and the dispenser of such favors!

Probably the most fascinating among ancient customs were the food taboos. These prohibitions were a godsend to old people, because they guaranteed them certain kinds of food. There are long lists of delicacies which tribal members were not permitted to eat, foods forbidden to warriors, to childbearing women, or children. For young Omaha Indian hunters, for instance, the tenderest parts of the buffalo were not considered healthy, and even a taste of marrowfat could unjoint their bones and soften their hearts. Among the Bushmen of South Africa, young girls were denied antelope meat for fear that if they ate it they would never conceive. For the Aruntas in Australia, wild turkey eggs could cause premature age and emu fat was thought to develop the penis abnormally; to Siberian Eskimos, reindeer milk flattened the breasts, and to South African Xosa, kidney meat caused sterility. In all these cases, foods that were forbidden to others were claimed by the old and eaten with gusto. Nobody can say whether or not such taboos were invented by old people, but they certainly worked to the elders' advantage.

When it came to controlling wealth or property, most aged contrived to hang on to their fortunes, in land, animals, money, and treasures. The Hebrew patriarchs, Abraham, Isaac, and Jacob,

were rich old men to the end; the Lord had blessed them with
"flocks, herds, silver, gold, men servants and maid servants and
camels and asses."

But land and food are merely the obvious possibilities. There
are far subtler ways elders have used to keep themselves at the
heartbeat of their cultures. As natural leaders, they long mono-
polized governing and decision-making roles. Old people more
often relied on their wits and wisdom than on property or physical
power. Age itself has very often been the key qualification for
high position. For example, among the Australian Dieri tribe great
councils of elders ruled. Old men made the important decisions
for their people. For Albanians, the idea of law has been so closely
associated with old age that their very word for "arbitration" also
means "seniority." To become a chief, a member of the official
council, or the head of a club or secret society, one must by def-
inition be the possessor of wide experience and special knowledge.
The old qualify; thus they have dominated political, judicial, and
civil positions in many places.

Age itself sometimes went unquestioned as giving the right to
authority. To command without it was impossible, or an embarrassment. Margaret Mead tells us of a twenty-seven-year-old
Samoan chieftain who complained bitterly of the discomforts of his
unnatural situation. The poor young men was forced to act old, to
"walk gravely and with measured step." He could not dance or play
games with the younger people, and had to keep company with the
aged, guarding his every word and gesture. No one dared address
him by his first name or take issue with anything he said. His hair
turned white after only four years as chief, a rare thing among
Samoans who, unlike Caucasians, seldom go gray until late in
life.[8]

Throughout history, the old kept the peace, punished criminals,
and settled civil disputes. Their job was to serve tradition and
ancient custom, and for some, like the Polar Eskimos, custom held
the world together and kept the offending powers at bay. The aged
were the upholders of the status quo. Their decisions were heeded
because their punishments were heavy.

Elder leadership often controlled the severest initiatory rites of
secret societies. As the guardians of secret rites, without which no

youth could enter adulthood or take up his position in life, the elders' strength was absolute. No young person could afford to resist or even question the ordeals imposed. The young were obliged to accept every kind of humiliation and hardship to gain manhood, and all under direction of the elders.

There are many legends and stories about old peoples' powers. Some societies made heroes of them: it was believed they controlled the weather, talked to wild animals, charmed food from the hands of enemies, even made themselves young again at will. They have been the interpreters of puzzling phenomena and have been called medicine men, seers, magicians, priests, wise men. Memory, for a preliterate people, was a great treasure. How little it mattered whether the body which sheltered such a lucid mind was frail. It was the skill or gift of recall that was indispensable. Those endowed with that ability were cherished as the custodians of priceless knowledge.

Sometimes, as among the Eskimos, old peoples' narratives were seen to be the wisdom of their fathers speaking through them. Such narrators preserved the earliest versions of the Creation and other lore of their ancestors. Often their dreams explained the magic formulas for living well. To tell such secrets to the young men was to give them the most generous of presents.

Ancient Hopi could describe complicated land boundaries and the sites of shrines from memory. Some knew the exact and only day for planting the crops, a handful possessed knowledge of the remedies for diseases, and still fewer were entrusted with the interpretations of dreams. Others could become advisors to the depressed or sorrowful. When such wise ancients died, it was much more than a personal loss; everyone wondered if some of the accumulated wisdom of the ages would be buried with them forever.

The Incas thought of their aged as living recording systems. Trobriand Islanders saw them as the key to learning. They were the storehouses of scientific knowledge: the local ferns, plants, mushrooms, insect species, and birds were identified by them.

And who but the old could qualify for shamanistic practices? For the Indians of Paraguay, a decaying body was often believed to acquire fetishistic powers, since the aged were closer to communication with the spirit world. For some, growing old made the call to magic irresistible. Experience had taught them not only how to appear all-knowing, but also how to explain away a mishap or make use of chance elements not under their control. Many a wily old shaman has interpreted his failures to better effect than his successes. For example, in 1840, a prophet of the Creek Indians was supposed to relieve a great drought by making rain. The canny old fellow performed his ceremony and then announced that since his success was assured, he must immediately desist and work alternate charms to avoid flooding. He cleverly manipulated back and forth for as long as necessary until the rains came.

The homage afforded old people by a society is a complex matter. Perhaps it is more a combination of forces involving certain important rituals and the fear of disregarding them than simply some natural instinct of love or pity. And there is little doubt too that different cultures provide different opportunities for old people. But above all, some form of esteem for old age is seen worldwide. Prestige and power for the elderly are almost universal. They have been an influential and valued segment of the population whose contribution has never been doubted. The old alone have held the keys to the traditions of the past and they alone could give shape to the future.

Yet today in America we can see little of this. Of course, we Westerners no longer solicit the services of seers, magicians, or ancients to recite the history of the tribe. But are not our needs for wise women and wise men as great as ever? Where are *our* experts in the problems of life? With the exception perhaps of our relatively few distinguished old men and women, our Supreme Court, senators, our rich or famous aged, it is lamentable that our elders are hardly ever consulted in day-to-day experience. Ordinary old people are now so separated from the various centers of society that they are seldom heard from and even less often heeded. Yet what substitutes have been found for the seasoned, the rational, the experienced human being? What substitutes for perspective, for clarity, for understanding? Never before in history have there been so many who have lived on to qualify so well for the tasks at hand. Among us we have generations of older Americans who have seen more change in the world than anyone could ever have imagined. But their talents are now rusting like so many beached vessels on the shore. Seldom has any group gone so unnoticed, so unattended, so neglected as the aging in our nation today. Our challenge then is clear—to devise new means for drawing them back into life, to build a society in which they can become active participants once again.

3.
Where Has Everybody Gone?

In America we preserve no delicacies for the old—no ostrich eggs, marrowfat, or antelope steak. How *do* we provide for them? What bounty do we offer? We have developed our own customs, evolved our own distinct patterns, and created a complex institution through which such privileges could derive. The very rituals which add structure and texture to our daily lives also provide the means for gaining such advantages. Through these ceremonies we come to expect the gratification and satisfaction that are the fruits of a life's work and devotion.

In our country and in much of industrial Western Europe, there has been no more important institution in the lives of old people than the family. For our elders that's about *all* there is, the only social relationship which the old man or old woman may legitimately claim. And within the family's secure boundaries, the old once flourished.

European settlers on this continent brought with them the customs of their lands, reverence for the Scriptures, and the solemn belief in the duties demanded of man by God. The old presided—patriarchs and matriarchs in the position of honor among children, grandchildren, and great-grandchildren. In the colonial settlements these patterns took hold and became American in style, reborn on native soil.

It was the patriarch who ruled such a family; women and children took subordinate positions and were subject to the judgment and wisdom of the elder male. Yet each person knew exactly where he or she belonged and his or her particular role. Above all, there was consistency throughout a lifetime. Family ties came first and foremost—through adulthood and marriage—and embraced generations. For the aging members of the clan, this meant increasing authority, more respect, and great power in their later years.

It was a system which sociologists term "the extended family," literally meaning the organization of blood relatives into relationships mutually rewarding for everyone. The arrangement was particularly suited to rural life where the family was self-supporting. Foods and household goods were produced and consumed with little surplus. The family was a successful, self-sufficient economic unit where a number of children supplied the labor required: sons for farm work, daughters for domestic tasks. It also served as the principal social institution: Sundays after church were occasions for family festivity. Education was also a family undertaking, and Bible study at home was so commonplace that the King James Bible continued to be the best-selling book in America through the end of the nineteenth century.

Even when a son married (and was helped by the father to acquire a farm of his own), he usually remained dependent upon the elder man. Father and son helped one another bring in the crops and shared farm work. As for daughters, their babies were often delivered by grandma, whose help and advice was sought in rearing children. Meanwhile, the older couple became more influential than ever in the community, continually active at local meetings, making plans affecting the townships.

Unfortunately, the stability of remaining close together created tension more often than it did bliss. The family with several generations living under one roof could hardly be free from strife. Old people might well be victimized within this structure and often were. But as a system, it was well defined. It was simply "the way things were."

But by the early nineteenth century, all eyes were turned west, and many people went off to carve out their own destinies far from family and friends. This splitting apart led to what sociologists term the "conjugal" family, as opposed to the extended family. It has prevailed in America to this day.

In contrast to the extended family, the conjugal family unit consists of a much smaller group with special loyalties—husband, wife, and immature children. Consider what this means for the older members of the group, how much more tenuous it is to depend upon one or two persons, rather than consulting with grandfathers, uncles, and the clan in general. An even more fundamental change was the radical separation of the generations. On marriage, each son and daughter, each sister and brother, would now belong to a different and separate family, feeling stronger obligations to the new family than to the old. What resulted was akin to divorce from the family to which one had been born!

Where did this leave the older person within the system? During its gradual growth, the conjugal family maintained filial loyalties and duty to kin. But as America grew into an urban, industrial society, the conjugal family shrank and hardened into itself, with older kin dwelling in a no-man's-land where they have no claims to participation or support.

Once massively relocated in the cities, the family's size dwindled even further. It soon became apparent that having many children was no longer the asset it had been on the farm, but merely meant more mouths to feed. Factories were filled with women and their children who (before the passage of child labor laws) were used to supplement family income. Well into the 1930s it was the father who would most often seek out employment for his wife or offspring, since their earnings were needed for family survival.

Through this change in family life, the fabric of our society was being rewoven into an entirely new pattern. No longer was the father the provider whose authority went unchallenged. Family members were now being judged by the outside world and by alien standards. Children employed in the factory or in the office received promotions based on efficiency and excellence, determined on the job and by their employers alone. Father and Mother had nothing to say about it.

And so family loyalties became threatened and parental authority challenged. Young people grew more confident as they grew less dependent. The fast-growing American industrial system provided opportunity, and children often surpassed their parents, becoming more educated, more skilled, and more wealthy. They were native to American ways, while many of their parents were immigrant "greenhorns" who had flocked to our shores by the tens of millions since the 1880s. It was not long before the foundations of family structure were being destroyed. True, the family continued to be the principal preparation for adulthood, housing and feeding the child, and mediating between the economy and the individuals. But it could no longer monopolize the life of the young. The father was often out of the home, employed by others. The disciplining of the children soon fell to the mother. Children saw new possibilities for life on the outside. This left little common ground between parent and child. Obligations to family remained, as they do today, but because of a vague sense of duty and sacrifice, rather than true devotion. Adult youngsters, especially married ones, developed the right and the superior duty to "lead their own lives."

An even more devastating blow fell when the mother's arduous and endless household tasks, previously distributed among children as daily chores, began to be taken over by modern appliances. These labor-saving gadgets have diminished the immediate needs for work within the family, additionally releasing the mother from her full-time domestic role.

With so many of its functions taken over by factory, office, church, school and government, the family's influence over relations between the young and old has been steadily deteriorating. Small wonder that U.S. Census Bureau statistics provide evidence of the continuous drop in the size of American households. The average in 1950 was 3.39 persons; in 1960 it was 3.3; and in 1974 it had dropped below 3 persons. The *New York Times* attributes this trend to the fact that increasingly the young and the old are living apart and alone.[1]

Perhaps even more crucial is that the conjugal structure of the American family has fostered the belief in adulthood, the need to break away from the nuclear family unit, to leave home and live far away. Our emphasis is upon "physical separation," as sociologist Talcott Parsons tells us.[2] In sending our children off to college, whether it be ten miles away or three thousand, we are assigning them to the life of the dormitory rather than the family home. It is an emotional weaning, allowing no proximity for extended periods. We develop the adult status of the young man or woman by instilling in them the ability to live alone, without the assistance of family.

Some may argue that such developments have produced a better atmosphere within the family. They speak of new potential for unity and affection without the repressive, authoritarian aspects of traditional family life. It is a condition within which closer ties can evolve, deeper relationships be maintained, and a truer appreciation of individual and generational differences comprehended and accepted. Gerontologist Gordon F. Strieb predicts in a forecast article for the turn of the twenty-first century that more older couples will be living apart from their adult children, demonstrating what he calls "intimacy at a distance." However, he believes that there will be considerable contact between older parents and their adult children, and continuing patterns of reciprocal aid (most of it, however, from parent to child, not vice versa).[3]

Many experts agree that older family members, particularly the "postparental couple," are not isolated in our society but are a part of a new modified form of extended kin structure. Lillian E. Troll, a psychologist at Wayne State University, claims that Talcott Parsons' prediction of twenty years ago—that old people would be isolated—has not come true. Recent research demonstrates that a large percentage (84 percent) of those over sixty-five have at least one offspring within their vicinity or no more than an hour's drive away. There is visiting once a week or more between the two groups, or telephone or written communication. Geographic distances in America no longer constitute the obstacles they once did.[4]

Yet one must wonder at such statistics. What do categories like "residential propinquity," "mutual aid," or "the number of contact hours" catalogued by sociologists really tell us about the relationships between married children and their aging parents? Very, very little. And the professors are the first to admit it. Such measurements simply do not get at the heart of the matter. They cannot tell us about the quality of the intimacy or even hint at the pleasure or lack of it in such meetings. The very need to arrange the meetings, the artificial structure of such "visiting," whether it be across the country or across the county, puts an additional strain on filial relations.

But in such studies the subsidiary facts are revealing. They can offer us deeper insights into the real situation facing elder Americans. For example, most studies show that over the course of the years it is on the female side that links are maintained, if they exist at all. Daughters, not sons, remain close to their parents, and it is their widowed mothers who are most often taken into a household. And often, as anthropologist Sheila Johnson observes, *that* daughter is an only child who has been close to her mother throughout childhood.[5] Sons, as a rule, have been so completely "weaned" from the family of their origin that once married they seldom turn back, and their new loyalty to the conjugal group often extends to their wives' parents and relations rather than to their own. But women's closeness to their mothers reflects the more traditional side of family life. The rift has already been completed for the men; will female loyalties too be thoroughly eroded by rapid changes in the lifestyle of the young?

Consider another aspect of filial duty—the extent to which parents and children offer one another assistance. Many sociologists think this is crucial to estimate family closeness and unity. Aid can be in the form of money, or services like baby sitting, shopping, or house-cleaning. Matilda Riley and Anne Foner found that the "proportion of old people who *give* help to their children tends to exceed the proportion who *receive* help from their children." (Italics mine)[6] Predominantly then, the flow is from *old* to *young,* it seems, for as long as the elder parents remain able.

There are less data available about exchanges of money and services *to* the old *from* the young. This is complicated by the disruptive effects families suffer from occupational migration among young professionals. Each year thousands of engineers, architects, lawyers, ministers, professors, and their conjugal families move to various assignments in different parts of this nation for stints of several years. Despite telephone company advertisements to the contrary, the occasional long-distance phone call to Mom and Dad has really become the symbol of this familial rupture. And perhaps even more touching and upsetting is that achievement has so surpassed family loyalty in our culture that statistics show many parents value their children's "success" above their presence and accept separation as necessary and proper.

Social security benefits have created the worst confusion of all when it comes to financial aid to parents from their adult children. Regular financial support is now virtually out of the hands of the younger generation and has become an industrial or governmental rather than family responsibility. Legal responsibilities are unclear, and moral responsibilities are being bitterly contested. Some old people firmly maintain their right to financial support from their grown children; others just as firmly deny such assistance. At one time the pressures exerted by relatives, neighbors, and communities, as well as the fear of criticism, were a powerful push to "do the right thing by the old folks." But what were once major inducements for young people to offer such financial support have virtually disappeared, since today family members are scattered all over the country.

Only recently has social research explored the subject of the diminished role of the grandparent, and found distinct changes in the makeup of this group. Apparently, earlier marriages and child-bearing patterns have made the grandparent younger than ever before. Many are in their early forties and actively participating in the working world. Despite this vitality, their involvement with the rearing of their grandchildren is minimal and their influence upon them virtually nil. Theirs is so peripheral a role in the American family that any participation by grandparents in the process of education or discipline is often regarded as interference. The dominant or stern grandparent, at one time accepted, is now looked upon with suspicion. Parents fear such intervention and consider it likely to do psychological harm to the child. So firmly has the conjugal family maintained its exclusive authority to decide what is right for its offspring that the modern grandparent is literally shut out. As a result, many American children are growing up without intimacy or even contact with their older relatives. Those liv-

ing great distances away from them can remember them very
faintly, if at all, and the time remembered is often that "one Christmas when they were very little."

Anthropologist Margaret Mead grew up in a household which
included her paternal grandmother, whom she adored, and she
considered this a key influence upon her life. She lamented the
frequent lack of such relationships for our young today. What has
become of that special wonder and closeness children once felt
toward grandparents? Where is the wise counselor, that transmitter
of secret knowledge and love once so much a part of each child's
life? Long gone and perhaps lost forever. And how interesting to
learn that the new breed, who have never known such relationships,
are far less interested in or sympathetic to the problems of the old.
They also have more firmly rooted prejudices against the aged, and
a distaste for infirmities.

American grandparents reflect this ambiguous position. They are
"glad to see them come and glad to see them go,"[7] openly preferring the younger children because the older ones "get bored" and
"won't bother with us at all."[8] Once grandparents were strong dis-
ciplinary forces and major influences; then they became indulgent
friends and teachers; finally merely occasional visitors and givers of
gifts. What a falling off!

What does it all add up to? An all-pervasive uneasiness among
the old; terror at the thought of dependency, shame at the idea of
being in need and becoming a financial burden to their children.
Such fears are the most striking characteristic of the aging in
America today. They are a direct consequence of the prevailing cultural view of both young and old that "independence" is the supreme
state of being. This is perhaps a chronic American disease—mis-
taking self-sufficiency for that much more exalted state known as
independence. To be free does not mean to be isolated or divorced
from all human responsibility. Individual independence is far
more complex than that. In the following pages we will assault the
very foundations of such muddled thinking.

What hurts more than every other development in the American
family situation is estrangement: the feeling of being dumped by
the very people on whom one relies the most. For as the younger
family moves away from the older, they lose the intimacy, the

sense of common experience, and mutual understanding. No amount of long-distance telephoning or visiting can recover it.

Is it any wonder that older people everywhere are asking, Where has everyone gone? As an institution in urban America, the family has clearly failed them, left them out in the cold, and they find themselves forced to seek new and meaningful ways to spend the rest of their lives.

It's clear that there can be no turning back since forecasts for the year 2000 confirm the ruthless trends. Along with a longer life expectancy (approximately sixty-eight years estimated for males and seventy-five for females) we shall see smaller families, fewer grandchildren, many more women in the work force, and more of both sexes in earlier retirement. Older couples will prefer to live separately, either remaining in their own homes or settling in the various tropical retirement colonies of Florida and the Southwest. There will be more permissive sexual norms, more tolerance for occasional affairs, and more remarriage among the widowed or divorced. Disenchantment with the marital state will grow, with middle-class, middle-aged husbands and wives finding their relationships unsatisfactory, their lives together "devitalized" and "passive." Divorces among these people will be more common than ever.[9] All of this can only mean further disruption between parents and their adult children. Besides the emotional turmoil, it means new conflicts in the transfer of property and in providing financial assistance.

So the picture emerges; the contemporary development of what Ruth Benedict delineated as the family, "Genus Americanum," a group of individualists, both in youth and maturity, all worshipers of free choice, with a reverence for privacy and for seeking out their own destinies. The old among them are no whiners lamenting what once was, but people determined to recognize their own situation in America today, and to find every conceivable means for changing that intolerable state, not only for themselves right now, but for their young (though very soon to be old) descendants as well.

4.
The Road to
Activism

Have we reached that moment in history when old people can become a dynamic political power? And, more crucial, how do we go about building a mass movement?

Older Americans have come of political age with a power to be heard in their own right. There are crusaders today who call this a period of revolution in a movement for liberation from agism. Jack Ossofsky, executive director of the National Council on Aging, tells us that "as the 1960s were a time of civil rights," and "the 1970s emphasized women's rights," so will the 1980s "be a time for the rights of the aged."[1]

There's nothing new about older citizens attempting to redress their grievances by going actively into politics—this has been happening since the early 1930s—but undeniably, we see significant new elements in the situation today, and they could dramatically alter the political picture.

Anybody who reads the newspapers knows that there are far greater numbers of older people to be accounted for today. The Center for Democratic Institutions made the unlikely forecast for that magic year 2000—one-half of the U.S. population will be over fifty and one-third over sixty-five.[2] But we needn't look that far ahead. Today the number of persons over sixty-five is close to 24 million, 11 percent of the American people. This 24 million hardly resemble those who came before them. No plug-chewing, rocking-chair porchsitters these! No butterchurning, crocheting, jam-makers! Here's a group who has, over the last several decades, been steadily subjected to a regular series of insults and depri-vations. A growing number of these people see themselves caught in an assault, a revolutionary blast against the structure of their daily lives. What began for them as a mounting fear later turned to misery and despair over their helplessness. Steadily a rage has grown at their continuing losses. Emerging now is their determin-ation to act, a new militancy that has set apart current efforts from the many earlier attempts at political recognition by old people. It's a new political consciousness, what Tom Booker, the executive director of the Houston Housing Authority, calls "savvy."[3] Here is a sophisticated, vocal, informed group: a generation of people engaged in a bitter fight for survival in American society.

Nor should this surprise us. Living in America through the 1930s, 1940s, 1950s, and particularly the 1960s, they have seen every sacred cow of their youth slaughtered. They have been wit-ness to the many postwar crusades, the growing momentum of the Black movement with its mass marches on Washington, the revolts of the other minorities, the antiwar rallies of the students, the war on poverty, and most currently the liberation of women and the push for the rights of homosexuals. They have heard the cries of dis-satisfaction and distress from every sector of society. As for their own cause, it too has seen its mini-triumphs, and from each of these, along with the growing swell of revolutionary change in the rest of American life, they have learned important lessons.

But first, who are these 24 million Americans? And where are they? Ninety percent of them are white, about 7 percent black. The rest represent the other ethnic groups. Their numbers are largest in New York, California, Pennsylvania, Florida, Illinois and Texas, though smaller numbers are to be found in Arkansas, Iowa, Mis-souri, Kansas and Nebraska. According to United States Depart-ment of Commerce figures, nearly 60 percent are women, many of whom are widowed or divorced, and living alone. Men over sixty-five, on the other hand, are mostly married and living with their spouses.

Probably even more significant is the addition of another, larger group which gerontologist Bernice Neugarten of the University of Chicago calls "the young-old" and which she says have enormous potential as agents of social change. The young-old are people from age fifty-five on. They are healthier, more educated, more affluent, more active politically, and more free of family responsibilities than the same groups in the past. Neugarten points out that ever since the Social Security Act designated sixty-five as the economic marker for "old age," it has arbitrarily become the indicator of a person's social and psychological state as well. With the lowering of the age of retirement, however, fifty-five is beginning to be a meaningful lower age limit, and the 1970 census figures already reflect a significant drop in the proportion of men over fifty-five in the labor force. Certainly with the new eligibility for social security benefits at age sixty-two and the government's recent delineation of age sixty for eligibility for a variety of services covered by the Older Americans Act, the stereotypes are beginning to yield to the new reality. The young-olds are a moving force among us and will undoubtedly wield their influence in the coming decades.

These young-olds, of course, overlap with those sixty-five and over; together, the groups are estimated to take in over 20 percent of the total population (currently 46 million people), and their proportion is expected to remain stable over the next twenty or thirty years. Women outnumber men, though not as dramatically as in the older group. According to the 1970 census only 50 percent of these women are still married and living with spouses who head their households, as compared with 80 percent of the men in this age group who head their families. What this tells us is that in this younger group more males are surviving. In the sixty-five and over group, more women are alone.

One of the fascinating details about the young-old is that one in three at age sixty still has at least one parent living. Neugarten observes that this usually contributes to their sense of youthfulness. This group has strong needs for opportunities to participate in community affairs and for meaningful activities in terms of self-realization. It is estimated that by 1980 the average fifty-five-year-old, already far more educated than his father, will be a high school graduate. The Carnegie Commission predicts that many will also have explored higher education in some form. The once notable differences in education between young and old continue to be reduced; and this group of young-old will articulate its needs for a wider range of options, making its demands heard in order to improve the quality of all our lives.[4]

Increased numbers are one thing, but the radical changes in attitudes may prove as important. There is less timidity, shame, and fear, and a growing confidence in the right to pursue one's share of America's wealth. People are no longer willing to accept the inevitable "shelving" of the human being when his "time comes." The psychology which once fostered dogged loyalty to employer and to company has been held up to ridicule, even deplored and denounced. Gone is the ritual gratitude, the gold watch, and retirement dinner. Such passivity is gone in a new generation of aggressive citizens and unionized workers, willing to challenge industry and examine their rights as human beings.

From the time the 89th Congress passed the Older Americans Act in 1965 (virtually a Bill of Rights for the aging) to the passage of the newest legislation against forced retirement in 1978, growing numbers turned to the courts to question age discrimination on the part of employers. According to Carin Ann Claus, in charge of age-bias complaints at the United States Labor Department, hundreds of federal court cases were brought by individuals challenging their employers on their right to continue on the job. The number of such complaints doubled since 1972. In 1974 there were over three thousand filed, and about sixteen hundred employees received damages totaling over $6 million. This included a $2 million settlement by Standard Oil of California to 160 employees who were laid off because the corporation needed to reduce its labor force and made selections strictly on the basis of age.[5] In May of 1974 *Newsweek* reported that Standard Oil was getting rid of older, higher-priced workers and replacing them with younger, lower-paid ones. The court's decision forced it to rehire 120 workers, provide them with back pay, and reinstate them in the company's pension plan, insurance, and stock pension plans.[6]

Another case involved the Greyhound Bus Lines, questioning the legality of a bus company's refusal to assign a man as a driver if he was over thirty-five years of age. Greyhound had taken the position that the human body begins to degenerate at the age of thirty-five, thus making it unfit for high-risk responsibilities. The Labor Department argued that the company contradicted itself, since it employed many drivers in their sixties doing a perfectly good job.

In one case tried in a St. Louis District Court, a test pilot named Phillip W. Houghton, well over fifty, was termed, according to the Labor Department testimony, "more healthy today than he was ten years ago." Was it legal to dismiss him? The issue was plain: Can an employer establish an age limit for a physically demanding job, or must he consider the specific abilities relating to the job when he hires, fires, or promotes employees?

There were cases posing other questions: Is it discriminatory for an advertisement to read: Wanted: recent college graduates? Or does this violate age-bias statutes? Can a company refuse training or promotion to an individual on the basis of age? Is the company within its rights to decide, for example, that training a man of forty-five is not economically feasible, and thus choose a twenty-five-year-old instead? These questions challenged the biggest industrial companies in the nation. But possibly the most complex of all, and the most urgent, was the one involving mandatory retirements, now clearly prohibited in the private sector by new federal laws.

Attitudes have changed in areas beyond business and industry. Frank Nelson, a professor at the University of Hawaii, complaining that "old people have been pushed around long enough," challenged that institution by refusing to retire at age sixty-five. "I had no intention of spending the rest of my life cutting glass bottles," he said. The State Circuit Court in 1973 upheld his right to do so, pointing to the fact that for other state employees the legal retirement age is seventy.[7]

It was not long ago that respectable people knew that they must "put something by" for their old age lest they end their days in the poorhouse. They believed that government intervention was charity and a scandal to any self-respecting person. In a letter to President Gerald Ford, lamenting the inflation that had reduced him financially, eighty-year-old Joe E. Hardy of Sun City, Arizona, expressed this attitude:

When I was a boy, we lived seven miles north of Pilot Point, Texas, on a farm. It was a great event in my life when I got to go to town with my father, riding the old wagon. . . . As we passed the county poor farm, we could see the old people sitting on the lawn in front of the house. My father would whisper, "Those people, when they were young did not save anything for their old age." I was determined not to sit in front of the county poor farm when I became old. . . .[8]

Yet the unprecedented number of federal laws, executive orders, and new appropriations aimed to benefit the elderly in the last decade have made such former attitudes irrelevant. The continuing existence of a committee such as the Senate Special Committee on the Aging, which has been renewed annually since 1961 with little or no opposition in Congress, testifies to the federal government's firm commitment to the problems confronting its older citizens. Even the proudest of our American individualists recognize the permanence of such federal intervention.[9]

We have increased numbers and changed attitudes, but what about prevailing conditions? The financial position of older people has always been a dependent one, in our own society and in others. However, recent events have clearly threatened the security of the group and the strain is beginning to show. Substantial numbers now living on fixed incomes find themselves caught by galloping inflation, which, though hard on everyone, means a pauper's existence for them, instead of a comfortable retirement. Many had been accustomed to a certain affluence, and now find themselves poor, even desperately poor, for the first time in their lives, with no solutions at hand.

Such people are undernourished, skipping meals, or buying what is cheapest at the markets: day-old chicken backs and necks, or marrow bones for soup. Some are badly clothed and living in substandard housing. Others face long-term illnesses which, because of incredible increases in medical costs, drain them of their last resources. Still others, attempting to save themselves by seeking jobs, are deemed "too old" or "unemployable."

All over America reports detail the many indignities facing this new breed of poor. In Miami Beach, a city in which 16 percent of the population is over sixty-five, police had reported that by 1975 shoplifting by old people had become a serious problem. Supermarket managers catch older women stealing little packages of food—meat, cheese, or small cans of tuna—hiding them in their underclothing. The authorities added that it is always in small quantities and merely what is needed for the next meal. Some of these "criminals" are arrogant and defiant, proudly maintaining that they are entitled to what they take because they have given the store their business in better days. Senior citizen groups in the area have recently brought in legal aid for those apprehended.

Others are bitter about their diminished incomes. A retired Los Angeles school teacher lamented that his $500 a month income, accumulated from pension and savings, ten years earlier had seemed a source of security to him. Today it hardly covered his bills. Hundreds of thousands are in this position today, and it is a good deal worse for the millions who are entirely dependent on social security. Ed Meagher, a *Los Angeles Times* staff writer, reported in April 1974 that though social security benefits had increased 80.7 percent since 1966, 29.7 percent of the 22 million over sixty-five recipients were receiving below-poverty-level incomes because of inflation. There are more social security recipients in the below-poverty level now than there were in 1969. Then the poverty level was designated at $1,850 for a single person and $2,400 for a couple. A survey in Los Angeles County conducted at that time by United Way, Inc., found that 15 percent of the approximately 1 million people over sixty living there were under the poverty line. And Meagher pointed out that these figures did not account for the many "balancing precariously on the tightrope of fixed incomes and rising prices, with constant threat of uncovered medical costs, auto, or household repairs."[10]

Others suffer from rent boosts. Despairing widows, for example, who have lived in the same place for fifteen years with such initial rents as $30 a month watch their one-room apartments upped from $85 to $150 or more while they remain on their fixed incomes of $200 per month. Not since the Great Depression have so many been so cruelly beset by money troubles.

Another, perhaps greater, woe plagues the old today—the danger they face in the central cities. We are shocked by increasing reports of muggings, robberies, beatings, murders, and even rapes of old people in New York, Detroit, Chicago, Los Angeles, and other urban centers. Such brutal acts often require long planning and surveillance, and police find that the $50 and $60 amounts generally in the possession of aged victims can hardly be considered the sole motive for such crimes. The *New York Times* has reported in recent years hundreds of such attacks on the aged by youths throughout Brooklyn and the South Bronx, most of them occurring in the victims' apartments.

In May 1975, a seventy-six-year-old woman was raped and murdered in Los Angeles in the twenty-third such incident within a year. All the victims of the so-called Wilshire-area rapist were elderly women living alone. Dr. Martin Reiser, the Los Angeles Police Department's director of behavioral sciences, says that such rapists are generally "very young, highly disturbed, with overwhelming rage at and resentment of females, particularly the elderly female figure who may have been very significant in early childhood. The elderly victim comes to be a symbol of the rapist's frustration." Reiser further notes the vulnerability of old people; their slower responses and poor sight and hearing make them easy targets for such disturbed personalities.[11]

Such incidents have put urban elderly into a state of continuing fear, making them prisoners in their homes. As a result they are even more isolated from friends and family; community life, whatever is left of it, is wholly unavailable to them. The continuing difficulties of daily existence for many isolated old has forced their mere survival to become an issue. An incident which occurred during the winter of 1974 in Milwaukee demonstrates this. It seems that while the temperature outside was one degree above zero, the Wisconsin Public Service Corporation turned off the gas at the home of Harold Radke in nearby Peshtigo, because he had not paid his bill in three months. The seventy-one-year-old bachelor's body was found frozen on the floor. Apparently, he'd been remiss earlier that year, at which time his brother in Idaho had paid the bill, telling the company that if there was any trouble again he was to be contacted. Though the company denied any record of this, they did have on record that the brother had paid the earlier bill. The collection manager who had ordered Radke's heat turned off admitted that he'd been out of town over the weekend.

It becomes evident that conditions have indeed become desperate for great numbers of older citizens in this nation. Thus, there is no telling how far a solidly founded, grassroots, activist organization could go if it caught the imagination of Americans growing old today.

But we may well ask, Is such a movement possible? There have been scores of movements, near misses, and outright failures. How can we hope to succeed now? Despite several historic attempts to organize effectively, the political influence of the aging in this country continues to be marginal. Beginning with enormous enthusiasm and energy, older citizens' groups often end up ephemeral, politically unrealistic, ridden with dissension and strife, and mostly ineffectual. New messiahs appear by the generation, each promising his own brand of salvation. How can we believe that *this* is the time for liberation?

Let's review the growth and development of such movements of the past, to study their accomplishments as well as their errors. From the turn of the century on, there have been many attempts to gain greater security for old people. By 1920, 50 percent of the population was already residing in urban settings, and the sense of support of the rural family, the continuity of the rural community, the comforting care associated with this atmosphere were already disappearing. Thus early groups like the Fraternal Order of Eagles (FOE) or Abraham Epstein's American Association for Old Age Security spearheaded old age pension bills which they sought to introduce into every state legislature in the nation. Their literature continually reiterated the fact that masses of aged people were living at or below the poverty line and that many had no relatives or offspring to turn to for help. These publications were helpful in breaking down the ideological objections to old age pensions, making them more respectable to the public in general.

But it was not until the 1930s, after this country plunged into depression, that the aged population (their jobs eliminated, businesses ruined, and savings wiped out) entered politics as a pressure group. These were independent people who had worked hard and saved in the tradition of free enterprise taught by the American economic system. It was the first time in history that masses of them were attracted to social action and saw a separate movement for their special interest crystallizing into a political force.

This belated action for the aged is unique to the American scene. As historian Abraham Holzman has pointed out, labor and socialist movements in most European countries participated far earlier and more effectively in the development of such legislation. Combined with generally stronger family bonds and a higher regard for their aged, this retained for the old of Europe a better position in society, at least during that period.[12]

Undoubtedly, the best known of such early American political groups was the Townsend movement, which at its peak boasted a membership of 1 million. It was the most appealing panacea of the depression decade, offering full employment and promising $200 a month for the aging. Its slogan was "$200 a month at sixty." The campaign grew in California, spurred by large numbers of recent migrants highly concentrated within one area of the state. Without such a concentration the movement might not have caught fire as swiftly and forcibly as it did. Townsendites in Southern California could see immediate results when, assembled, they filled the Rose Bowl in Pasadena.

Regarding its origins, there is a much-quoted story about its leader, Dr. Francis E. Townsend, who, like St. Paul, was struck by a vision. A displaced midwesterner, Townsend was born in a log cabin in Illinois and had had a checkered career as a miner in Colorado, a teamster in Washington, a country school teacher in Kansas, and a stove salesman in Nebraska. At the age of thirty-one he enrolled in the Omaha Medical College, later practicing medicine in the frontier of western South Dakota. By 1919, he'd moved to Long Beach, California, to continue his career as a doctor and dabble in real estate as well. With the crash in 1929, he found himself near bankruptcy at the age of sixty-two, when his position of medical assistant was terminated in a change of hospital administration.

The legend goes that the aging doctor, lively, intelligent, and still immensely energetic, one morning gazed out of his window and was startled by the sight of three haggard old women, stooped with age, rummaging for food in the garbage cans outside. Appalled by this sight, Townsend exploded:

A torrent of invective tore out of me, the big blast of all the bitterness that had been building in me for years. I swore and I ranted, and I let my voice bellow with the wild hatred I had for things as they were. My wife came a-running.

"Doctor! Doctor!" She's always called me Doctor, . . . "Oh, you mustn't shout like that. All the neighbors will hear you!"

"I want all the neighbors to hear me!" I roared defiantly. "I want God Almighty to hear me! I'm going to shout till the whole country hears!"[13]

Townsend never acknowledged this tale, not even in his biography written ten years later. It is quite likely that it had been conceived for publicity purposes, and it certainly became a useful propaganda device.

Townsend's famous letter to the *Long Beach Press Telegraph* on September 30, 1933, presented succinctly what he saw as the "cause" for the Great Depression and its "cure." Overproduction, he maintained, caused it, and increased consumption was the only cure. His proposal was to retire all those over sixty, providing them with pensions of $150 a month (later this was amended to $200) on the specific condition that the money must not remain in their hands, but must be spent within each payment period. This would keep the money in circulation and maintain the buying level so that goods produced would be goods consumed, thus insuring the labor force against unemployment.

His estimate of the cost of such a plan was between $2 billion and $3 billion, and this was to be raised by means of a sales tax which he called "the easiest tax in the world to collect." This too was later reconsidered when Townsend began to see the sales tax as regressive in nature; he substituted first what he called "transaction sales tax" and later a "gross income tax."

The very size of the pension can only be appreciated when contrasted with income figures for 1935. An estimated 87 percent of all U.S. families were earning around $2500 annually. Obviously, this plan was attractive to millions of Americans; it suited the economic scene of that moment, what Holzman calls "a similarity of ideas with the existing socio-ideological climate."[14] After several years of severe depression, America was desperately in search of new schemes to bolster the economy. Townsend's plan would provide jobs for the young as well as pensions for the old, thus avoiding the label of "old people's handout," a particularly sensitive issue at the time. The Townsendites maintained that by providing $200 per month pensions to retired Americans and requiring that they be promptly spent, money would be circulated and thus ensure a return to full employment. By spending $2400 per year, each man would be "buying" one new job. After all, hadn't British economist John Maynard Keynes stressed that a crisis of abundance was as possible as a crisis of poverty? Hadn't President Roosevelt and his New Deal brought this idea into the public view?

Above all, the plan offered social and psychological security to thousands in a generation which felt itself being pushed into a corner. It offered hope in a period when America's faith was shaken to its core. It removed the sense of personal guilt or failure from the individual by placing the responsibility for the situation upon a complex set of economic forces wholly out of his control. These were the people, it shouted, who built America and who should never find themselves pushed aside, but who must instead become the "distributor custodians" of its national wealth. They must be assured of their proper role in social and cultural affairs.

Townsend also skillfully managed to appeal to what was considered a conservative group, one suspicious of bureaucracy and government intervention. Despite what may seem like radical elements, the Townsendites were never revolutionists. Ever respectable and recommending the need to work within the system, Dr. Townsend depended upon the populistic backgrounds of the many midwesterners who joined him.

But the good doctor seemed to be a greater rhetorician and propagandist than anything else. His speeches and articles are characterized by a demogogic reliance on his heroic connections with the American pioneering past, describing the many ordeals and the stamina required by our forebears on the frontier. And it was not too long before the movement publication ran features prominently featuring Townsend among photographs of Washington, Jefferson, and especially Lincoln. There was a strong religious element in the group too, and indeed many of Townsend's spokesmen were ministers. The next logical step was the elevation of the hero to prophet. The Townsendites were hardly shy about this either. Townsend spoke of himself as a "fisher of men" and drew the parallel between Jesus' and his movement.[15]

Undoubtedly he believed in his plan and was a skilled orator, but he was certainly no economist. When asked to elaborate on his initial statements, he was quoted by the *New York Times* in 1935 as saying "the greatest value of our plan is its simplicity. . . . I don't want to depart from that. People can understand it." Unfortunately, economists soon demonstrated how unfeasible it actually was. It would *not* increase purchasing power, because it merely put into the hands of one group the money which it was taking away from another. And by retiring older workers whose employers were not likely to replace them immediately, it was likely to diminish the number of jobs available instead of increasing them. The plan, unworkable despite enormous popularity, was now doomed to failure.

But the popularity of the Townsend movement demonstrated for the first time that older Americans had entered the political arena and that they would continue to play a role in American politics. As Holzman has pointed out, the group "fashioned an articulate self-consciousness among many of the aged members of the population." So, despite the flamboyance of its leadership and its tendency to fall in with the corruption of the times[16]—all of which contributed substantially to its eventual exposure and downfall—this group influenced several of the pension plans later proposed on the state and national level. The Townsend movement was the mere political infancy of such old age pressure groups.

Simultaneously, but coming out of a whole other tradition and with an entirely different emphasis, and once again in California, was a group known as End Poverty In California. The state gave EPIC, as it came to be called, added impetus because of the many displaced and older persons arriving daily at its borders and settling. This organization was spearheaded by the prolific and well-known socialist writer, Upton Sinclair. Long associated with utopian ideas to combat the "evils of the money system" Sinclair founded a program considered so radical it had Democrats as well as Republicans shouting "crackpot," "Red," and "Bolshevik." At its heart was a twelve-point platform which would take a million Californians off relief and put them to work on unused farm lands to grow their own food. Others would operate factories at state expense. The idea of the plan was "production for use." Actually it proposed a method of bartering through which the state would complete the transaction for the exchange of goods. Sinclair, the fiery radical and a popular figure and hero of sorts, was prevailed upon to switch parties from Socialist to Democrat in order to compete in the primaries. He astonished everyone by winning handily.

The tenth plank in his platform was the plan for old age pensions. He demanded $50 a month for all needy persons over sixty who'd been living in the state of California at least three years. Sinclair realized too late the appeal and power of that particular proposal. His EPIC was actually reaching for a far wider group, and his major proposals involved shifting the tax burden from the small income to the high income groups to ease the plight of the low-income population. But Sinclair talked directly to older people and in his *I, Governor of California* and *How I Ended Poverty,* he promised to become their champion.

Unfortunately when once he'd won the primary and taken triumphant control of the Democratic party, his troubles really began. Most of the influential Democrats began to desert the EPIC cause in droves as a result of a smear campaign so destructive that it has hardly been equalled since. Such slogans as "Epileptic," "End California in Poverty," "Easy Pickings in California" and "End Poverty, Introduce Communism" were widely circulated, describing Sinclair as an atheist, a free lover, and even a mental case— in short, a danger to decent folk everywhere.

As though all this were not enough, Sinclair then made the great mistake of dropping the old age pension proposals as a prominent feature of his platform. This was more of a disaster than he estimated because his enemies picked it up as a demonstration of his cynicism. But Sinclair was merely an idealist who did not wish to favor one interest group over another and thus to serve all the victims of the depression, young and old.

Still another tactical error was his admitted lack of sympathy with the immensely popular Townsendite cause. Though Sinclair soon realized the political folly of this and attempted to reverse himself, it was too late. He had made several overtures before and after the elections to Townsend himself. But since Sinclair had been quoted as calling the plan a "complete delusion" and their tax provision "an abomination," he could hardly expect them to rally to his support. Sinclair was badly defeated in the 1934 election. But his EPIC movement didn't fold up for a long time after that. By 1935, EPIC had once more put all its efforts into the battle for old age pensions, moving deeper into other related questions concerning the legality of various investigative techniques in the administration of pension benefits. But by then courting the Townsendites for support meant sure defeat for Sinclair and his associates. By this time Townsend had completely rejected what he considered dangerous socialist ideas and formed a coalition with such figures as Gerald L. K. Smith, Father Charles E. Coughlin, and William Lamke. These were outspoken, violent haters of President Roosevelt, notorious racists, and anti-Communists. H. L. Menken even called the Reverend Smith "the greatest rabble-rouser on earth since Apostolic times."[17]

Smith had been much involved with another scheme for redistribution of wealth masterminded by Huey Long of Louisiana. Long's proposal was to eliminate great fortunes and turn them over to lower income families as well as give pensions to the old. It had great attraction. By February 1935, it could claim more than twenty-seven thousand clubs and mailing lists of over 7 million. Long, an incredibly skilled demagogue, had such political clout he was even feared by President Roosevelt, and had the Democrats in near panic at the thought of his heading a third party.

Townsend toured the country with these men, attacking the New Deal as "an alien and communistic trend"[18] and trying to rally support for a third party which could defeat Roosevelt. It was an unholy alliance indeed and caused much dissension among the Townsendites, especially when in 1936 Roosevelt was so triumphantly victorious.

The Townsendite movement had in the long run contributed substantially to the demise of the EPIC group, and partisan politics even more to the defeat of them both. But there was certainly one thing that had been established firmly and decisively: politicians could never again be unaware of the extent to which the depressed condition of the aged might generate a threat to their political futures.

Meanwhile, pension movements were springing up throughout the nation. Along with the frustration born of defeat in earlier political efforts came growing public awareness of the deteriorated position of older Americans. In Colorado, in Arkansas, North Dakota, Ohio, Oklahoma, Texas, and Washington, there were various schemes for boosting pension payments. The Colorado Bonanza, for example, was an intensive signature campaign launched by disappointed Townsendites to raise payments and lower the age limits for recipients. By 1938, the drive was widespread in Colorado and the state had so overreacted by raising assistance payments that it went into heavy debt. State politicians, both Democrats and Republicans, voiced alarm at the political machine which had been built up in the name of old age pensions. Roosevelt himself, in a speech marking the third anniversary of the Social Security Act, warned about "shortcuts to Utopia and fantastic financial schemes."[19]

One of the most sensational and colorful of such statewide pension plans takes us yet again to California. It came to be called "Ham 'n Eggs." Like its predecessors, it too was characterized by forceful personalities—first Robert Noble and then the Allen Brothers and Roy G. Owens. Dashing, magnetic, and highly skilled in oratory, Noble was a former radio announcer and real estate salesman, as unscrupulous as he was ambitious. He flirted with all the existing groups: EPIC, the Townsendites, and even the Huey Long movement until that collapsed. What's more, he had been accused of desertion from the United States Navy and had a criminal record. Still later he was associated with a pro-Nazi organization and prosecuted for sedition in 1944. Noble was searching for something new, something of his own, a movement where he could be the star.

Ingeniously, he adapted a 1932 plan of Yale economist Irving Fisher for stimulating the economy. By circulating a time-dated stamp scrip to all unemployed over fifty years old, Noble would get production moving again. Naturally, he gained an enormous following and soon had thousands of dues-paying members.

Just then the Allen Brothers stepped in to take charge. Willis and

Lawrence Allen knew a profitable venture when they saw it and were even better at being charlatans than Noble. They maneuvered him out of power, putting their own people into positions of authority. Among these were Raymond D. Fritz, an outspoken Nazi and anti-Semite; Sherman Bainbridge, who had shouted "We want our ham and eggs" at a public rally, thereby dubbing the movement with its popular name; and Roy G. Owens, a self-styled engineer and economist, chief spokesman for the group and much given to cultism in his remedies for the country's economic ills. Owens wrote a bill called the Retirement Life Payments Act and upped the pension proposals to $30 a week, coining the instantly sensational slogan "Thirty Dollars Every Thursday."

Despite much criticism for its lack of sophistication (especially from the irate economist Fisher, who considered their application a perversion of his theories and utterly simple-minded), Ham 'n Eggs continued to flourish. By October 1939, the movement claimed 362,000 members and over a million supporters.

But sensationalism pervaded every action of the group, accompanied by a Bible-thumping devotionalism. One incident involving the suicide of a sixty-two-year-old man in San Diego illustrates their shenanigans. Archie Price, penniless and desperate, had killed himself in a public park, leaving a suicide note which said, "Too young to receive an old-age pension and too old to find work." He was buried in a potter's field. Ham 'n Eggs staged an indignant march of over 7000 participants, calling this the death of a martyr for a sacred cause. Sheridan Downey, then candidate for United State senator, formerly associated with Sinclair's EPIC and eager to align himself with the fast-growing Ham 'n Eggs movement, defined this sacred cause as "the right of senior citizens to dignity, to security, to life." Price's body was exhumed from its pauper's grave and reburied in an elegant service amid lamentations and eulogies. These tactics brought much publicity to the group.

Despite the unsavory character of its leadership (Noble and the Allen brothers were constantly in power plays for control of the movement) and the defeat of their proposal in the 1938 gubernatorial election, the movement grew, gaining support from the state's most ambitious politicians, many of whom were swept into office as a result of their allegiance to the Ham 'n Egger's cause. By

1939 they were strong enough to demand that a special election be called to resubmit a streamlined version of their initiative. The rhetoric continued as it had before, theatrical and vulgar, but highly successful at recruiting masses of Californians. It even took on an ugly anti-Semitic note by comparing the "international bankers" of today with the "money demogogues" of ancient times who had "crucified the Redeemer" and were once again viciously enslaving humanity.[20]

The movement was threatened only after steady attacks by the California newspapers, the California Bankers Association, various citizen's committees, by 138 economists from all the institutions of higher learning in California, by organized labor and by Governor Culbert L. Olsen (the very governor they had helped to elect), all pointing to the impracticality, unworkability, and even unconstitutionality of the measure.

In desperation the group stepped up the pace with bigger rallies and noisier shows. And, in a move which analysts have since considered the very strategy which may finally have exposed the dishonesty and recklessness of its leaders, they offered to speed up the plan for redemption of their scrip money from fifty-two weeks to thirty days. This meant reducing the earning potential of the scrip to a mere twelve cents on the dollar as opposed to the initial $1.02. Disaster! On election day the Ham 'n Eggs amendment did not carry in a single county in the state. It lost by over a million votes.

Within the Ham 'n Eggs group was a young man named George McLain, who was to become the single most important figure in pension politics for the next decade. After associating with several reform movements in Los Angeles, and then running unsuccessfully for office, McLain was hired by the Allen Brothers to reorganize and coordinate their vast membership. It was said that in this capacity of district manager he'd worked wonders and acted "as a genius of organization." A proud Californian, and descended from a well-to-do family that had been reduced to poverty by the depression, McLain determined to devote himself to avenging the fate of his ruined father. His father, as a paving contractor, had given himself "to the development of his state and his country," but when bankrupted was subjected to indignities, heartache, and harassment in his attempts to obtain pension assistance.[21] His father's loss of self-respect along with a once lucrative business was what McLain most deplored, and his stated aim was to battle against such injustices.

By 1940 McLain had broken with the Ham 'n Eggers, and associated himself with a new group then known as Citizens' Pension Association, which he subsequently revamped into Old Age Payments Campaign Committee, and yet again to the Citizens' Committee for Old Age Pensions, the California Institute of Social Welfare, the California League of Senior Citizens, and finally (after his death), it was to become the National Senior Citizens' League, which is functioning even today.

From modest beginnings in 1941, McLain steadily expanded his following by broadcasting a radio series, campaigning for political action and for $60 monthly for sixty-year-olds, while attacking the California state legislature for "making life more miserable" for citizens receiving old age benefits. By 1943, Governor Earl Warren had appointed McLain to a prestigious committee for old age pensions. The movement was expanding rapidly. Its *California Pension Advocate* now claimed 8,000 subscribers and billboards advertising the Citizens Committee had been plastered up and down the California landscape.

Not unlike his predecessors, McLain had built an organization characterized by one-man leadership and one-way communication, that is, his radio broadcasts. He was accused of high-handed methods, manipulation, and opportunism, yet he was entirely devoted to his cause.

A pervasive theme in the McLain organization (and one much criticized) was that of the alienation of old people in the United States, the discarding, even the persecution of the aging by upcoming generations. The loss of social status and esteem, he felt, was most damaging, a prophetic insight in light of conditions existing today. In 1956 his official statement summed up this sentiment:

> There has been a slowly growing appreciation of the fact that old people require more than economic security in order to live a normal life. There is greater recognition that any person, regardless of age, must continue to be a functioning and integral part of his community. He has the need to continue in his own behalf and in the interests of society as long as he is able to do so. . . .[22]

Thus he paved the way to discussion of the validity and constitutionality of forced retirement laws.

The McLain publicity also had its propaganda aspects, its patriotic zeal in phrasing, its references to the mothers and fathers of a nation to whom the young were indebted. The sign which hung at his headquarters read: "Through these portals pass the builders of a Nation. . . . They shall not be forgotten."[23] He accused the young of turning away from their parents, implying that they were betraying their country and heritage as well: "The country you built is now ours, we may dole out enough of its goods to keep you alive, but we do it solely out of generosity, not because we owe you anything."[24] McLain's tactics are perhaps most questionable here.

Yet the achievements of his movement are substantial. He had maintained a political lobby to consistently serve the interests of his membership. For the first time causes of the aged were vigorously pursued in the California legislature, resulting in the passage of many laws liberalizing benefits for older Californians. McLain's efforts in Sacramento and later in Washington continued uninterrupted. In the 1948 election, he had gained prominence when a constitutional amendment to liberalize the Old Age Security Act in California was passed. That the measure was repealed the very next year and that McLain never again succeeded in any election is hardly of importance, because McLain's popularity and political clout continued strong through Governor Edmund Brown Sr.'s terms in the 60s and until his death in 1965.

Plainly, politicking for the rights of older citizens is not new. Despite the notoriety, skullduggery, and sensationalism of "Pied Pipers" during those turbulent years, each movement has made its contribution. The old have been organized, active, and on the march in the past. We are not starting from scratch. They have shown us the potential, if not the means. We today must rekindle this spirit, while devising more sophisticated methods to realize our aims.

5.
The New Militancy of the Old

Most of us, while this early political activism was stirring among the aged, were dancing the Charleston, the Shag, the Big Apple, the Cha Cha Cha, or the Lindy, depending upon which decade we grew up in. In that fairyland existence known as youth, we hardly noticed the cross-country antics of the placard-carrying Townsendites, the Ham 'n Eggers, or the EPIC protesters. Preoccupied with growing up, getting launched, getting married, starting families, building careers, we took very little interest in that distant, remote process: growing old.

So it's all history to us today. But as we too come into our later years, we may well wonder how we can make use of what has gone before. Let's now sort among the usable and the unfeasible; there is much to be learned and adopted, as well as much to be avoided and discarded.

If anything at all has been established, it is that a mass movement of older Americans is not only a possibility, but has been a fact several times over. Age consciousness in this nation continues to emerge as a real, growing phenomenon. Established, too, is the fact that our numbers will grow and that these statistics of our generation are dramatically in our favor. In 1974 the American Association for the Advancement of Science ran a symposium entitled, "The 1990s and Beyond: A Gerontocracy?" In recognition of these growing numbers, experts looking towards the turn of the century now talk of the potential of "senior power" and the rule of the aged.

Yet there is much disagreement among political scientists as to what effects these vast numbers alone can have. We are told they mean little unless they can be mobilized into a cohesive voting block. Gerontologist Robert H. Binstock of Brandeis University says that today there simply is no "aging vote," and that "age is not an important variable for explaining voting swings."[1] Other analysts have noted over the years that voting behavior of older citizens has shown little if any consistency.

Confirming this view is Angus Campbell of the University of Michigan Survey Research Center, who has studied voting behavior over the last several decades. He points out that the 11 percent of the population over sixty-five includes individuals of all races, religions, both sexes, and of rural and urban origin, all with highly disparate economic needs:

> Because each age cohort includes people who differ profoundly in many important conditions of life, it is not likely that any age group will be very homogeneous in its attitudes. The evidence which national surveys provide in fact demonstrates that attitudinal differences between age groups are far less impressive than those within age groups.[2]

To weld such people into a cohesive group has been in the past, and is likely to remain, an obstacle.

Furthermore, Binstock argues, political surveys have demonstrated that substantial numbers of older people (up to 65 percent) simply *do not conceive of themselves as old or aging;* they consider old-age issues as irrelevant (as least for the moment) and are unwilling to align themselves with such causes. If they react at all, it is often negatively. Many today are facing problems of housing, health care, safety, transportation, and income, but do not associate these new difficulties with aging. To some extent this avoidance is dictated by the fear of being patronized or pitied; age is a "negative identity" which may actually be considered by some a "deviant" form of behavior. This presents a challenge to today's activists: to stamp out negative attitudes in favor of a new independent social identity based on age consciousness and group solidarity. (Problems on the subject of personal identity will be discussed more fully in chapter 6.) But those referred to earlier as the young-old—the fifty to sixty-five category—figure solidly in meeting this challenge. Some have spoken of the new group's "retirement identity." With so many retiring so early, common experiences should help engender homogeneity in voting behavior; this new group needs only to identify and unite itself.

Another obstacle to building a powerful voting block has been that older people were once spread across the nation, thus dissipating their effectiveness in elections. As dispersed minorities, they often threw their votes to one major party or the other, with neither party specifically representing their needs. This situation may be changing too. John Schmidhauser at the University of Iowa has observed that in certain regions the aged are strategically located for influencing the vote.[3] In California, Florida, rural Iowa, Missouri, and Nebraska, concentrations of elderly citizens can make their voting behavior influential in local and county elections.

The conservatism of older groups in America is seen as a real problem in mobilizing support for radical programs. Stereotyped as "set in their ways," uncompromising, unwilling to change, and tending to hang on to outmoded ideas, the group is regarded as unmoveable—hardly a potential for activism. Yet there is little evidence supporting these stereotypes. Sociologists and psychologists tell us that older people are as capable of adjusting to variable social situations and accepting new ideas as younger ones. What is referred to as conservatism may merely be the tendency to be more careful, reflective, and thoughtful in the process of making decisions. Such caution and deliberation, often based on the experience of a lifetime, can contribute to a society which lacks historical perspective, and one in which youthful leadership is prized, often with more zeal than reason.

If older citizens seem fixed in their voting patterns and consistent in their preferences, they may be reflecting a more serious difficulty: the tendency to identify strongly with one party, voting for a party rather than people or issues. Accounting for such loyalties are the length of association with a particular group and the prestige and status that accompanies such an association. (The large numbers loyal to the Republican party, for example, are often cited as evidence for "old people's conservatism." This is noteworthy because the Democratic party's legislative record shows it has supported far more positive programs for the elderly than has the Republican party.[4] Yet the vast majority of today's older voters entered the electorate when the Republican party was the more influential of the two. Their identification might demonstrate loyalty rather than adherence to policy. For upcoming generations, whose first voting experiences were often involved with the Democrats, the picture could look significantly different.)

Another devastating criticism leveled at the aging over several decades is that they have a limited conception of the public interest—that they are unwilling to support programs for the public good which do not involve their own welfare, even that they are unsympathetic to the needs of the community. For example, old people are often cited as the major opposition to local school bond initiatives in their efforts to keep real estate taxes from rising. Yet this charge must be viewed in a larger framework. Along with fixed incomes, pensions, and the sharp reduction of income most experience at retirement, there is continuing inflation, particularly threatening to those who see no possible change in their income levels. It is hardly to be expected that such people would advocate increased public expenditures.

But the social system which disengages the older person also perpetrates a kind of psychological retreat from it; this engenders an isolation from society, encouraging detachment and disinterest. The classic work of Elaine M. Cumming and William E. Henry, *Growing Old: The Process of Disengagement,*[5] explains that older people go through an inevitable process in which many of the relationships with other members of society are severed, and those that remain are altered in quality. There is a decline in the number of people one interacts with and in the frequency of such encounters. Patterns of relationships between older people and their society are altered, since they no longer actively contribute to it. Finally, distinct personality changes occur in the aging as they become more preoccupied with self. In short, the "disengagement" theory maintains that as people age, the different roles assumed by an individual, the effect of these roles on others, and the number of personal contacts an individual has will decrease through time. There is a two-way process here: the individual is withdrawing from society, and society is so structured that it is served by this withdrawal and even fosters it for the benefit of the system. The last stage in this disengagement is, of course, death.

The trouble with this theory is that the study upon which it was based was conducted in Kansas City in the late 1950s, sampling only 275 people who were restricted in terms of class, race, and religion. They were white Americans, generally over fifty, 75 percent Protestant and 25 percent Catholic. No Jews, Orientals, Blacks, or Latin Americans were surveyed. They hardly are representative of the varied aims and energies of a pluralistic aging population in the 1980s. There are those who waited for, even long for, disengagement; there are also those who consider is a blow to their whole life's structure. To consider the person who has no wish to disengage from his or her activities in society as suffering from a form of maladjustment is to miss the point: that a diversity in the forms of aging is no less prevalent than the many varieties of lifestyle observable in adolescents and younger adults.

Which brings us to the crux of the matter. Any new movement, or the conglomerate of several movements, must build upon this diversity by incorporating into the action older people, who have different needs and hold differing philosophies of life. The America that has nurtured such diversity in its young must become the America which maintains it into later life. Not only must it accommodate every taste and every lifestyle, it must avoid partisanship. The lessons of the past have demonstrated this. Upton Sinclair's association with socialist causes led to unscrupulous, unprincipled attacks upon his EPIC structure as a "Red plot." Dr. Townsend's machinations and political bed-hopping with rightist groups brought upon the movement disillusionment from his vast membership and shouts of "collaborationism" in an America at the point of war with fascism. Such alliances can only complicate issues. The major challenge is to stay in the political arena to carry out one's expressed aims effectively, without being pushed into loyalty to either the Republican or Democratic parties. The issues upon which candidates stand and how they relate to older citizens must alone determine the position an organization for the aged will take.

History has alerted us to the Pied Piper syndrome, and the messiah movements: new and clever spokesmen offer to lead vast numbers into the light, and even unto the Promised Land. Such demagoguery will not serve, since it usually involves a corruption as characterized by Robert Noble or the Allen brothers. Today there must be safeguards against such antics within the democratic structures of the organizations.

Literally hundreds of organizations in America today are effectively involved in making decisions concerning the aged and their future welfare. In 1971 the White House Conference on Aging, recognizing the importance of such peripheral groups, extended over four hundred invitations to their representatives to solicit contributions to the cause. However, for the vast majority of these groups, only when their own major aims happen to coincide with age-related problems do they conduct intensive activity to effect a change.

Actually only about a dozen organizations can be considered *exclusively* absorbed in aging issues. These may be termed "pressure groups." Of the dozen, three organizations can be termed "mass movements," with a fourth gaining steady attention and an active membership. In June 1975, *New York Times* writer Nancy Hicks reported in a front page story on the growing sophistication of such organizations in the handling of their lobbyists in Washington.[6]

Probably the largest of all is the American Association of Retired Persons, which as of November 1979 reported membership of 13 million. The AARP includes the National Retired Teachers Association, which, though it retains a separate identity, is run by the same professional staff and maintains the same program and political stance. Actually the NRTA was the parent organization of the two. It had been founded in 1947 by Ethel Percy Andrus, a retired school teacher who had gained national prominence through her associations with the National Education Association and who became its crusading president. The NRTA's early goals were essentially apolitical, with emphasis placed upon what Henry J. Pratt has called "individual uplift" and "social betterment."[7] Dr. Andrus worked devotedly to improve the national image of older citizens; she believed that private enterprise could and should provide for most of the material needs of its former employees. The organization did have some legislative aims even then: the demand for higher state pensions for teachers and federal tax breaks for those already in retirement. But Dr. Andrus was convinced that each issue could be dealt with separately to relieve the growing financial anxieties of older Americans.

By 1955, while searching for low-cost health and accident insurance coverage for twenty thousand retired school teachers, Dr. Andrus encountered a sympathetic insurance broker named Leonard Davis of Poughkeepsie, New York. Davis had more than a casual interest in age-related insurance, and after some statistical research into the subject he was convinced, along with Dr. Andrus, that earlier assumptions of the insurance industry regarding the financial feasibility of low-cost policies were dead wrong. He put up $50,000 of his own capital, and thus persuaded Continental Casuality Company of New York State, followed by the Colonial Penn Group, to write a policy to cover NRTA membership. (Davis was quite correct in his prediction, and the investment has made him a wealthy man. In *The Washington Post* estimate, insurance held by NRTA-AARP membership by 1972 was valued over $184 million.[8])

The response was instantaneous and NRTA offices were deluged with five thousand applicants within several months. Dr. Andrus felt she had made a breakthrough. And the United States Department of Health, Education and Welfare officially approved of the plan, calling it a "significant social achievement." From this point on, as insurance demands increased and began to come from sources outside the teaching profession, the realization grew that a broader organization whose framework could serve all older citizens was needed. So in Washington D.C. on July 1, 1958, Dr. Andrus filed for a nonprofit membership corporation to be known as the American Association of Retired Persons. It has grown tremendously, and is easily the largest organization of its kind in the country. Membership grew from 150,000 in 1959 to 13 million in 1979.

The group's motto states, "Seek to satisfy the mind and heart, helping older people to create new patterns of independence, purpose and dignity." Specifically, the AARP makes available to its members "concrete tangible answers to as many pressing everyday needs as possible."[9] The organization has widened its services to include health insurance, discount drugs, sensibly priced travel group tours, discount book buying arrangements, driver improvement courses, and an institute of lifetime learning. Its membership receives its publications *AARP News Bulletin, Modern Maturity,* and *Dynamic Years,* reporting on community-service projects and the ever-changing legislative picture.

The vastly expanded organization retains its association with the Colonial Penn Insurance Group, which has provided counsel over the years, along with specified supplemental monies to offset the cost of administering its insurance programs. The influence of the insurance company is notable and entirely open (the masthead of the *AARP News Bulletin* clearly makes reference to its support by the firm), yet there are those currently questioning the legitimacy of such arrangements. The association undoubtedly places some limitation upon the group if it presumes to represent or to speak for the needs of *all* old people.

Political scientists have tended to picture the average member of the AARP as a former white-collar or professional person with distinctly conservative leanings. The organization has had an informal tie with the Republican party, specifically with the Nixon-Ford Administration. Its leaders have protested this image, describing their membership as representative of a cross-section of Americans, but the stereotype seems to stick. It might well come to be the major obstacle to the AARP's unchallenged image as the organization for every retired person.

The organization's social outlook has, in fact, been in favor of industry and management. This was well illustrated in 1959, when the Forand proposal on health care was before the House Committee on Ways and Means.[10] An alternate plan to Forand's was devised and presented by Ethel Andrus, calling for formation of a trusteeship staffed by representatives from the American Medical Association, American Hospital Association, and the United States Chamber of Commerce, among others, to administer a program by soliciting bids from competing insurance companies. And in 1965, the AARP was not an active spokesman for Medicare, presumably because it involved government instead of private industry.

Yet it should be noted that in recent years, and particularly during the able leadership of Bernard Nash from 1970 to 1976, the group has gained greater acceptance by Democrats as well as Republicans in Washington as a nonpartisan organization. However, it would seem that the AARP has distinct reservations about activism on a large scale. "I am worried about the protest image of the elderly," Bernard Nash was quoted as saying in reference to a march in Washington in June 1975 by three thousand members of the National Council of Senior Citizens to picket for subsidized housing. He added:

> Most older persons are not standing around with their hands out. . . . They desire an opportunity for first class citizenship to use a lifetime of experience to serve the community. I am alarmed at some organizations that show older persons (as) militant, demanding and self-seeking.[11]

The National Council of Senior Citizens, whose current membership is recorded at about 3 million, faces a problem not unlike that of the AARP. But this organization originated in the bosom of organized labor and is closely aligned with it. With the help of Walter Reuther and other leaders of the United Auto Workers, it was started for the specific purpose of assisting in the passage of the Medicare program. Richard Harris reports that Representative Aime Forand, a Democrat from Rhode Island and a prominent early supporter of health care legislation for the elderly, spearheaded the move:

> At the (1961) White House Conference on the Aging, Forand had gotten into a discussion with several union leaders who were considering whether it was desirable to organize older people to work for Medicare. Some of the men he talked to opposed the idea on the grounds it would inevitably lead to a kind of Townsend Movement. Among those who held this position was Nelson Cruikshank, head of the AFL-CIO's Department of Social Security.

> Then, in the summer of 1961, the two men who ran programs for retired workers in the AFL-CIO—Charles Odell of the United Auto Workers and James Cuff O'Brien of the United Steel Workers—decided to go ahead with the project on a part-time basis, despite the opposition of Cruikshank and other labor leaders. They presuaded their unions to put up small amounts of money and prevailed on Forand to lend his name as Chairman.[12]

It was not the first time that the labor movement had taken an interest in the affairs of the elderly. As early as 1916 Samuel Gompers had expressed an interest in providing governmental provisions for the aged, and in the 1930s while the Social Security Act was being shaped, the AFL solidly supported all proposals for the aged. However, organized labor was not lured into the early popular movements. Though a few union members joined the Townsendites, the AFL and the CIO were much involved in their own differences regarding pensions and social security disposition, and never offered endorsement for outside groups.

But in 1946 the unions jointly supported the Wayne-Murray-Dingel Bill, which aimed at expanding the Social Security Act, especially in the area of health insurance. The bill, however, met tremendous opposition, particularly in relation to its health care additions, and it never succeeded in getting out of committee. This was a considerable defeat. Meanwhile, the legendary individualist John L. Lewis of the United Mine Worker's Union, had managed to force the mine owners to grant a royalty on every ton of coal mined. This was to become part of a welfare fund from which pensions for the aged would be drawn. Strong demands and collective bargaining on the part of the unions for pension provisions resulted.

When the Social Security Act was amended in 1950, the UAW-CIO leaders took the credit, claiming that employers were so threatened by union successes in getting pension plans that they sought a more liberal social security law as a defense against further demands.[13]

Therefore, the National Council of Senior Citizens has been credited with a significant role in the passage of Medicare legislation. It has stayed active in national politics and grown both in membership and aims. Now it has over three thousand affiliated senior citizens clubs, composed of trade union, religious, ethnic, and social welfare groups.

The organization received its initial financial backing, though meager, as well as its professional staff (part-time on loan from the UAW) from the labor movement. By the late 1960s, the organization became self-supporting through membership dues. The group provides many valuable services like those offered by the AARP, and prints its own news organ. But its origin in the labor movement has meant stereotpyes for its membership. Despite efforts of its national leadership to broaden its image, a typical member is seen as blue-collar worker from the most heavily industrialized northeastern section of the nation, and usually sympathetic towards the Democratic Party. Moreover, its leadership has been consistently drawn from labor union sources and the movement reflects the style and rhetoric of its leaders who are given to calling one another "brother."[14]

As the organization became increasingly engaged in political issues and candidates, its steady if informal cooperation with the Democratic party has increased. Since 1964, the NCSC has supported various campaign affiliates representing presidential and congressional candidates, particularly those endorsed by organized labor. It has established a permanent action group known as Concerned Seniors for Better Government. Thus, despite its enormous growth and greater acceptance, the NCSC today faces the same difficulty with which the AARP group is attempting to cope: How to offer a convincing heterogeneity which truly speaks for *all* the aging in American society?

Yet another mass membership group, known as National Association of Retired Federal Employees (NARFE), has served the special needs of retired federal government employees. In 1978, this organization had a membership of about 275,000. Centered (since its founding in 1921) in the Washington metropolitan area, it has consistently pressed for greater benefits and cost-of-living increases for federal retirees.

Despite this, and in contrast with the ever-expanding AARP and NCSC, the federal employees group has shown less dramatic growth. This seems to be related to its less vigorous approach and to its specific attention to day-to-day problems of membership, with little concern for the broader social and economic implications of aging today. The group continues to wield considerable influence, however, as the publisher of *Retirement Life,* read by growing numbers outside of, as well as within, the NARFE.

There are many others active in the politics of aging. Trade groups like the American Association of Homes for the Aging, which is federated through all the states, and the National Council of Health Care Services, comprised of a group of commercial enterprises in the nursing home business, are just two examples. Supported by contributions and dues from affiliates, these groups preoccupy themselves with issues involving long-term care for the aged and the conditions affecting such care. Activities thus involve pressuring congressmen and government officials to maintain conditions favorable to the industry, which has not been something for Americans to be especially proud of.

Yet another trade association is the National Association of State Units on Aging (NASUA). This is composed of administrators from state government agencies who are supported by funds under the Older Americans Act of 1965 to provide technical and supervisory assistance to grant-in-aid programs throughout the states. A professional organization, The Gerontological Society, is also involved in developing new policies. Behavioral scientists, biologists, physiologists, social workers, architects, nurses, and administrators are united to pool their specialized resources. The society has taken legislative positions on many issues facing older Americans.

The National Council on the Aging (NCOA) works with other organizations (mostly public and private health, social work, and community action agencies), as a central national resource for planning, consultation, and training as well as producing communications and publications devoted to older people's problems. It evolved with the assistance of a Ford Foundation grant in the late 1950s. In the 1960s it developed ties with the NCSC and organized labor to help negotiate grants from the Department of Labor and the Office of Economic Opportunity.

Among the newer groups is the National Caucus on the Black Aged, a coalition of professionals, both black and white, which has joined enthusiastically in political lobbying for older black people. They have, in recent years, participated in aging conferences, met with administrators, and testified before congressional committees hearing old age issues.

Indeed, these groups and others on state and local levels are much in evidence in the political arena. They provide access to congressmen, public officials, and sometimes even the White House for millions of older Americans. Through them, aging issues can be exploited in the media, whether it be to expose conditions in nursing homes or discuss the effects of inflation on a fixed income population. As the main interpreters of the current interests of the aging, these mass membership organizations have the unique opportunity to make demands on politicians in what Binstock has termed the "electoral bluff."[15] They thus act as spokesmen interpreting the special needs of the older citizen to the politicians, who, not wishing to offend any powerful interest groups, are responsive to such pressures.

This is not an inconsiderable achievement. The growth and stability of such contemporary groups demonstrates the progress made since the razzle-dazzle days of Francis Townsend. Today's organizations have broadened their bases with less dependence upon charismatic leaders or on specific legislative issues. Their bureaucratic structures help to assure their administrative continuity. This was clearly demonstrated in the AARP when in 1967 its guiding founder Ethel Andrus died, and the group was able to revitalize itself, determined to continue her work. NCSC, having coalesced for the purpose of passing Medicare legislation, has continued even more forcefully with broader issues.

Significantly, leadership and administrative skill have been found among the young as well as the old. The prejudices which once understandably dictated the employment of older people *only* within older people's organizations have given way to the practicality demanded by the frenetic, changing pace of our complex political structure. The top elective positions of NCSC and AARP are now limited to those over 65 years of age, while the more pressured directorial commissions are open to younger men and women. (Bernard Nash and William Hutton both, when they undertook these jobs, were in their mid-forties.)

But the lesson that has been learned, and has sustained contemporary movements, is the groups' ability to balance for their memberships immediate benefits against long-range aims. Payment of annual dues offers immediate rewards of services like group travel fares, drug discounts, legal aid, group insurance. These are advantages for members as well as a means for providing generous support and income for their administration. The Townsendites saw this only too late: they did make attempts to offer benefits to their waning membership with items like Dr. Townsend's Old Fashioned Horehound Drops and Dr. Townsend's Toilet Soap, but they could not rescue a declining and defeated movement.

This steady source of income has provided the newer groups with solidity and permitted them to make heavier commitments to the building of public policy for the populations they represent. And in this role, they have come to be more accepted. The movements of the 1930s, '40s, and even the '50s met with opposition and angry public opinion on every front; their leaders were denounced as quack economists, crusading idealists, charlatans, and opportunists. The climate today has substantially changed. These organizations have gained a respected position as power-brokers in dealing with government agencies.

This new, receptive political climate is part of a massive change termed "interest group liberalism" by political scientists. In his 1969 book, *The End of Liberalism*[16] Theodore Lowi pointed out that interest groups representing specific sectors of the population —Blacks, Chicanos, women, Indians, and older people—rather than the assorted citizenry at large, were now the most influential in framing public policy. According to this concept, the public interest was best implemented through conflict and compromise between such pressure groups and the continuing impact they made upon legislators. During the Kennedy Administration such participation became viable as it had never been before. Groups which involved themselves actively in shaping national policy were rewarded, giving acceptance to the view that this is the essence of "participatory democracy." For the aging organizations, as for other interest groups, it meant opportunity, approval, and recognition on a scale unimaginable earlier.

Despite the great change and progress, we may ask once again, Where does this leave the majority of older Americans? Just what are the future prospects for more than 24 million citizens who are growing old in this country today? More than 5 million remain in poverty or hardly above the poverty level. Of the luckier ones, many more suffer from depression, live in isolation and fear, reluctantly accepting themselves as an "unwanted breed."

In fact, no matter how successful aging organizations appear to be, political analysts have repeatedly observed that their activities in national politics are "hardly militant or radical." In 1972, Binstock admitted that "their efforts do not reflect a vigorous pursuit of major changes that could bring about substantial amelioration to the problems of the disadvantaged aged."[17] At the American Academy symposium in 1974 he draws the following conclusion:

> If one looks briefly to forms of power other than voting and interest groups, are there alternatives for increased senior power in national politics? No, not very strong ones, *unless there are sweeping changes in the nature of American society.*[18] (Italics mine.)

Sweeping changes in the nature of American society! It is to such basic change in our lives that this book is dedicated; not just in the political but in the personal sphere as well. Until recently, political organizations for the aged simply have not addressed themselves to revolutionary questions.

A new group making just such a political appeal is the Gray Panthers. Whether it can have a lasting impact upon the life of older citizens in America is yet to be seen. Certainly it represents a departure from the other groups in that it can be described as *radical* in its approach and *militant* in its methods. Deploring an atmosphere which has alienated the old from our society, the Panthers are attacking rejection, exploitation, ridicule, loneliness, and abuse of the old in every form.

A recent cover story in *Esquire,* pretending at humor, printed such drivel as this:

> Face it, Americans hate old people because old people in America are eminently hateful. They whine, intrude, make you feel guilty, pretend they're senile, wear blue hair and pointy glasses and use the excuse of old age as a murder weapon. Accordingly, younger Americans retaliate by creating detention centers like nursing homes and Miami Beach to get the old out of sight. This is, for now, a splendid solution. But there are more young people today than ever before, which means there will be a God-awful number of old people in a few years. And what's even more awful is that one of them will be *you.*[19]

It sums up the kind of frivolous irresponsibility and sadism which passes for wit among the supposedly swinging and liberally tolerant audience of young adults.

Such twaddle is one form of a far more subtle and serious ailment. The Panthers have labeled it "agism," a form of discrimination as invidious as racism or sexism. Agism is defined as a "destructive force" by which a person is judged unsuitable by chronological age alone for professional, social, and cultural pursuits. In comparing the two as discriminatory phenomena, the Panthers liken agism to racism because:

1. Both are built-in responses of our society to persons and groups considered to be inferior.
2. Both deprive certain persons and groups of status, the right to control their own destinies, and the access to power, with the end result of powerlessness.
3. Both result in social and economic discrimination and deprivation.
4. Both deprive American society of the contribution of many competent and creative persons who are needed to deal with our vast and complex problems. This is a great social loss.
5. Both result in individual alienation, despair and hostility.
6. To be eliminated, both will require mobilization and commitment of national political processes and public and private institutions.[20]

Agism is "a societal illness' which permeates Western culture and its institutions, and essentially is the cause of attitudes and values which are self-perpetuating, thus supportive of the disease itself. The Gray Panthers feel they must focus first upon such basic issues in order to identify the symptoms in America today and only then to attempt their cure.

The organization was founded in 1970 by a group of six Greater New York Area people about to retire from various national, religious, and social service organizations, who discovered themselves facing retirement-reduced income and loss of contact with associates. The Gray Panthers at once displayed the vigorous militant stance they have taken ever since. From the start, the group's founders challenged the stereotype of the disengaged, uninterested retiree by devising a coalition of young (primarily attracting college students) as well as old members in driving for a strong power base. Pointing out that both groups suffer age discrimination at the hands of society, they offered to throw their weight towards a new alliance. Their strong position against the Vietnam War, their sympathetic attitudes towards those avoiding the draft, and their support of the nonviolent war resister gained them considerable loyalty among radical youth. In fact, in November 1971 during a conference in Washington on the plight of elderly Blacks, one of their number led a march to the gates of the White House with demands to end the war. Fannie Jefferson was arrested and released two days later only after the intervention of Arthur Flemming, chairperson of the then up-coming White House Conference on Aging.

The guiding spirit of the Panthers is a little woman over seventy named Margaret ("Maggie") Kuhn. She has unceasingly presented a walloping case for the movement. The Gray Panthers, she has said, are "a liberation group" out to "shake up society, to humanize it for everyone. . . . If we do that, we will make it easier for any age group." Maggie Kuhn talks the language of revolution. "The young and the old are natural allies in a revolution for new freedom and against wrinkled babyhood." The latter is a condition she describes as ". . . playing cards, shuffleboard, bingo or games all day long. Not growing, not exploring selfhood, not putting anything back into the community.

"This society," she goes on, "has never faced in any human way just what any kind of dependency means." She then quotes Alvin Toffler, the author of the best seller *Future Shock,* who recommends that old people today ought to be trying on the future for size. "No idea ought to be too extreme, or too radical. We've got nothing to lose. We've got a brain trust."[21]

So strong is the rhetoric from revolutionary movements that Ms. Kuhn insists her group is "not into service" but into action and "social change." The Panthers recommend to their membership the works of Saul Alinsky, an outspoken radical who openly deplores the liberal approach to reform. In *Reveille for Radicals,* Alinsky, in distinguishing between the liberal and the radical characters, tells us:

Since there are always at least two sides to every question and all justice on one side involves a certain degree of injustice to the other side, liberals are hesitant to act. Their opinions are studded with "but on the other hand." Caught on the horns of this dilemma they are paralyzed into immobility. They become utterly incapable of action. They discuss and discuss and end in disgust.

But the radical, continues Alinsky,

. . . does not sit frozen by cold objectivity. He sees injustice and strikes at it with hot passion. He is a man of decision and action. . . .[22]

Theirs, say the Panthers, is a coalition of groups acting with companionate goals as forces for liberation and self-determination. Existing groups with similar aims must not be regarded as competitors; on the contrary, they are to be seen as "co-conspirators" in a joint effort towards liberation. Once the Panthers have identified such groups, they must then "go underground" to infiltrate and radicalize them.

As spirited revolutionists, the Gray Panthers challenge rather than try to reform institutions that they accuse of oppressing people through their "agist" policies. Such institutions are "afflicted with a deep insidious paternalism offering little or no voice to the recipients in the governance and planning of their programs."[23] More service for the elderly is no solution, the group points out, since it ignores the basic lack of humanity behind such service systems. Their aim is to humanize the systems themselves.

"Gray Panthers" was not adopted immediately as the name of the movement. It was originally (and far less dramatically) dubbed "The Coalition of Older and Younger Adults." Then, in the spring of 1972, during an interview WPIX-TV in New York, the producer thought the term "Gray Panthers" far better highlighted the activist approach of the feisty new group. At first, its founders hardly considered it seriously; it was just a "fun name" to separate the doers from the sitters. "We hassled (with) the name for a year and a half" because of its associations with the violent Black Panthers group, explains Maggie Kuhn. "We wanted to show we were taking a stand—rocking the system—not just giving lip service. We decided that if the word 'Panthers' did turn some people off, we were glad. They weren't going to do much radical action anyway. . . ."[24] In any case, the press took up the name and it stuck; by May 1972 the national media did likewise and the movement has been gaining momentum since.

Unlike the AARP and the NCSC, the Panther organizational structure is minimal and informal; there is no apparatus for joining or card-carrying, no dues are required. It is composed of associates of local chapters and councils loosely and flexibly tied together by common goals. This informal structure is based on the "network principle"—people are social beings who meet people who meet others, reaching out into a community in a helterskelter way in which no formally structured organization could hope to recruit. Human beings naturally develop such networks, they tell us, growing into larger ones. Leadership is multiple, flexible, informal, and involves all kinds of people with a highly sophisticated division of labor. As Maggie Kuhn puts it, "When you think of the human resources old people represent in our society, it is kind of arrogant to assume that an elected slate of officers have all the knowledge or insight. Leadership is a dynamic thing, the ability to release responses in others, to develop a following." Thus a spokesperson becomes an "enabler" who releases experience in others.

The network principle, as the Panthers define it, should provide for a broadly based movement, rotating leadership so necessary for continuity in such an organization. At a workshop held at the Ethel Percy Andrus Gerontology Center at the University of Southern California in March 1975, Maggie Kuhn demonstrated the Panther organizational and training techniques. There, in cooperation with Tish Sommers, a representative of the women's liberation movement's newly organized Task Force on Older Women, (one of those groups with companionate goals) she called for participation from the assembled group of retirees, social workers, and professionals, in what she refers to as a teaching-learning situation, where "getting involved" and "unlearning the patterns of silence" were basic aims. Kuhn managed to engage the entire group in a conversation as natural as one held in one's own home, explaining that only in developing such skills in public speaking could their influence reach out to networks of people everywhere.

A technique borrowed from the women's movement, is that of consciousness-raising. Older people, they point out, must be made aware of society's pervasive view of them as "obsolescent," much like last year's automobile. Older people must recognize their own poor estimate of themselves, since it is often based on society's view; they must come to grips with self-hatred and self-rejection. Why, for example, should a man or woman want to lie about his or her age? Why should they feel complimented when they are thought younger than they actually are? Such re-examination can revolutionize attitudes. (We shall further discuss this in later chapters.) To implement their discoveries in consciousness-raising, Panther projects have suggested taking oral histories, with young people interviewing older ones. The exchanges have been a learning and developmental process and a revelation for both age groups.

The search for new lifestyles is reflected in Panther recommendations for solutions to the highly complex housing problems faced by most elderly people in this country. Maggie Kuhn, in an interview with the Center for the Study of Democratic Institutions, condemned the retirement community as "a plastic world, not a living world, one which isolates older people from the rest of life and from any interaction with society. . . ," a place to which people go because there are even less attractive alternatives, but which is no solution at all.[25] Instead, she proposed co-operative living arrangements where the same facility might be used for people of all ages, but with a particular concentration of people over sixty and under thirty. In the Panthers' home state of Pennsylvania such a plan has actually been devised but financial problems have stymied its enactment. Similar experimental housing projects are sponsored by Quaker groups in Philadelphia, where old mansions have been remodeled into attractive multiple units and installed with a generous mixture of age groups. In one such "life center," retired people, students, and divorced women with children live cooperatively, each benefiting from the presence of the others.

The Panthers attack other major issues facing old people with the same innovative approach. In late 1973 they merged with the Retired Professional Action Group, a subsidiary of Ralph

Nader's Public Citizen's Group, another activist organization which had attracted much national attention for its probes of nursing home abuses, pension plan systems, and forced retirement laws. The RPAG had just released results of an investigation of the hearing aids industry, demonstrating that there were exhorbitant profits in sales. Physicians, they pointed out, had virtually abdicated their responsibility to the deaf in this country by referring them almost exclusively to hearing aids manufacturers for advice and counseling. There were so many companies producing so many types of equipment that many old people found themselves confused and were consequently easy targets for victimization by unscrupulous dealers. In the RPAG campaign, young and old in five states joined forces for legislative action to check such abuses.

The Panthers have since taken on the American Medical Association by holding a demonstration in front of the group's national convention in Chicago (in June 1974) to attack the myth that "Americans have the best health care system in the world." And outside the organization's Atlantic City convention site they staged "guerilla theater" with a white-coated "doctor" auctioning off several old people. Their leaflets read: "How Much Is An Old Life Worth? What Did You Bid?"[26] The AMA *has* been guilty of gross neglect when it comes to older Americans—Panther demands have stressed the need for a "health care" system as opposed to the "disease care" system now in existence.

Panthers have tackled banking interests to demand free financial counseling services and free checking accounts; they have petitioned the public utilities for lower rates; they have even organized aging members of the clergy at Princeton Theological Seminary. They attempted to get a better mass transportation system in Philadelphia. To gain attention and "shake up the system," a Gray Panther suffering from lupus appeared at transportation authority hearings. The incurable inflammation of the nerves and blood vessels had left ulcerated lesions visible all over her legs. She carried with her a wooden box which was the exact size of the first step one encounters on local buses, demonstrating how impossible boarding any bus had become for people with infirmities of this sort, and that the use of mass transportation was virtually an impossibility for them. Her appearance certainly got the Panthers, now numbering over 10,000, the attention they sought (even though the tactics were reminiscent of the sensational days of earlier movements). And the group has had press and media people begging for more.

On the Dick Cavett Show, that generally unflappable TV personality literally jumped with applause when Maggie Kuhn delivered a stinging condemnation of an America where the "young are cut off from their own history, from their family groups, and old people are isolated and lonely." "Where" she went on, "technology has weakened family ties, destroyed neighborhoods" and "robbed us of the capacity to care for one another, to be truly human."

The Panthers have consistently stressed the role of the media in their campaigns for very particular reasons. Maggie Kuhn pointed out (to Chris Ames on KNX-FM Radio in Los Angeles) that the movement has "been intertwined with the electronic world from the beginning." The media are the key to their operation and success, a way for people everywhere who are cut off and alone to plug into the new possibilities for action.

Effective? For the moment, yes. Certainly while there are cover stories, newspaper editorials, invitations to meet with the President for mini-summit conferences—and as long as the Panthers get good TV ratings. Yet what happens when the media exhaust the subject, and their viewers, tiring of the tirades of the Panthers, tune out? What then, when their shock value has worn off?

Considering the network structure of which the organization is so proud, one wonders whether it will find other means of gaining attention or will wind up with its members left talking to one another—back to powerlessness. Outside of their own quarterly publication, the *Gray Panther Network,* it is difficult to imagine how national unity could be maintained without media attention. But many would argue that the real work for older Americans is happening *behind* the scenes, in the backrooms of the state capitols and in Washington, and that all the rest is mere fluff.

Even more critical is the question of whether the Panther stance, the activism and mod style which have characterized them, will antagonize too many? Have their incisive criticisms of American life and their "third world loyalties" offended? In short, can a movement hope to attract the vast numbers of diverse types of people aging in America today with their "wrinkled radicalism" approach? And is it the business of such a group to take a stand in *every* political fight, however remote from immediate old-age problems? (For example, their September '76 platform included planks for scaling down military spending, providing full employment and fighting world hunger.) The movement needs everybody it can get to achieve its goals. To gain that mass following it must combine the solidity of an AARP or NCSC with its own vital message of social change.

But whether or not the Panthers have staying power is not the issue. What is to the point is that they have provided a forceful outcry, airing ideas which can hardly be discarded with yesterday's newspaper. Their political thinking leads us to the *deeper,* more intimate problems to be grasped before activism can hope to succeed. Their success confirms what we have all known for some time: that American society has critically failed its growing numbers of old people, and that, even more crucial, unless the present and coming older generations act definitively to repair the devastation, there is little future here for any of us.

Part 2.

What Can We Do About It?

6.
The Search for Self

No self-respecting revolution can begin and end in the political arena. Vital as it may be to attack the issues in order to get legislation passed, and to fight the battles in state capitals and in Washington, this is only a fraction of the task. A far more intense upheaval is that which we face personally and internally. We must first cope with ourselves, the individuals we older Americans have become, in order to find the place we seek in the future of our country.

In the past we have fought old age. What we must do now is to fight *for* our old age—for our *right* to old age! We must fight for our right to the new choices and freedoms it entitles us to! This means freedom from routine, from rituals, and from the competition and hostility which are so characteristic of the earlier stages of our family and working lives. This means our right to open our lives to new thoughts, new arts, new skills. The right to fulfillment and meaning should be ours, not for just the first forty years, but for the *whole* of our lives. But instead of moving into a new realm with age we are phased out—shoved into the world of "nonpersons."

A new kind of alienation is developing in our country. It is alienation from the mainstream of our society, by which people are defined out of existence by seemingly impersonal and inhuman forces. A new type of outsider is evolving, as separate and

79

certainly as unequal as any of our now highly mobilized minorities. There are vast numbers of this new breed, and they are multiplying at an astonishing rate. These outsiders come in every color and every religion; they are instantly recognizable, yet they go virtually unnoticed. Like Blacks in Ralph Ellison's novel *Invisible Man,* who were easy targets for discrimination because they wore their difference on their faces and were ironically dubbed by the author *invisible* Americans, symbolizing their utter powerlessness in our society, so are our old people today.

Though they are everywhere around us, they are the unseen. If noticed at all, they are shunned. They are seldom taken seriously. A busy America confidently assumes that whatever knowledge they have is obsolete, that they have little to contribute, and that their power is nonexistent.

This phenomenon has been documented by researchers in gerontology. In 1965 Arnold Rose[1] use the term "subculture" in speaking of the aging and made distinct comparisons with American minority groups: Blacks, Indians, Mexican-Americans, etc. He predicted that older Americans will increasingly assume the characteristics of such groups. As a vast alienated minority (already larger than the entire Black population of America), their exclusion from contact with the majority culture has resulted in a turning inwards towards what he calls "self-segregation." We see them concentrated in groups in the central cities and in the "retirement communities" of Florida, California, and Arizona. They gradually come to depend only on one another, visiting with one another, eating with one another, telephoning one another. The chasm grows, until over 24 million people have taken on all the negative characteristics of a minority subcultural group.

Typical of a beaten-down minority, older Americans accept and are dominated by the image which the majority culture has imposed on them. They see themselves as they are seen, and it is a depressing portrait of general physical and psychological decline.

The myths and stereotypes which characterize aging Americans are familiar to us all: they dislike innovation, they are rigid, they seek only to maintain the "old ways" at all costs; or, they are irascible, cantankerous, and impatient; or, they are unproductive, preferring to withdraw from business and family life, and display little interest and less capability in making decisions; or, they are in "second childhood," moving from responsibility to complete dependency; or, their sex drive, much ridiculed, particularly by the media, is considered indecent or patronized as "cute" when it is not a subject for gross comedy.

Life in America is riddled with such outmoded stereotypes of old age. A self-image acquired through these distortions, simplifications, and exaggerations can only create a damaged ego, an unsure, limited, and handicapped individual. This describes the average older person in America today.

It is hardly surprising that Arnold Rose uses the term "group self-hatred" to describe this subculture. Much like the ethnic minorities, the aging have come to hate in themselves what the majority culture scorns and rejects, resenting the changes in their bodies, studying their faces for wrinkles, plucking out those first gray hairs. Even worse, they have come to doubt their continuing capabilities, to question their skills, and to distrust their own judgment. They have seen themselves reflected in the eyes of the young, have read the distaste in their expression, and have tactfully removed themselves from view. Like King Lear, they have willingly ceded authority to youth as being the more able, the more fit, the more right, and consequently have relinquished the power to control their own destinies.

Since old age is deplored, it is also greatly feared. Despite its inevitability, it is a state one must avoid. Many refuse to talk about it. Some do not allow themselves to be found in the company of anyone "over age," as though it were a communicable disease. But most commonly, Americans simply deny it—friends may age, parents and children and relatives may age, but in one's own mirror all remains forever youthfully serene. This stubborn resistance to identification with aging is visible at every level of American life, from the simple to the sophisticated.

This stance is one which many believe necessary for survival. To admit to being old is to admit defeat. Old age *is* defeat itself, and therefore should be denied, fought off. Not to do so denotes cowardice or a lack of spirit.

Simplistic perhaps, yet it is such a pervasive attitude that it goes unquestioned. It is in youth alone that one can possess beauty. How can a lined skin engage the eye? In youth alone there is excitement, spirit, and surprise, after which life can only grow stale and repetitive. Or so goes the popular myth.

Consider the long ago liberated and sophisticated writer Clair Booth Luce, who writes in the *Ladies' Home Journal* about a basically "disagreeable subject." She recommends to her readers that they cheat old age by aiming first and foremost at the goal of a "youthful appearance," and only secondarily at a "youthful spirit":

> Only last week you plucked out that hideous gray hair, and this morning there is another. And your scales tell you that somewhere along the line you've put on seven pounds—all in the wrong places. Might as well admit it: Some subtle, unfavorable change is taking place in that dear, familiar image in the mirror. It's beginning to look more like mother.[2]

Over sixty herself, she chatters on with cheery, chin-up admiration about older people who are "young at heart" and "refuse to grow old."

Clearly she is not alone. The popular press spews out How To Stay Young and How to Stop the Clock propaganda by the ton. Periodically, *Harper's Bazaar* devotes a special issue to aging. In its August 1975 issue, "How You Can Feel Fantastic From 40 On," the magazine cover displayed the perfect complexion of Princess Grace of Monaco and inside featured women whose over-forty faces were lovingly photographed by fashion's slickest magicians to reveal little trace of age lines. The spread on revitalizing over-forty hair showed society women whose supershiny silkysoft tresses could not be distinguished from those of the svelte young models in the book's advertising.[3]

But one comes to expect all this fantasy from *Ladies' Home Journal, Vogue, Harper's Bazaar, McCall's* and the others. Reality seldom invades Madison Avenue editorial conferences. And much of this nonsense can be dismissed as concerning only the jetsetting, cafe society superstars, or the aging beauty, male or female, whose looks are his or her fortune, and who must maintain a career by them.

But what about the many millions who find that getting old threatens them in their jobs, menaces them in their marriages, terrifies them in their daily encounters with the rejecting world? Consider the kind of services they receive in medicine, dentistry, in social work, and in psychiatry. If biological breakdown is inevitable and "natural," what can the scientists and medical workers do to help? It is useless to think we can hope to stabilize an aging body. This is where the negative image of old age does its greatest damage. Anyone who has accompanied an older person on visits to the doctor or consulted the doctor regularly in the interests of that person knows the skepticism with which complaints are greeted. Much is discounted on the basis that "old people need to complain," that they exaggerate, and that they are forgetful about taking prescribed medication. This negative and patronizing attitude can be found among the very best practitioners.

Even greater damage can be done in the ways many older Americans deny their age. They desperately try to conceal their awful secret, and become the willing dupes of swindlers and quacks. Vulnerable to misleading advertisements, get-rich-quick and make-money-at-home schemes, and other frauds, they are exploited, coerced, and often humiliated. Despite their reduced economic position, their social security, their pensions, and their return on investments and savings amount to a considerable market which attracts the most unscrupulous tricksters. Victimization of older Americans has been so widespread that the U.S. Senate's Special Committee on Aging has held periodic hearings over the last decade to bring some of the more scurrilous swindles to light.

In 1967 Senator Harrison A. Williams estimated that Americans over sixty-five control a purchasing power of about $40 billion a year. Though inflation undoubtedly has cut into this figure since then, there remains a sizable sum of spending power. Add to this the purchasing power of the "young-old," and a vast potential consumer market emerges—and not unobserved by the business world. But since the older group often lives in isolation, wanting desperately to be back in the swim of things, it provides the most fertile territory for the pitchmen. According to the Senate report, Americans are being bilked for "worthless nostrums, ineffectual and potentially dangerous devices, treatments given by unqualified practitioners, food fads and unneeded diet supplements, and other alluring products or services that make misleading promises of cure or end to pain."[4] The annual bill for this scandalous deception was estimated *at that time* (1967) at a minimum of $1 billion.

Among the most lucrative are the schemes which claim to provide the miraculous cure, instant health, sheer revitalization—the Fountain of Youth. One of the most popular of such nostrums is mere seawater. Sterilized and concentrated it has been touted as a panacea, claiming to rejuvenate, to "step up manly vigor," relieve arthritis, and prevent loss of virility, baldness, gray hair, anemia, cancer, diabetes, and even Parkinson's Disease, among others. The argument is that nutrients are "totally missing from our farmland, so that meat and potatoes, vegetables, are often sadly lacking in vital chemicals," but that they are now provided by the forty-four chemicals present in bottled seawater.

There are the hundreds of other products which purport to make the old healthier, more radiant, more athletic, more sexy, and above all more beautiful. They all sell for handsome profits—the sex pills known as "Stagg Bullets" or "Genuine Passionola," guaranteed to overcome impotency; the yogurt which insures the consumer that he will live to be a hundred; and the worthless obesity remedies that are often dangerous to the health and addictive. Add to this the gadgets, the "health machines" that are advertised to help "pep up the body and the mind"—the vibrators, the sun lamps, the slimming and the trimming devices offering "forces unknown to science" that will cure wrinkles and rejuvenate thinning hair!

Arthritis, a disease which many older people suffer from and for which there is no cure yet known, is an area of easy pickings for the quacks. There are bogus clinics operating throughout the country, administering treatments of alfalfa tea, distilled water, body baths in extreme water temperatures, and the exposure to beds of uranium ore. Copper bracelets are sold for up to $50 each, and mittens lined with radioactive uranium ore are sold at $65 a pair: these items are said to reduce inflammation. Millions are spent annually on such fruitless remedies by desperate sufferers.[5]

Then there are the social frauds. The promises of popularity, the "dance your way into somebody's heart" routines. The dance studio, long associated with shady possibilities, discovered the great potential in the older market some years ago. Sweet-talking, high-pressure salespeople have aimed their promises quite selectively at the lonely old. Their flattery, their personal approaches to the vanity of these unhappy people have served them well, and the victims have been taken by the thousands. One sales scheme is the "lifetime membership," through which a studio contracts to furnish several thousands of hours of dance instruction, to be paid in advance. (Some studios even sell "multiple lifetime memberships," whatever those could be.) It was reported at the Senate committee hearings that one seventy-one-year-old widow mortgaged her house to pay up the $32,600 total for her "several" memberships, even while she lay in a hospital bed with a knee injury from which her doctors thought she might never walk again.[6]

Such madness and vanity might seem merely laughable—but desperation and emotional starvation loom up to spoil the comedy. There are only the few cases that have been investigated; consider the countless numbers whose humiliation silences their grievances.

The same terror of the infirmities of age figures in sales of dentures, hearing aids, and eyeglasses. Mail order and fly-by-night outfits rather than regular medical channels profit because of customers' limited resources; but often they pay more for unqualified people who produce inferior work in ill-fitting appliances. These "specialists" maintain that there is no need to see a proper dentist, for instance, that dentures can be fitted better by those who manufacture them.

The possibilities for swindle in the hearing aids business are even grander, since loss of hearing is the kind of infirmity felt to be particularly compromising to a self-image. Many never admit to it, and struggle to maintain an illusion. Among those who do purchase equipment, many have fared little better. An elderly person, for example, was sold two sets of hearing aids: the first, costing $700, was for herself alone, while the second, an additional $600, was a "special device to be hooked to her television set."

Undoubtedly, however, the juiciest frauds are perpetrated by the wrinkle quacks. The willing victims are those older people who see youth as life itself, and who will go to any lengths to recapture youth, often at the expense of life. E. J. Kahn describes some of the wilder schemes caught by the Inspection Service of the United States Post Office.[7] He details the incredible career of Cora Galenti, a self-styled facial rejuvenator who averaged $3,000 a patient, cash in advance, over a thirty-year period. This colorful, highly successful, six-times married lady, who'd had no medical, scientific, or even cosmetological training, used an extraordinary method: the repeated application of 100-proof carbolic acid solution to the faces of her eager clients! This acid is often used in disinfecting toilets and drains, and is highly toxic even when diluted; it had been used by doctors to remove warts, but always cautiously—and certainly never on the face. Severe burns and a loss of pigmentation, and most often weltlike keloid scars could result. The acid could enter the bloodstream through the skin to damage the kidneys and the bladder. When the burns were bad enough, shock, toxemia, or septic infection could cause death. If and when such burns began to heal, there was indeed a tendency for the face to swell, which resulted in a smoother, somewhat tighter look to the skin. This was the "new face for the old" that Cora Galenti hawked.

The case of Cora Galenti is not an isolated one. In the 1920s a Kansan named John Romulus Brinkey's scheme for rejuvenation involved the implantation of goat glands. It made him rich and famous. Currently, the fashionable Rumanian, Dr. Ana Aslan, of the Bucharest Geriatric Institute, claims that her regenerative formula has been tried by one hundred thousand people in 144 Rumanian clinics, including such celebrities as the late Charles de Gaulle and Nikita Krushchev. Known as Gerovital H3, which is essentially novacaine with a few preservative ingredients added, it is said to forestall degeneration by producing hormones which elevate the mood and submerge the depressive tendency so common in older people.

An expensive but much talked-about treatment is known as "cell therapy." Originally developed by the Swiss doctor Paul Niehans, it consists of the injection of sterilized and refined cells from the organs of unborn lambs. Though the process was kept highly secret, the theory held that cells from different parts of the animal's body are considered particularly effective in the cure of specific ailments. For example, placental cells were specific for angina and high blood pressure, hypothalamus cells a cure for impotency, and heart cells aided in diseases of the heart. Although Dr. Niehans died in 1971, Ellen Switzer reported in 1974 that his clinic was still attracting a large clientele and that cell therapy was growing more popular, particularly in England and Germany, where dried rather than fresh cells are used, thus reducing the immediate need for the slaughterhouse.[8]

The huge cosmetic firms in America are not far behind in their research. Hampered by more stringent government drug controls, they currently reject the Aslan/Niehans type of approach because interference with the formulation of hormones or their stimulation may be too risky. The current rejuvenation fad in this country is to be found in the potentially miraculous properties of vitamin E, both in terms of retarding changes associated with pigmentation in aging, and in prolonging life. The latter claims are based on experiments with mice, which, fed vitamin E daily allegedly lived 25 percent longer. Extensively marked already for its antioxidant value in deodorants, vitamin E is touted as the new "youth pill," yet scientists remain highly skeptical, maintaining that mice are not men, and that human aging processes are certainly no "single oxidative process" that can be remedied by massive doses of vitamin E, which in fact can be harmful.

Such research will inevitably proceed, and who knows what progress will be made by the turn of the century? Yet for those of us presently expecting up to twenty-five more years of life, how quixotic, how futile this pursuit of youth seems! In the same way as we may rejoice at the sight of astronauts walking on the moon, so man's aspirations toward immortality may move us. But the real question for us is, How can these efforts to prolong youth and life figure in our daily existence? In the past, fear and desperation alone have dictated our frenzied pace. Only after a reexamination of ourselves can we construct what should be the major, not the waning, portion of our lives. First we must become visible, throw off disguises, come out of the shadows, and walk into the light. We must begin to exist as mature individuals, not as masquerading versions of our former youthful selves. To be seen differently by society, we must first see ourselves differently.

Consider the revolutionary impact upon our society when Black Americans woke up to the fact that their own self-image had been cultivated by the majority white culture. As late as the 1950s, from the moment of their first exposure to first-grade primers, black, brown, and all minority children had rarely seen themselves truly represented in the popular press. They learned with us to admire the human ideal as it was pictured in school, in comic strips, in newspapers and magazines, and most of all, in the movies. Always white, this ideal was often blonde and blue-eyed, with straight hair and thin lips. No amount of hair-straightening, skin-bleaching, or cosmetics could put things right. It wasn't until Black became Beautiful on bumperstickers and the most popular hairstyle in the country was the natural that a dumbfounded but admiring America saw a new kind of person emerging.

Yet *older* Americans today still are trapped in the image imposed by the majority. Since the majority usually prefers to ignore their existence, they remain invisible. If we thumb through the advertisements in the slick magazines, we'll scarcely find a single photograph of an older person. Startling was the sight, in a special supplement, "Fashions of the Times," of a handsome seventy-five-year-old woman modeling the clothing of her choice, loose-fitting, brightly colored, handwoven cotten tents. An expert in the Japanese tea ceremony, and interested in Zen meditation, chanting, and prayer, this slightly offbeat woman is described as "fearless about fashion," one who never buys "clothes for style," and who "hates diamond and furs." And the writer hastily explains, "The fact that she is seventy-five seems completely irrelevant in context with her life."[9]

But how rare is even such bizarre attention. Where are pictures of the scores of grayhaired, wrinkled women who *do* buy the diamonds and furs? They remain unseen, above all in the full-page, full-colored advertisements peddling those wares. And where are the people whose contours have naturally grown thicker with age? Where in the marketplace are the innovations in clothing for their bodies? Better to deny that such figures exist: the once-slim body must be retained despite nature's inclination!

While To Be Old remains synonymous with To Be Ugly, there is little hope of breaking through the defeatist but popular stance.

For the subliminal message purveyed by every skin cream, hair coloring, girdle, and bra ad for as long as anyone can remember is—"old is ugly." The subculture of the aging which Arnold Rose delineated over ten years ago is today an alienated, segregated, isolated, and devalued group whose treatment *Time* once quoted the Nobel prize novelist Saul Bellow as likening to a "kind of totalitarian cruelty" similar to "Hitler's attitude towards the Jews." He added ruefully, "It is as though the aged were an alien race to which the young will never belong."[10] How can the young ever conceive belonging to that "race" when the aged themselves refuse to admit it?

Here then is our first task: to begin the search for ourselves. We must learn to discover the natural beauty in faces with laugh lines, to find satisfaction in less angular, fuller bodies, in gray hair, in slower movements and an easier carriage.

Beauty has eternally been a complicated state of body and mind. Its composition remains a mystery. In light of this new consciousness of ourselves, consider the image which can and will emerge: the beauty to be found in composed features, in a calm demeanor and serene presence; the grace of smooth, deliberate movement so characteristic of the dignity of older people; the subtlety in expression; that sparkle which only comes with experience and wisdom; the sexual appeal of those so knowledgable in the art. We must search out in ourselves the beauty that is there. We must see it and appreciate it.

First then, we need a physical rediscovery—the demand that our own standard of beauty be recognized—to be followed by an even more exacting task—the reclamation of the psyche. This means, first, liberation from the myths that have enslaved and victimized the minds of older people and have produced the vast, isolated, subservient and submissive group we now have. The old have unquestioningly accepted society's judgment in such vital matters as the impairment of their learning abilities, the inability to perform new tasks, the incapacity to solve problems, the inflexibility in making decisions, even the inevitability of memory loss. This image has persisted despite mounting evidence from psychologists demonstrating that age alone does not account for such changes. As Clark Tibbits reports, the literature is rich in studies searching for visible changes in the central nervous system, perceptual capacities, and the continuing ability to organize and use information. Scientific experiments into intellectual and motor performance, changes in speed of intake or output in learning, memory, or creative thought all seem to demonstrate that any decline occurring in the normal aging process is "highly differential and very gradual." In fact, many of these skills improve with age, notably reasoning and oratorical abilities. The evidence shows that mental competence may well remain unchanged as late as the seventies or eighties.[11]

Shura Saul, a practicing gerontologist, has pointed out that environmental stress (fear of failure) is far more often responsible for inhibition or slowed responses,[12] a viewpoint shared by many psychologists. So, this situation is most often a circular one where performance and ability are reduced by circumstances themselves. For example, young minority secretaries, when tested at employment agencies (often by members of their own race), may do competent speed-typing and shorthand, only to find that in a hostile, all-white environment on the job, their skills suddenly decline and sometimes evaporate altogether. Frightened, panicky people, young *and* old, do not perform well; yet for the aging such failure is immediately associated with deterioration and senility.

"The reclamation of the psyche" finds many battles to be fought. One is the recovery of the vital roles that we have openly relinquished to the young, thus abdicating our position of leadership. For example, we discussed earlier the willing abandonment by Americans of their roles as grandparents. Margaret Mead regards this chiefly as the result of our fanatic preoccupation with independence and privacy. She writes:

> We have reached the point where we think the only thing we can do for our children is to stay out of their hair and the only thing we can do for our daughters-in-law is to see as little of them as possible.[13]

She laments that the old devote most of their energies to "looking cheerful" and "not being a burden." Why have old people denied their proper roles? Is it not that the majority culture has scorned these roles as superfluous? Young parents, considered all-wise, were not to be interfered with by the old folks with their old ideas.

And we can see the disastrous results for the generations which have come of age without the guardianship or companionship of grandparents. These new generations show little interest in older people, and seem to have no stomach for infirmity or frailty of any kind. Are these to be considered a new breed, a higher step in the evolution of the human species? Or are they more likely just casualties of a chaotic social change, who lack perspective, even humanity, precisely because they have never themselves experienced an intimate relationship with the other generations around them? And the other generations are indeed their connections to mankind.

This is but one major role lost to the old in our time. Others must be recaptured in the community, business, government, religion, and the arts. But we must first cast aside what is basically a bankrupt lifestyle, a style which condemns us to live a lie.

To begin with, fathers cannot continue to be merely brothers to their sons, or mothers their daughters' sisters. Instead of pretending that we are no different from the young, we older persons must affirm our right to be different, and demonstrate it. The eminent psychiatrist Carl G. Jung, in a now classic essay, observed that people would scarcely reach seventy or eighty if such longevity had no special meaning for the species:

> The afternoon of human life must also have a significance of its own and cannot be merely a pitiful appendage to life's morning. The significance of the morning undoubtedly lies in the development of the individual, our entrenchment in the outer world, the propagation of our kind and the care of our children. This is the obvious purpose of nature. But when this purpose has been attained—and even more than attained—shall the earning of money, the extension of conquests and the expansion of life go steadily on beyond the bounds of all reason and sense? Whoever carries over into the afternoon the law of the morning—that is, the aims of nature—must pay for so doing with damage to his soul. . . .[14]

Jung saw even then the mistakes that have grown into our current problems. The propaganda of the youth culture has convinced us that youth is the best, if not all, that life has to offer. The hope that mankind has for youth does not recognize that both youth and middle age are caught in a web of biological and tribal rituals—courtship, mating, childrearing, and providing for a family—and that it is only after years of conformity and service that the prospect presents itself for the creation of a free spirit. It is very likely that the old are mankind's real hope. But many never recognize their potential for a newfound freedom, and those who do, find limited opportunities to make use of that potential in America today.

How often do we read of women in "empty nest" depression, or of fifty-year-old business executives having nervous breakdowns? These people are merely reflecting a culture that encourages mastery through action, progress, and success. For forty or fifty years they find little time for the inner self. They dash about in all directions, never once pausing until that dreadful crashing moment when "old age" is upon them. Emptiness, depression, and helplessness accumulated over half a lifetime fall upon their heads and they are wholly unprepared to face the moment. Jung, noting this phenomenon, wonders why we provide no colleges for forty-year-olds, much like those for our young, to prepare them for their coming life as elders and its demands—for the afternoon of life as well as the morning.

Psychologists have only recently begun serious study of lifelong habits in the uses of time, its meaningfulness and its meaninglessness. Just as certain activities may naturally please one participant and repel another, so certain actions may seem altogether rewarding in one stage of life while exasperating and futile in another. Charlotte Buhler has pointed out that from ages forty to sixty, many people show a distinct tendency to search for inner order or equilibrium and integratedness, and that such an examination of values can lead to an emotional crisis.[15] For those who have systematically avoided such questions, it is at these times, when the children have left home, or when a new younger talent usurps a promotion, that shattering discoveries are made. What often follows is a loss of direction and purpose, and worse, a realization that the efforts of half a lifetime may be utterly useless for the coming years. For these people aging is a kind of condemnation, a circle of hell in which they must remain unheeded spectators while the dynamic world proceeds without them.

Until people such as these understand that a meaningful life is not inextricably bound to the obsessive preoccupation with success and wealth and the American work ethic, and turn themselves towards questions of self-expression, fulfillment, and free choice for the individual of all ages, there can be little hope for revolutionary change.

We've already seen that age consciousness is growing steadily among older people, and with it a new awareness of its political potential. This must go hand-in-hand with the development of personal pride and the dignity of becoming a mature individual.

7.
Body Worship: What's Fit, What's Fad

Of the many popular assumptions we accept, probably the most deleterious for the aging is the supposition that the human body is merely a machine—an ingenious, efficient device, but just a mechanism. For older people, the analogy is positively destructive, because it suggests that, like a machine, the very *use* of the body deteriorates it.

There are indeed many parallels between machines and people: both need fuel or food to function; both must be attended and maintained to operate smoothly; and both show "wear and tear," tend to "run down," and finally just plain "wear out."

Folksy talk, but harmful and patently untrue. According to the British gerontologist Irene Gore, every single thing we have learned from biological research since World War II has demonstrated just how superficial this idea is.[1] The machine, automobile, dishwasher, or diesel engine, once manufactured, is the sum total of what has been constructed and no more. The materials therein will serve just as long as their matter allows, and good care and treatment preserve them. But *these* are inorganic contraptions, dead substances incapable of renewing themselves. For them, use does cause their deterioration.

The human being is a *living* organism, existing in "a state of dynamic equilibrium." Unlike machines, we are not merely the matter which is put together at our birth, a genetic accident, un-

95

changing and static. We are growing, reproducing, renewing, responding beings through the entire span of our lives. In order to survive, our bodies are constantly in production. The human body is an ever-resourceful entity, always sensitive to its own needs. In a process called metabolism, we "synthesize" matter in continuing chemical activity, renewing and revitalizing its functions throughout life.

There isn't a machine invented yet that can repair itself. We heal our fractures, grow new skin over our wounds, adapt to all sorts of conditions—cold, hunger, polluted air, lack of space. We defend ourselves against disease with complicated immunological systems. What human being was ever so limited as a machine? Such mechanisms transport us, wash our dishes or our clothes, even do higher mathematics; but can they be taught a new skill or trained to perform a function other than what they were designed for? Can they surprise us or delight us with hidden talent? Can they make us laugh?

So, such mechanistic rubbish about our bodies only reduces and demeans us. We must refuse to accept it. As Dr. Gore stresses, it can lead us to the fallacious conclusion that the best course for the aging is to preserve themselves, to slow down, ease up, prevent that wear and tear and stave off deterioration, in hopes of prolonging their lives.

But inactivity, sluggishness, and bodily sloth can have the opposite effect. The human organism must maintain itself, *must use, move, and act—to be and stay whole.* Physical activity is part of being alive, a natural stimulus to which our whole person responds. Without it the body stagnates. It is not simply a matter of preventing flabbiness or tightening muscles—it involves all our bodily functions: proper digestion, good circulation, deep breathing, muscular control, balance, easy movement of the joints, and so on. This is not just a program for staying alive, but one for living—an individually planned program, designed and adjusted for each of us.

This is probably the first time in human history that we have a choice as to *how* we shall age. Earlier generations, threatened by famine, epidemics, wars, poor hygiene, or poor nutrition, labored till their dying day, and in most parts of the world people still do.

Our own society, despite continuing setbacks, has largely freed itself of such threats. As a nation of "retirees," for instance, we can choose between activity and inactivity. We alone can decide between a sedentary, automated daily life, or one which remains physically demanding. The direction is clear, though the path may differ for each person.

Recent medical research studying fitness for older people tells us that even if you've spent the better part of your life inert, doing nothing for your body, you can still profit handsomely from exercise in later life. To demonstrate this Herbert deVries experimented with 112 people whose ages ranged from fifty-one to eighty-seven years as part of a two-year study financed by the Administration of Aging of the U.S. Department of Health, Education and Welfare. He went to Laguna Hills Leisure World, a large, affluent retirement community in Southern California, to choose his sample —a group of upper-middle class Caucasian males who had never been athletic and who, in fact, came to the program with some skepticism and resistance. *Time* magazine, impressed with the progress of forty-six participants in the initial phases of the study, reported that "within six weeks the difference between the exercisers and the nonexercising group of twenty-six men in the same age range was profound," and that the "bodies of septuagenarians" acted like those of "forty-year-olds." When tested, deVries' subjects showed an average of "4.9 percent drop in body fat, a 6 percent reduction in diastolic blood pressure, a 9.2 percent rise in maximum oxygen consumption (the best single index of vigor, according to deVries), and a 7.2 percent increase in the strength of their arms. . . ."[2]

As the program progressed the gains were even more noticeable. At eighteen and forty-two week intervals, repeated tests on the group, now much enlarged, continued to show steady gains in strength, endurance, and agility. So much so that deVries feels he has conclusively demonstrated not only that "controlled exercises can be both safe and beneficial for older people" by improving their basic bodily functions, but more significantly that those who had been "least active in youth and middle age" could "benefit most from such exercise programs."[3]

During this same period Lawrence Frankel was conducting

similar programs in and around industrial Charleston, West Virginia. The *Preventive Care* participants, as they were called, differed from deVries' group in that they were both men and women and were selected from low-income families, many of whom admitted to never having participated in any sports in their entire lives. Several were found to have serious medical problems such as emphysema and heart disease. Yet after ten weeks of carefully supervised, individually planned activity, testing on stationary bicycles revealed dramatic changes in performance capacity. Frankel's program began to be known as "recycling old people into new," because participants soon walked better, danced better, even laughed more.[4]

Some record-setting older athletes began strenuous physical exercise late in life, often after years of sedentary patterns. George Leonard describes the wonderful accomplishments of Paul Spangler of San Luis Obispo, California, who, starting ten years ago, is now close to eighty and running six miles in forty-five minutes. And he keeps beating his own record. Leonard refers to the "fastest growing and most exciting field in sports—Masters Track and Field":

> The feats of the Masters-men and women of ages forty to one hundred plus—are drastically altering current medical ideas on aging. They are shattering the stereotyped thinking that goes with such terms as "middle aged" and "senior citizen." And they are forcing us to realize that standard definitions of human potential have probably been set ridiculously low all along the line.[5]

Pole vaulters, high jumpers, Senior Olympics champion runners, and javelin and discus throwers from around the globe are similarly demonstrating that physical fitness is fitting at every age.[6]

Scores of physical education specialists have come to similar conclusions for every age group. Leonard Morehouse, the exercise physiologist who directs the Human Performance Laboratory at UCLA, confirms this view in his popular book, *Total Fitness*. "An inactive life," he says, "is a slow form of suicide. The right kind of exercise buys years." Longevity may not be the ultimate result of exercise, but evidence demonstrates that "if we don't exercise regularly we are hurting ourselves—lessening our capacity for living, reducing the number of active years in our lives, and probably shortening our life span."[7]

Not ten years ago, we Americans were accused of being the world's heaviest smokers and drinkers, the flabbiest, most indolent, idlest, most indulged adults on earth. That has certainly changed. Americans of every age are jogging, swimming, playing tennis, running track, doing yoga exercises and pumping their bicycles. The trouble with most of the advice in these physical fitness programs is that many of their authors ardently worship the *young* body above all, convincing their readers to keep their youth and "not look their age." So they are of little help to us. What we do, we do to cultivate our bodies, for our growth and our pleasure alone—not in some nostalgic, vain search for the youthful physiques of our past. We must cull out what is important to our group from the reams of literature being churned out. We must isolate what suits our own bodies, ruthlessly discarding the rest to those who want to believe in the fantasy of preserving their youth forever.

There is much to be learned from current work in the field, if we read such research, not to prevent ourselves from growing older, or even to prolong life, but with the attitude of maintaining *good* living for all the time we are alive. These new books can alert us to some dangers we face in everyday living and ways we can fight physical hazards that threaten the health of our mature years.

For example, consider the whole question of nervous stress. Fitness experts insist that developing the ability to relax is a vital skill in which we must train ourselves, a tool through which we can improve the quality of our lives. Difficulties in countless daily situations, pressures, anxieties, and crises can cause the muscles of the body to tense up, with aches and pains in the neck, back, and arms. Such distresses can also increase blood pressure and cause adrenalin to flow into the bloodstream. Nervous stress is a destructive force that can cause many serious illnesses, particularly in our most vulnerable years.

One early researcher in relaxation methods was a Chicago doctor named Edmund Jacobson, who in the 1930s demonstrated the effects of stress on diseases like asthma, high blood pressure, and some disorders of the stomach and colon. Jacobson pioneered the idea that nervous tension, though certainly a part of the normal action of the human system, was also a great destroyer when out of control. Enlisting the help of Bell Telephone Laboratory engineers, he devised instruments to measure electrical changes in muscle tension levels. He thus furnished the means for evaluating the nervous system's activity even when an individual was supposedly at rest. Jacobson then went on to prove mechanically what had long been suspected: that controlled exercise could do a great deal to relieve such tensions.[8]

Specific use of Jacobson's devices was made by deVries in the late 1960s with his older group from Leisure World. By putting these electronic meters to work in his own laboratory, he noted that as his group exercised and their physical condition improved, so did their ability to relax. He concluded that the relaxed older individual thinks and works better and has far fewer health problems.

Since then other investigators have been probing causes and effects. Hans Seyle of the University of Montreal, one of the foremost experts in the field, has emphasized the havoc nervous tension plays with the body. Through experiments with animals, he has demonstrated that stressful conditions, extremes of temperature, loud noises, and frustrations for extended periods of time developed dysfunctions like peptic ulcers and enlarged adrenal glands.[9]

Recent research has called particular attention to the role of stress in the development of coronary heart disease, now commonly referred to as America's number one killer. Such research has alerted us to why exercise helps alleviate such strains on the system. Every year some 700,000 Americans, young and old, die of heart attack, which in large proportion afflicts them through coronary atherosclerosis—a process in which fatty deposits line the walls of arteries and eventually narrow and choke them. Such "atheromas" are formed primarily of cholesterol or saturated fats, and since tensions, among many other factors, tend to elevate the blood cholesterol level, continuing pressures can contribute to their accumulation and final calcification and "hardening" of the arteries. Modern man responds to the many frustrations in life the way he does to danger itself, in what M. F. Graham has called the "fight or flight mechanism."[10] This means recurrent secretions of adrenalin increase blood pressure, to make for a higher pulse rate and a tighter muscle tension, thus providing for the expression of such rages, conflicts, and fears. The trouble is that in our world the natural outlets for such stresses are mostly inhibited. We repress, suppress, swallow what irks us, seldom "working out" the extra supplies delivered to our bloodstream for such emergencies. The result is a vicious cycle of more tension and more anxiety. Eventually, scar tissue replaces fatty matter, and finally calcification occurs—a blockage which can cut off blood supply and life itself.

Contemporary cardiologists have found in exercise the perfect substitute for the primitive reaction of "fighting it out," a readily available and natural means for altering the seemingly unalterable patterns of contemporary life. Nowadays doctors speak of "trained" and "untrained" hearts. The trained one responds to activity easily because it has a larger capacity, the ability to pump more blood with each beat. The untrained one must increase its beat rate to accomplish the additional work. It was once thought that the trained or "athlete's heart," a muscle which tended to enlarge with continued workouts, could become a hazard, or even "use itself up." On the contrary, the increase in size, which is actually quite minimal, can achieve more work with fewer beats. So this trained mechanism is merely the *proper* development of our potential cardiac reserve. This is demonstrated after heavy exercise, when the beat rate of even the best trained heart accelerates. Recovery for this individual is much more rapid and the effort proves invigorating instead of exhausting, the latter being a common reaction of the untrained specimen.

If exercise alone cannot be considered the one and only answer to atherosclerosis and heart attack, it is at least the best known method of checking these conditions. This is but one major medical problem facing us. Exercise has been found to have beneficial effects on all sorts of serious disturbances—respiratory, hormonal, coordinational, digestive—in short, it can have a profound effect on our total bodily function. Since older people are particularly prone to such infirmities, this is clearly news for us.

But the most obvious effects of exercise might prove the most crucial. Stronger muscles provide a stronger skeleton, one which supports the spine with firmness and security. From exercise we derive postural gains, the ability to align the structural foundation, to gain a poised stature, and to distribute weight. Correct posture can be a liberation, for it means escape from aches and pain. Another byproduct of exercise is untroubled mobility, that protector of independence; while we can get about with ease and agility, our lives are our own. Fear of falling is critical for many aged, because once immobilized, a human being is weakened further by inactivity in slow convalescence. It's a fearful cycle of inactivity, lower resistance to infection and diminished vitality. Physical solidity and stability on one's feet derive from steady exercise and are the best insurance against injuries from falling and bone breakage.

Best of all, continuous and controlled physical exertion brings an easy release for the tired body by inducing sleep, "the innocent sleep," as Shakespeare said, "that knits up the raveled sleeve of care." To very many older people who fight a continuing battle with insomnia, this particular byproduct can be the decisive one.

Exercise is only one of the preoccupations of current research. Books abound on the ill effects of smoking, for example, or backache and its prevention, or stomach troubles. An enormous literature has grown up around the foods we choose and our habits in eating them. Library shelves are groaning with schemes for battling obesity, for weight loss, for eliminating cholesterol, for avoiding constipation, diarrhea, heartburn, and hemorrhoids. Surrounding us are vegetarians, health food devotees, yogurt enthusiasts, and vitamin poppers—all striving for prevention, management, or cure through "natural" eating.

Again the question arises, What benefit is there for older people in such food fads and fashions? Certainly the importance of nutrition goes unquestioned The balanced diet is ever a necessity, in youth as in age. It must supply us with all the substances we need for maintaining our health and for providing energy and vigor. A well-nourished person is one who has supplied sufficient protein, roughage, vitamins, and minerals for his daily needs, and who keeps to a minimum his consumption of starchy and sweet foods. This generally means a balanced diet, including meat, poultry, fish, salad, vegetables, fresh fruits, cheese, milk (and plenty of fluids), eggs—all in moderate quantities and all properly chewed.

But the latest literature reminds us that eating enough or even "plenty" is not necessarily nourishing oneself. One can become obese and undernourished at the same time, the two are not mutually exclusive. And for older people even mild obesity puts additional and unnecessary strain on the heart while reducing mobility and agility. As Jean Mayer has pointed out in discussing obesity and the aging, "Even in the absence of any visible improvement in muscular strength, a weight reduction also decreases the probability of further locomotor disabilities consequent to arthritis, cardiovascular disorders, or accident."[11] When doctors such as the popular David Reuben attack American eating habits as the cause of our susceptability to degenerative diseases and the shocking state of our general health in later years, we must keep in touch with such research. It could prove of great interest to older Americans.[12]

There are many for whom these and other nutritional schemes are providing digestive relief; and others for whom they have brought about a renewed interest in balancing their diets and avoiding obesity. This is all to the good. Certainly, as we have already noted, there are far too many old people living alone in America today who are undernourished. The reasons for this are many and varied, with emphasis upon the growing financial problems plaguing them (to be discussed fully in chapter 10). Also note that those cooking for just one person often regard it as dreary or an unnecessary nuisance. They may grab a morsel, a bite at this and that, seldom sitting down to a nourishing hot meal. Such aversions and negligence may relate to early associations; eating has been, for most, a social occasion, part of a continuing ritual in family life. There are older women, for example, who at earlier stages of their lives were acclaimed as cooks and hostesses, but who now consider the process tedious and excessive altogether, preferring to buy prepared foods instead.

Supermarkets are guilty of making purchases for one far too difficult. Prepackaging requires that most items be bought in larger quantities than any one person can possibly consume. There is hardly a thought given by merchants to the "one person" food buyer. Considering the great numbers of older people currently shopping for themselves alone, this is a revealing oversight. It tells us again how invisible older people are among us. In such a commercial country as ours a new market as potential as this one should be taken up by some enterprising food packer. Yet there is little to be found on the shelves answering the need. Old people are often reduced to settling for small jars of baby food instead, a symbolic defeat, rife with irony and pathos.

But of all the proposals and programs for food cures, most important to old people are warnings about the continuing abuse of drugs. Since the aging are particularly victimized by a tendency for doctors to overprescribe, this is a welcome contribution. Henry G. Bieler, a doctor himself, has written of the untold damage to the human system done by excessive use of such drugs, tranquilizers, and corticoids. He takes the position that the new potent miracle drugs, while ostensibly acting as "quick cures," cause reactions, additional disorders, long-standing conditions of dysfunction, sometimes even tragic damage to the body. We are much victimized, he feels, by medical fads and fashions. Just as cod liver oil was once the panacea for all childhood ills, so penicillin became the wonder cure for every conceivable disturbance in the postwar generation. Without underestimating the value of this and other remarkable and powerful drugs in the treatment of staphyloccocal infections and other diseases, Bieler feels that it, along with more recently developed antibiotics, have been prescribed far too freely by doctors, sometimes with disastrous results. He reminds us of the shocking postwar Thalidomide incident affecting European and American pregnant women and its tragic aftermath of deformed infants. An example, he says, of hasty, miracle-drug thinking.

Bieler sees the human body as "breathtaking in its intricacy" and believes it capable of using the foods it digests therapeutically. Some foods, he feels, are indeed harmful, and an improper diet can *cause* disease. It is through a proper diet alone that a sick person will be restored to health, he says. Bieler's book describes at length the various body-restoring properties of certain foods and the chemical processes through which food therapy works.[13]

Food cures like Bieler's and Reuben's—and there are many—are generally greeted with skepticism from orthodox medical practitioners. Yet their claims are not altogether dismissed; not enough is yet known about the exact role of nutrition in the development of chronic and degenerative diseases. Scientists can ill-afford to dismiss any possibilities, and such research may some day provide dramatic breakthroughs for the maintenance of the body. Certainly, the successes these doctors claim with their own patients have been quite remarkable.

Let's look into the steps we might take now for our physical selves. To build our body's power, to become active participants in mobilizing our health, will take reeducation, not just of the muscles but of the whole being. Thus we need to maintain, or in some cases even regain the bodies we possess. We need to care for them as lovingly as we care for our most precious possessions. This implies not just the *preservation* of the body, but the provisioning of it with sustenance, support and above all, affirmation. It means the development of pride in the *current* physical self, and the ability to look with pleasure at its strengths. As for its weaknesses, they too must be sought out, so that we can determine what contributions we can best make for our current welfare, and for our continued vitality and endurance.

For some of us such prescriptions will be more easily acceptable than for others. For the thousands of passionate tennis buffs, the dawn-to-dusk golfers, the eager bowlers, the devoted joggers, hikers, climbers, swimmers, sailors and dancers, physical fitness comes easy. As a result of lifetime habits, they are enjoying themselves and providing marvelously and naturally for their bodies as they grow older. Theirs is the easy path of pleasure and fitness together. As long as they are alerted to their *current* potentials and do not choose to compete with their *former* selves, pushing at their limits to achieve better scores and proof of their continuing prowess, they will be serving themselves and their bodies well.

But what about the many who have always abhorred such activities, and who now, less than ever, want to get out and do something about it? Where is fitness to be sought and how can their bodies be successfully maintained?

Nowadays there are thousands finding solutions to their physical fitness problems. After a thorough medical checkup, (which *must* precede every sort of exercise regimen) people, for example, may ride stationary bicycles mile after mile right in the warmth of their homes, while reading a book or watching television. Some have made exercise a social occasion by joining a weekly class; others merely routinized it by working out at a gymnasium several hours a week. Some people have taken to walking, instead of plunking themselves into their autos to go on errands.

Many types of exercises have been designed specifically to suit the needs of older groups, often assisted by federal and state funding. In Iowa, for example, David K. Leslie and John W. McLure developed a series of special movements and routines which were not the usual sort of calisthenics, the kind for building biceps or weightlifting, but were instead "a slow-paced series of exercises which would not only be fun but which would tone up muscles, improve joint articulation, promote relaxation, help rid people of constipation and give a sense of well-being." At TOES (The Oaknoll Exercise Society), several Ph.D. students in physical education from the University of Iowa conducted exercise programs for fifteen senior citizens organizations. TOES-type programs have mushroomed in many of the nearby counties; they have even been developed especially for a series of half-hour television programs on the local educational channel.

The movements are easy and varied, emphasizing flexibility, agility, and awareness of the body rather than cardiovascular fitness. They extend fingers, stretch palms, flex wrists, shrug shoulders, roll heads, goosestep legs, curl toes, and even cross eyes and make funny faces—everything to tone up the muscles and keep the body agile.[14]

We have already mentioned Herbert deVries and Lawrence Frankel's extensive experimentation with groups of fifty-, sixty-, and seventy-year-olds. From this they have developed programs for fitness and renewed vigor in age. DeVries' exercises are comprised of three elements: first, the endurance group, to condition the heart, lungs, and blood vessels, and to relax the body; second, those which strengthen muscles and thus improve posture; and third, those for expanding joint mobility to avoid aches and pains.

As for Frankel, his focus is on building flexibilty and agility as the strongest measure for "preventive care."

Across the nation many systems are being designed or adjusted for our current needs. The great success reported by the Sage group of California (see chapter 8) in adapting the Feldenkrais exercises for older people is a case in point. Moshe Feldenkrais, an Israeli doctor, believes that there are vast untapped areas of human capability, and that with certain kinds of exercise we can gain access to a higher kind of perfectibility, revitalizing the nervous system entirely. The technique teaches people to convert conflict into energy, into easy bodily action, to make less motion accomplish more. Many of his exercises seem simple; yet to succeed at them, we are told, takes many repetitions. This is because their aim is to feed new information into the brain, thereby expanding its efficiency. Very possibly it is because Feldenkrais' exercises challenge the self-image, now so depressed by the gloom associated with aging in our nation, that they have added value for our group. "When your body is held confidently," he has said, "your mood lightens."[15] So whether they be variations on Feldenkrais or the Alexander technique for bodily awareness, or the Mensendieck posture-correction system for a well-balanced carriage, or the Bluestone-Simon method for deep-stretching and breathing, they are increasingly available and adaptable for older people.

Other people have found more exotic and diverting outlets, such as exercise systems from the Orient. Perhaps the most popular of these is the yoga system, more specifically the Hatha Yoga system of bodily control. Actually a complex way of life founded in ancient Hindu and Buddhistic teachings, Yoga stresses the union, equality, and balance of body, mind and spirit, and presents many ways to achieve this. However, what many Americans have found particularly relevant to the Western way of life are the benefits provided by the "asanas" of Hatha Yoga—its therapeutic postures, along with its breathing, relaxation, and meditative techniques.

The word Hatha (from Sanskrit, *Ha* meaning "Sun", and *Tha* meaning "Moon,") implies the attempted balance of the positive and negative pulls of the body. The classic postures, many of which are patterned after the movements or stances of animals, are generally held for short periods of time. The great asset to older participants is that yoga does not include any quick movements; all its practices are meant to be done very slowly, with grace and without strain. The body stretches naturally to its own capacity, avoiding any violent pulls or dislocations.

And yoga teaches techniques in breathing deeply, that of filling our lungs to their fullest. These breathing exercises are performed before each session and are considered a vital part of the exercise. The "bellows" breath *(bhastrika),* an exercise to warm up the body, tones up the nervous system and generally produces a sense of exhilaration. This is done through a series of quick inhalations and exhalations that contract the abdominal muscles. Another one is the *cleansing* breath (kapalabhati), which clears the nasal passages and sinuses. One takes a deep breath, filling the lungs, and exhales through shorter, more abrupt movements of the abdomen, thus emptying the sinuses and nose of unwanted mucus deposits.

There are gentle activities: head and neck rolling, scalp massage, arm, leg and spine stretching exercises, techniques for relaxing the eyes and facial muscles. All are geared to restoring spinal flexibility, to encouraging fluidity and ease of movement, and to preventing the stiffening of muscles, particularly in the knee joints, where deposits tend to form, preventing proper flow of blood. Yoga techniques aim for total relaxation, for inducing sleep, for reducing back pain, and for learning to listen to body rhythms.[16]

Still others have discovered the remarkable possibilities in Tai Chi Chuan, an ancient Chinese discipline practiced in Taiwan and mainland China. These graceful movements were developed by Chang San Fung, a fourteenth century Taoist monk, who was inspired to create the movements after watching the contest between an entrapped bird and a snake. Centuries before, however, in the time of Confucius, exercises based on animal movements were known to have been performed in China. Today Tai Chi is a combination of easy, pleasurable, slow, graceful steps which condition and stabilize the body, making use of the entire organism. As the Taoists have observed, the body, much like stagnant water, can become contaminated when it is not in motion.

In fact, it stands virtually as an invitation to parasitic and infectious matter. Thus the 108 forms of the 37 basic movements of Tai Chi consciously engage the whole body, the hands, fists, fingers, elbows, palms, buttocks, even the soles of the feet. And these moves are beautiful to watch; balance and motion are interwoven at an almost hypnotic pace.

Tai Chi has always been a great favorite of the Oriental old. For them it is as much a part of daily hygiene as bathing. In more traditional times and even in Communist China today, observers report that an early morning walk through the parks and gardens everywhere presents one with a daily display of old people practicing this art.

Tai Chi is totally different from yoga. Yoga attempts to hold extreme positions in a stable balance. Tai Chi stresses movement, the feeling of change from one stance to another, and it is highly regarded for the internal silence that comes with this concentrated external activity. That's probably why it has such enormous appeal among older Oriental people. For Western participants it has a number of advantages; most novices immediately observe that the motions it employs engage muscles seldom used. Tai Chi postures combine one's physical efforts in such a new way that the immediate results are often painfully charley-horsed upper limbs or upper arms. Circular arm and hip rotations, knee circling, tiger crouches, monkey stretches, and stances like the horse posture (spread legs, bent knees, buttocks pushed forward, spine erect) account for these initial reactions. We Westerners are unaccustomed to using our muscles in these particular ways. But once they become adept, Tai Chi enthusiasts feel that they are surer on their feet, more balanced, altogether more solidly rooted. In fact, the remarkable aspect of this "wise" exercise, as Edward Maisel calls it, is that each form is meant to be wholly satisfying in itself. Each circular or angular motion accomplishes a completeness, a conclusion to particular movements. These act to soothe and quiet the body. Since it is taught step-by-step, Tai Chi presents no pressure to push on, to memorize, or to complete the course of 108 postures. Each posture contains the whole, its pace slow, and performed in a silent atmosphere; it is to be savored for itself alone. In the posture known as the "empty step," the doer moves against the air, as it were, elegantly, slowly, in a progression of movements to nowhere. In the "white cranes flying," the palms are back and arms extended to resemble a bird's wings. The effects are dramatic, each a sort of achievement in itself.

So too with the breathing techniques of Tai Chi. From its former associations with the martial arts of Tai Chi Chuan, there remain various stances combined with sounds, groans, and animal roars to release air, then to open up the diaphragm and the lungs and fill them full. In Tai Chi breathing goes hand-in-hand with the exercises and postures because it is believed that only through them can we stimulate and regulate our breathing.[17]

There are numbers of other Oriental systems, wonderfully strange and vastly complicated, only now coming to the attention of interested Westerners. The Japanese Shiatzu, for example, is a health keeping art introduced during the eighteenth century. *Shi* (finger) and *atzu* (pressure) therapy is practiced widely in Japan today to overcome aches and pains, and more generally as a method of maintaining health and well-being. Acupressure, uses the direct pressure of fingers, hands, and palms to ease pain, remedy disorders, and transmit energy. It has been known to help overcome insomnia, cure headaches and pain in the lower back, neck, and shoulders, and even clear up cases of tennis elbow. Related to the Chinese practice of acupuncture and using the same meridian points of pressure developed for acupuncture, "shiatzu," is, however, a method of healing which is more accessible to laymen. With a little training in its techniques, anyone can practice them to give comfort to himself or to others.

What is most interesting about shiatzu is its discovery of the hands as tools for easing pain. Since the 657 pressure points identified by Oriental healers are related to one another, they can be used to keep the body in harmony with itself, preventing pathways from becoming blocked and from disrupting the flow of energy in the body. Acupressure restores that energy and thus helps preserve physical harmony.[18]

Techniques exist in forms and fashions for every twist and taste—the Aikidos, the Zen of Jogging, or the newest variations on yoga and Tai Chi Chuan, such as Kundalini Yoga or Tai Chi Chi. It is not so important *which* one we choose, but that we seek out the right one for our bodies, and that, after we check with our doctors, we tune into our body, listen to it, measure our health, and improve it, and along with it the quality of our lives. We must give up lamenting our losses, quit sitting before the mirror worshipping the ghost of bodies past. We should instead find the means, in one system or a combination of several, to sustain, serve, and build our mature physical selves now, in pleasure and in health.

8.
Body and Mind:
A Holistic View

If Carl Jung's afternoon of life is itself an independent phase, a separate time, and not merely an appendage to life's morning, we Americans need to seek it further. It has gone too long unidentified, too long unheeded and especially, too long untaught. But we have already seen how much easier it is to reject the "deculturation" forced on us by our society than to seek out new paths in the deeper search for ourselves.

Revolutionary developments in philosophy and psychology in the last several decades provide us with at least some direction to follow in this pilgrimage. In our country, young and old have suffered so many shocks in the twentieth century that many have already been driven to search for deeper meanings. We were once the traditional optimists, the noble Yankee crusaders, but in the post-World War II era Americans have repeatedly faced revelations and disclosures concerning human aggression, deception and brutality. It has left us disillusioned, and forced us to reexamine the very foundations of our existence.

Such eminent thinkers as Jean-Paul Sartre and Albert Camus burst upon us after World War II with concepts (long familiar to European intellectuals from Kierkegaard and Heidegger's philosophy) like the "alienation of man" and the "absurdity of human life," with their discussions of dread, despair, self-deception, with reminders that in our modern world choices in life are ever before us, but that we are seldom knowledgeable enough to anticipate their consequences until too late. Many Americans were ready to listen, and ready to learn.

The existentialists were merely rephrasing fundamental questions about our place in the cosmos and about life on this earth, questions that had been asked by philosophers throughout the centuries. Erasmus, the fifteenth-century Dutch theologian and humanist, in writing of free will, had spoken in these very terms, of man's crucial choices, and his decision as to whether or not he wishes to be "saved." But postwar existentialism was a contemporary statement, a new humanism which, in emphasizing the individual rather than the remote religious and secular systems which surround him, had great appeal to a population that had recently discovered treachery and tragedy in the world.

Much influenced by these Europeans, what has been dubbed the "new psychology," "humanistic psychology," a "third force in psychology," or the "Human Potential Movement," has been gaining steadily in impact and influence in this country. It has emerged in opposition to the two major schools long dominating traditional psychology in the United States—the behaviorism of Harvard professor B. F. Skinner and the psychoanalytic therapy of Sigmund Freud. One of its founders, Abraham Maslow, saw a great gap in the practices of American psychology, a chasm for the vast numbers of people who were striving for meaning in their lives away from the "absurdity" engulfing them. Our psychology, he pointed out, was so preoccupied with mental illness that it had little to say about mental health.

"What must it be like," he speculated, "to be a creative, fully functioning, happy human being?"[1] The discipline of psychology, he maintained, had never seriously taken up the question.

Behavioristic psychology teaches that all we know about an organism is learned from what it does, how it performs—in short, its behavior. The school's experimental scheme was clear; it came from laboratory study of the learning process. The problems were defined in specific behavioral situations, not as "diseases" or "pathologies," but as "maladaptations" to society. The business of the therapist then was to change that pattern of behavior. Treatment, therefore, involved the study of events immediately preceding and following behavior problems to help facilitate change in such dysfunctions.

In order to investigate behavior, the subject is given a certain stimulus, usually an electric shock, and in turn offers a certain response. Behaviorists have worked in the laboratory, most often with rats as their subjects, to demonstrate that for many learning problems the stimulus-response theory operates consistently. The hungry rat will soon learn that the food pellet awaits him at the end of the maze. Thus a theory evolved concerning human "behavior modification," and its methods are commonly in use by speech therapists, by weight-watching and antismoking establishments, and by social workers, psychologists, and educators.

Behaviorists argue that since conditioning is the basis for the building and changing of habits, it can be altered in terms of rewards and punishments. The human being, therefore, is merely the sum of his behavior patterns, and as B. F. Skinner has said, to speak of the "inner man" is to speak of a sheer illusion.[2] But for the humanists this picture of the species as a bundle of animal responses to basic stimuli, ever malleable, ever controllable, is far too brutally mechanical.

The other dominant psychology, the Freudian school, while much more attentive to the mysteries within the human being, was searching the darker areas of the unconscious and the irrational in man, his frustrations, his hostilities, and his repressions. The assumptions underlying psychoanalytic therapy, though certainly revised and relaxed by contemporary practitioners, continued to involve the conflict between the "innate" drives of the individual and the demands of the society in which he lives. Often such demands of the unconscious, or the "id," were simply unacceptable, and thus forced out of conscious awareness by the ego. They might then reappear in disguised form, "sublimated" in creative channels, or surface as a type of "neurotic behavior" evidenced in phobias, compulsions, or uncontrollable temper tantrums. Psychoanalytic treatment attempted to sort out such conflicts through an extended process in which the patient is made conscious of, and able to confront, understand and interpret the sources of such neurotic behavior.

Yet the Freudians' concern was with neuroses, internal chaos, the study of the mentally crippled, the stunted, the immature, and it too could not provide a broad enough framework for emergent interests in the "normal" human being. The great Viennese himself had spoken of confining his work exclusively "to the ground floor and basement of the edifice called Man."[3] And Maslow, along with the many humanistic psychologists who have followed him, has continued to complain of this very limitation. In his view, Sigmund Freud had never really grasped the dominating concern of the twentieth century man: his search for meaning within the human condition.

That is what the "third force" psychology has confronted. It has searched for the *whole* man, not merely in terms of his responses to stimuli or his neuroses, but in the "coming together" of mind and body, the unique experience of life particular to the individual, and the complexities of that individual self from "basement to attic." The "holistic" approach seeks to balance the whole being—the emotional and feeling person with the rational and logical one—in a harmonious combination to produce "full humanness," or in Maslow's phrase "fulfillment of biological destiny." And it goes one step further: a complete psychological theory *must* involve the philosophy one lives by, and the whole cultural context within which one acts. The humanistic psychologist wants to retain the "image of man while systematically studying the human being."[4]

Now this is a tall order. Many insisted that the new school was trying to encompass far too much, was vague in structure and goals, impractical, and above all unscientific. For many years, its position was indeed marginal, with opposition coming from many universities and establishment psychologists all over the United States. Only a few years ago did that prestigious organization, the American Psychological Association, accept disciples of the school as members. Before this, the group had found it necessary to form its own organization, the Association of Humanistic Psychology, to publish its own journals and develop various "growth centers" around the world to put its theories into practice. Still, many were seen (and still are today) as bordering on the "far out" or the "kooky," attracting a variety of displaced persons in search of a psychological home. Esalen, at Big Sur, California, the best known of the domestic centers, was notorious for its general wildness, for group nudity, and for its "touch-me-feel-me" encounter groups.

Even more troublesome, perhaps, was the theoretical position the human potential psychologists took and their involvement with existential philosophy, which made it necessary for them to make a sweeping attack on science as a whole and the rigid boundaries it forced upon its researchers. Maslow felt that the scientific method had come to a "dead end" and was seriously in need of reevaluation. Science could tear things apart, he felt, but it could seldom serve us in creating a positive model. What was vitally needed was a new concept of the truly scientific. Maslow felt sure that his work fell properly within the realm of science, yet the highly subjective nature of relationships between persons found no place in the current format of scientific methodology. How could one be objective about "loneliness," or "doubt," or the "loss of identity," for example? He boldly called for a new, broader philosophy of science which would be more aware of its limitations, and above all more able to serve the psychologist in his innovative explorations of the whole man. "My thesis is, in general, that new developments in psychology are forcing a profound change in our philosophy of science, a change so extensive that we may be able to accept the basic religious questions as a proper part of the jurisdiction of science, once science is broadened and redefined."[5]

Despite such controversies, Maslow (and the many humanistic therapists who have since based their practices upon his conceptions) said much of interest to us as older Americans, particularly his view of human nature, that man is much more than his basic drives for life, safety, and security. The "higher" needs or "inner nature," unique in each of us, await our self-realization. How else, the humanists ask, can we explain away the persistent human preoccupation throughout history with such abstractions as beauty, truth, justice, and goodness? According to Maslow, "The possibilities of human nature have customarily been sold short." These higher needs are not, as the Freudians maintain, merely diversions or sublimations of baser drives, or cures for disease and disorder; they are instead our true inner nature pressing for "self-actualization" and a path to more complete enjoyment and a broader view of life. They are, says Maslow, that ever vital human search for meaning.[6]

This orientation towards discovery and growth of self seems most feasible for us as we age. Unlike the behaviorists' early conditioning theories and Freud's contention that after age fifty certain rigidities prevail and make psychoanalysis difficult or useless, the new psychology's developmental approach is applicable both for young and old. Every being must continually seek fulfillment whenever and wherever it can be found.

"The person who hasn't conquered or withstood and overcome continues to feel doubtful that he could: This is true not only for external dangers, it holds also for the ability to control and to delay one's own impulses and therefore to be unafraid of them," says Maslow.[7]

This fulfillment is seen by humanists in various ways. Kurt Goldstein, an early theorist, had called it "self-actualization." Carl Rogers has talked of the growth process through which a person's potential is best realized, and Charlotte Buhler has laid emphasis upon *values* which must be sought to give life meaning. Mike Murphy, the founder of the Esalen Institute, searches further, with references to unsuspected resources, new sensitivities, fresh ways to perceive the world and heighten the consciousness, all available to people but often untapped. Humanistic psychology and its allies—transpersonal psychology, psychosynthesis, transactional analysis, gestalt therapy, encounter, sensitivity training and the more commercial versions of these—are part of a growing effort to find new sources for fullfillment.

Humanists argue that current experimental research in science lends support for their ideas. Recent studies of the brain, for instance, show that the left hemisphere manages logic and linguistic skills, while the right is charged with intuitive or perceptual modes. Through biofeedback and other techniques, we can be attuned to our physiological processes—our heartbeat, our blood pressure, our muscular tensions, our brainwave patterns—but even more important, we can learn to control these processes. Experimental scientists now recognize such abilities as latent in most human beings. What Eastern gurus and mystics have accepted for centuries is finding new recognition even in the controlled atmosphere of the laboratory. Even such phenomena as extrasensory perception, no longer dismissed as quackery, are being studied.

Humanistic psychologists see revolutionary transformations in the coming decades for both man and society. For the upcoming old, still imprisoned in a clockwatching America and shackled to chronology, such ideas can become a liberating force.

In seeking the whole person, consider first the clinical observations made in the 1950s by Dr. Cecil Sheps, a specialist in preventative medicine. Chronologic age, he tell us, "differs markedly from biologic age and cannot be used as an indicator of functional capacity." The reason for this is that the organs of each person age at a different rate. Thus, instead of a uniform deterioration, a body can boast of a forty-five-year-old digestive system while its cardiovascular complex is the equivalent of that of a sixty-five-year-old.[8] So it is almost meaningless to ask, "How old is this person?" Nobody is the same biologic age throughout his body. One must restate the question: "How old is he in relation to his heart, or his bladder, or his mental functions?" The peak function, what is often referred to as "the prime of life," would be better determined by multiple measurements to see where an individual fits on the scale between birth and death.

Again, each style of life puts emphasis on its own sort of excellence. Sheps cites the example of a sprint runner who breaks records at eighteen years old or at the latest twenty-two; the marathon champions are sometimes as old as forty-five. So there can be no fixed estimate of peak achievement either. On life's scale, the rate of deterioration varies widely with the tasks involved.

The current research of Paul Baltes and K. Warner Shaie demonstrates that the once accepted notion that IQ tended to rise through youth and adolescence and begin a steady decline in the thirties and forties is "largely a myth." In many ways, they tell us, as in the storage of information, there is actually evidence of *improvement* in such functions with the coming of age. It is only in the *speed* of performance that decline is observable.[9]

They also raise the question of age bias in such testing. Since intelligence tests are generally designed for measuring performance in the schools, the emphasis may be wholly inappropriate for older people. There are decidedly intergenerational differences in study habits (memorization, for instance, was once highly prized and is now generally scorned as a pedagogical technique), differing levels of sophistication in taking exams, and varying goals and definitions of "achievement." Yet many of the psychology textbooks are still filled with data about the inverse relationship between age and intelligence. It wasn't until 1973, after a task force on aging reported to the American Psychological Association, that this outmoded idea about intelligence decline was officially shelved by that organization.

What Carl Eisdorfer has described as "learning strategy" in older people is simply very different from that of younger people. Less willing to take risks, not wanting to appear ignorant, and always in fear of ridicule, the older are apt to leave key questions unanswered and make a mistake rather than appear slow or inept. This has often been taken as an inability to learn. Naturally, until there is no special shame associated with trial and error for this group, such learning handicaps will persist. But older people can and do learn, and there is no telling how well the old could perform if more innovative educational resources were at their disposal. Study after study has shown that there is no decline in knowledge and reasoning ability with age.

Confusion is also common in the distinctions made between sickness and aging. The two may be frequent companions, but they are not inextricably bound. What, after all, is a "healthy" person? There are some people who live all their lives in pain and yet manage to ignore it and function well. Others find the very hint of it intolerable. To some extent, then, an individual's ability to cope with bodily dysfunction of one sort or another throughout life determines his state of mind in youth as well as age. Researchers tell us that old people seem to be less subject to acute illnesses, but are much more prone to chronic ones which can be inconvenient, uncomfortable, and limiting. Yet such restrictions need not necessarily alter their lives; there are today many medical adjustments possible for such ailments.

Another worry among older people has been loss of memory. One hears it most often in the anxious complaint that somebody's memory is "simply not as good as it once was." Here again science is discovering that the capacity to remember is about equal in young and old. What is taken as "loss of memory" is often due rather to inadequate learning in the first place, a sudden hearing loss, poorer vision, or an unawareness of the reduced psychomotor speed required to learn new skills.

It is simply not yet possible for us to know exactly what aging does to people psychologically. The question of how much harm is done by accepting despair, by associating aging with loss and pain, and by seeing nothing but misery ahead remains unanswered.

But the extent of physical damage this can cause may prove considerable. Lissy Jarvik, a UCLA professor of psychiatry, has recently seen a strong tie between intellectual decline and death. Doing longitudinal studies on aging identical twins, she finds that "there is mounting evidence that inactivity, both mental and physical, results in deterioration." An attitude of hopelessness, usually accompanying inactivity, can result in consequent intellectual decline. She most frequently finds critical loss and intellectual decline in the twin who dies first.[10]

Research seems to be questioning every psychological postulate about aging which we once matter-of-factly accepted. We must reconcile some of these contradictions, i.e., the discrepancies between, on the one hand, the ever-growing chance for longer life, our improved state of preservation in both mind and body and, on the other hand, our premature "obsolesence" as people. Such incongruities are gnawing away at us all. And there is discomfort with the alternatives left to us older persons. Our capability for enterprise often far exceeds our access to it.

It is in light of this deepening "winter of our discontent" that the new psychologies can awaken us. They tell us that we must "get in touch with what we are, to find out what there is in us to become." Many people focus upon basic needs and immediate satisfaction, move without direction through their chores in life with no interruptions and few distractions, and put no effort into developing their inner selves. Then they are quite abruptly deprived of their short-term cultural identities (as breadwinners, spouses, or parents, for instance) along with the status and associations accompanying such positions. They are left bewildered, uncertain, mere shadows of the personalities they once possessed.

Such individuals might well go after that "inner nature" as Maslow urges, the unique self which is in each of us to command (like our voices or our gestures), no matter what roles we may be forced to shed. People whose basic needs for food and shelter are taken care of must go on further to become self-fulfilling people, in search of unity and integration. In other times, the psychologist notes, these were our saints, our knights, or our mystics: the sort of people whose life work transcended their personal existence because they were able to rise above the routine. In our own time the results may be less dramatic. Yet such integration can lead us to a far more realistic view of oursleves and perhaps a superior appreciation of reality. External objects can then be seen in terms of the universe, not merely for their relevance or irrelevance to immediate concerns. "The mosquito," says Maslow, is a "wondrous object if it is *not* seen in terms of the harm it does to humans."

Certainly what can come out of all this is a new detachment, a new lens, a new focus, something altogether necessary for a fresh approach to experience. This new eye can bring with it total attention, a kind of absorption which is free from expediency or trivial, everyday purposes. Through it a person can reach what Maslow calls "peak experiences," encounters far richer than the average perception. This new focus is made possible through a release from anxiety, a greater openness, a fusion of all of one's creative energies into the moment, and the value to be found in it. This is the way humanistic psychology sees the emergence of the whole being:

> . . . an episode or a spurt in which powers of person come together in a particularly efficient and intensely enjoyable way, and in which he is more integrated and less split, more open for experience, more idiosyncratic, more perfectly expressive or spontaneous, or fully functioning, more creative, more humorous, more ego-transcending, more independent of his lower needs, etc. He becomes in these episodes more truly himself, more perfectly actualizing his potentialities, closer to the core of his Being, more fully human.[11]

Chronology is not important; such a whole being can emerge at any age.

Of course, Maslow is not alone in this quest. What he terms self-fulfillment is variously delineated by others. Erik Erickson's model is an "identity" search in five developmental stages, along with the various crises it faces in its formation. Alfred Adler's "creative self" makes a "style of life," and Carl Jung talks of the "psyche" which embraces all states, both conscious and unconscious. Kurt Goldstein discusses "self-actualization on the whole organism," an organism Carl Rogers sees in need of "positive regard" and "self regard." Whatever you call it, the attempt is to draw together and balance the whole being, both the limiting person who needs security and the searching person with creative needs.

Many of these ideas crystallize in the work of the late Roberto Assagioli, a Venetian born psychiatrist who practiced in Florence, Italy, and the U.S. Using methods similar to those of Maslow, Erikson, and Goldstein, he provided us with practical working techniques to make them accessible. His system, known as "psychosynthesis,"[12] sees man as naturally tending towards harmony within himself and power in the world around him. Like the other humanists, Assagioli started within the central being, the self, and moved out from it to a self-actualization of the personality, a process which fostered harmonious growth and steady development throughout life, realizing the latent potential in each human being.

He argued that psychological hygiene resembles physical hygiene, and that much as physical health depends upon certain basic factors (a good diet, cleanliness of person, breathable air,) so does psychological health. However, while these physical needs are recognized and attended to, psychological ones are mostly ignored, and "psychological poisons" of aggression, violence, fear, depression, and greed can pollute our immediate environment, making us close in upon ourselves.

He reminded us that while we are constantly searching for meaning and value in our lives, we are also facing daily choices and decisions. Most of us see such daily necessities as a serious business, an atmosphere in which anxiety and suffering are common elements. Paradoxical though it may sound, everything, even conflict, is *food* for the development of the individual. It is the stuff upon which the self grows, and much as the food we eat serves our bodies, so do impressions and experiences provide for the well-being of our whole existence. We mentally feed and breathe upon visual displays, on sound vibrations, on architectural proportions, on combinations of forms, on changes of color, on rhythms and various combinations of chords in music, on the apt turning of a phrase in conversation, on a change in mood, or on a beautiful line of poetry.

It is just such exposure and experience that is in most jeopardy when opportunities diminish and options close. Postretirement depression is not just the loss of a profession but of the personality as well, when stimulation of this sort is no longer available. What Assagioli offers us are active techniques for strengthening, cultivating, and transforming energies into positive, even joyous experiences. His techniques reach out towards Maslow's "peak experiences." Psychosynthesis may be seen as a dynamic conception of psychological life, which in dealing with the constant interplay and conflict of forces outside, unifies and harmonzies the personality so that it can utilize and control such "lived" experience. The future is always seen in terms of its dynamic role in the present, so it is inconceivable that the synthesized individual can ever be left wholly helpless, regardless of circumstances.

When Assagioli talked about loneliness, he considered it neither "ultimate" nor "essential." There certainly are times in life when this condition persists; in adolescence it is most acutely suffered, and it again looms large in the life of those whose spouses have recently died. Yet with appropriate methods, he finds, one can steadily develop skills to integrate the personality into larger groups, to blend it with society so that it prepares itself for inevitable changes in circumstance.

Among these methods are systematic exercises in the development of the will, in the expansion of the imaginative faculties, and in the process of what Assagioli calls "disidentification." Each day of our lives presents us, he says, with numbers of opportunities for such exercises in order to break former patterns and meaningless habits and reduce tension, haste, and compulsiveness. He uses the phrase "Make haste slowly" to signify a new attitude and approach to routine. His psychosynthesis techniques are complex and exacting; what follows is no more than an outline of a few of them.

The development of will, he says, is "one of the ignored areas of psychology." What we must develop is the "will to train the will," because this is the very core of synthesis. This involves uncovering the powerful unconscious motivations within us, and focusing these energies on what we truly value in the world. The active will must progress through other stages: *deliberation, decision, affirmation, planning,* and the *direction of execution.* The will must be honed into a dynamic instrument, persistent, enduring, and single-minded in its focus.

How is such training accomplished? Assagioli suggests relaxing into a comfortable position and picturing to oneself as vividly as possible all the unfortunate consequences connected with inadequate strength of will. This must be followed by a careful review of each potential loss. Then a list is written to itemize each one. He predicts such forecasts can bring on strong feelings of regret about the lack of proper action. Feelings of shame and dissatisfaction will cause a subsequent urge to avoid a repetition of such conduct and a growing desire to change.

Next, one is asked to picture the opposite situation, with all the benefits and satisfactions deriving from decisive use of the will. One must fully examine and analyze' acts which strengthen the desire to realize one's aims in life and gain the intiative to take such actions. Next, one must picture oneself the possessor of such a "strong persistent will," and moving so firmly in every act of decisiveness that one is able to concentrate every effort and resist intimidation. Here the focus is upon situations in which one has previously failed to exert a strong will. The job of this exercise is to make evident the possibilities that exist and how these can be used to advantage. It is a technique borrowed from the French theorist, Robert Desoille, called "rêve éveillé," which means essentially, "the waking dream." In psychosynthesis it becomes the "live it again, talk it out, write it down" method, the way to see and build the self anew.

Assagioli has exercises for imaginative growth, as well as for development of many deficient aspects of the personality. So widespread has desensitization to nature and art become in our modern world that many people proceed through life virtually blind and deaf to the beauty around them. The "motor power of the imagination" must be put into gear again. His specific techniques combine visualization, observation, and memorization to teach people how to evoke the imagination, to "open the doors again to the world" and thus retake command over their lives.

He recommends the continued concentration upon expansion of visual, tactile, auditory, kinesthetic, gustatory, and olefactory energies through specfic training or retraining. He starts with simple exercises in visualizing. Suppose you think of a blackboard, and on it appears a number—5 for example—this to be followed by the appearance of another—say 2. The idea is to visualize the combinations, dwelling upon their image until you've absorbed them, pronouncing them aloud: 52 for instance, and then proceding with the addition of each digit to alter the number: 524, 5248, 52486, etc. Each time you try you must aim to achieve a longer string in your memory.

Deceptively simple on paper, but try it visually! You'll find it requires conscious attention, but with practice it is indeed possible to make improvements, to advance in the ability to hold more in the active memory longer.

A form and color exercise asks the subject to see before him on the blackboard "a blue triangle, a yellow circle and a green square." After he can hold these in his visual memory, he is asked to change the order or layout of the group, or shift the colors onto other shapes. This takes fixed concentration, a determined will, and patience, but it can be very helpful in sharpening one's appreciation for painting or sculpture.

In an exercise called "mental photography," a person is asked to observe an image for a short time, an illustration on a postcard, a diagram, or an advertisement. He then must evoke in his imagination what he has just seen, recalling and describing as many details as he can. This technique tells us how much information we absorb, how long this takes, and how long such impressions stay with us. The display of the image can also be repeated several times for short intervals to improve skills in observation and memorization and to make the subject more sensitive to what is before him.

Auditory exercises suggest we distinguish the sounds of nature from the mind-clouding noises of construction work or traffic which often plague us. Evocations in the imagination of the sound of the ocean, waves breaking against cliffs, running water, church bells, the song of birds or wind in a forest are all attempts at creating auditory images. This can sharpen sensitivity to man-made sounds, particularly that combination of rhythm and harmony known as music. Assagioli has written extensively about the relationship between music and emotional states in life, but that is a discourse in itself. It is sufficient to point out here that enlivening or renewing such a sensitivity to sound (or to vision) can contribute to revitalizing the senses.

For evoking tactile awareness, one lightly strokes a piece of fur, passes one's hand over a glass of water, or notes the fit of one's clothing, the tightness of a belt or the pressure of a wristwatch. Tastes and smells can be evoked with similar exercises.

After initial retraining of the senses, psychosynthesis combines and integrates its exercises, growing more intricate and demanding. By incorporating signs, symbols, abstractions, and mythologies, Assagioli hopes to show in the new awareness "the unlimited possibilities" for development and self-realization in every person. From nature he draws upon symbols: mountains as they seem to us to rise in "ascent"; jewels as they show "light"; sunsets as they relate to shadow and darkness; animals, humans, and man-made objects as they call up various pictures, the lion as unfaltering strength, the mother as love and warmth, or the bridge as it spans the void. This is what he refers to as "spiritual psychosynthesis," the realm of the higher urges of the human psyche, where the creative imagination, intuition, and aspiration are in tune. These spiritual forces are as basic, as real, and as important to us as our material needs and Assagioli's exercises strive towards this higher awareness, or "superconsciousness."[13]

We have sparsely outlined the techniques offered by only one of the theorists working in the human potential area. In addition, Bruno Geba's "vitality training" teaches the reseeing, recentering and reintegrating of the self through practical breathing and relaxation exercises,[14] and already noted, Moshe Feldenkrais' method overcomes physical and emotional traumas by rebuilding the body.[15]

Right now methods are being put to the test for us with dramatic results. A California group known as SAGE (Senior Actualization and Growth Explorations), working in Berkeley and Los Angeles, has been employing the new humanistic psychologies—the Assagioli sensory awareness training, Gestalt dream therapy, bioenergetics, psychodrama, encounter techniques—the whole spectrum of the human potential movement, along with a generous sprinkling of more exotic Eastern disciplines—Tibetan Yoga, Chinese Tai Chi Chu'an, Indian meditational postures, and Sufi dancing. SAGE powerfully demonstrates that older people can, with proper support and guidance, experience a flowering, a period of growth, and beyond this, an augmentation of spirit.

Its dynamic founder, Dr. Gae Gaer Luce, began her crusade several years ago when she found, in seeking out solutions for her own aging mother, that few answers were to be had from "gerontologists and other specialists in aging." In frustration, she devised her own program, something "far out" by the usual standards for senior activities, which she describes as "an eclectic progression of exercises for self-development and preventive medicine that had never before been combined for any age group."

"We felt that people could grow as much at seventy-five as at twenty-five, she says,

> . . . if given the same conditions that inspire growth in the young —nurturance, support, challenge, freedom, and continued activity. Children use all parts of themselves continually, their muscles, bones, emotions, intelligence and spirit. Moreover, they are touched a great deal, and encouraged. They are allowed to experiment with themselves and play. In adulthood this abruptly stops, and challenge, nurturance, openness, and intimacy decline to the vanishing point after middle age. We tried to create an analogue of the situation that enhances learning in the child or young adult. . . .[16]

Ms. Luce advocates (exactly what we have seen here) that "massive cultural neglect and ignorance" accounts for many problems in older people today. Alter their circumstances and you could transcend all the expectations of our culture in a revitalization of body and spirit. The growth and success of Luce's groups since 1972 have demonstrated the need for and effectiveness of this program.

Hers is an approach to the *whole* person. People in their late sixties and seventies who are working simultaneously at many levels to reverse their own negative patterns in their bodies, minds, and emotions. Many have reported remarkable progress in combating long-standing medical problems like arthritis pains, insomnia, migraine headaches, high blood pressure, weight gains and losses, and in learning to compensate for hearing and sight losses. One early participant, who had come to the group after a surgical replacement of his hip by a piece of plastic fastened to his pelvis, inched about fearfully on a cane. He was so heavily sedated he had begun to lose his memory. At SAGE he learned balancing exercises and combined them with relaxation techniques. He soon began standing on one leg, and later functioned so well that he took on responsibilities as one of SAGE's instructors, going into nursing homes to help revitalize others.

Another participant describes being plagued by a tremendous feeling of tension, something she had never been without:

> . . . Bad pain in my shoulder and arm, almost constant. I had tried physical therapists, osteopaths, medical doctors. I even tried acupuncture. Nothing helped. I came here, and they told me deep breathing would help. How could just breathing deeply, relaxing completely on the outgoing breath before I took the next breath . . . how could that do anything? But it did it, and slowly I realized the pain was going way. And it's completely gone now. . . .[17]

A group member in Los Angeles feels it has given her a new attitude towards her deafness:

> I'm not so critical anymore. Losing your hearing is not so important after all. You still can touch, you still can see the beauty of the world. Life is lovely anyway![18]

But it is not only physical handicaps which SAGE is attacking. They aim at deeper targets like depression, feelings of isolation, dependency, and, most common, fear of death. And with the revitalization of bodies through graduated exercises comes renewed interest in sensory awareness, expressive movement, and a new willingness to explore personal relationships.

At the crux of the program is training in deep muscle relaxation. This is no easy accomplishment. Each person is taught first to relax the upper torso, particularly the face and neck, through the techniques of biofeedback, a recently discovered phenomenon by which man can learn to control his own biological and mental functioning. Biofeedback instruments receive physiological changes through sensors on the body and then amplify such signals in a visual or auditory display. A person can be lying still, eyes closed, concentrating on relaxing the muscles in a particular part of the anatomy. His earphones can bring the clicking signals which indicate contraction and tensing of such muscles, or their relaxation. Dr. Barbara Brown, of the UCLA Medical Center's Department of Psychiatry, who pioneered work in biofeedback research, believes the idea to be revolutionary:

> The interior universe of man, his inner space, can be opened for new exploration. As man learns more about his internal functioning, he will learn how to communicate information about the new horizons of the mind. But perhaps the greatest consequence will be the possibility that biofeedback will allow the individual to regain control of his own being and body. We can become aware of new feelings and how they relate to the interior self, and perhaps can become aware of the unexplainable, the self teaching the self to control the inner self. Bio-feedback is an experience: at the same time it may be the mind watching itself evolving. The personal, social and even psychic implications are enormous.[19]

The self teaches the self to control the *inner* self. SAGE has used biofeedback to dramatically alert people to the tensions which plague them. Many have responded immediately when faced with such mechanical evidence.

Another technique used at SAGE is "autogenic training," a relaxation method developed by a German neurologist in the early part of the century and only lately adapted for the English-speaking world. People are asked to repeat such thoughts as, "My right arm is heavy," or "My eyelids are drooping," until they become hypnotic in effect. Exercises like these can become the imaginative way towards revitalization and regeneration. Through them one SAGE disciple, for instance, has succeeded in lowering her blood pressure significantly.

Another, called "art therapy," aims to evoke emotions and encourage fantasy through explorations with clay, pastels, tempera paints, or chalk. Many participants report a wonderful new sense of freedom in such artistic excursions. Their reactions and excitement with such materials are similar to those of young children on their first experience with the medium.

Best of all, SAGE people come to know and care about one another while working together. After a time they feel comfortable, trusting, and willing to touch each other. Exercises at SAGE then include massages, administered by participants upon one another in various muscle areas. Foot massages seem to have wonderfully satisfying effects. Relationships involving physical contact help create new bonds between people, which so many older adults have retreated from or lost entirely. A Berkeley enthusiast at SAGE explains this exhilaration:

> Two things. One is purely physical. We love each other. We touch, we hug, we do all the things that I've long since almost forgotten except with my family, and see, this has unbelievable value for an individual. The other thing is that I think somehow or other the whole world is my new world. It's new in the sense of energy, of producing, of meeting friends on a new level. My family is so excited about it. It's almost too much and yet it's very real. I do honestly feel cosmic.[20]

In fact, SAGE's most important contribution of all may be that it exists, and that it functions well for the people it serves. It shows us just how effectively the new discoveries of psychology can be put to work for older Americans. Its vital California trainees and graduates, the newly "actualized," are going out to teach others what they have just learned. Such active spirits bring a new vision of older people into focus. They are full-time life builders, not helpless onlookers condemned to sit out their own decay while waiting for death.

9.
The Sexual Revolution

Considering that apathy surrounds most aspects of old peoples' problems today, it's striking to find that the subject of their sexuality has been taken up at all! Remarkably, the matter has been discussed and even subjected to physiological experimentation. This unexpected development is actually a byproduct of altogether fresh discoveries regarding sexual experience at any age.

Somewhat like the weather, human sexuality has been gossiped about, crowed over, and simply talked to death over the centuries, but no one has ever actually done much about it in terms of controlled scientific experiments. Scientists may have begun dissecting cadavers ages ago in their study of anatomy, but they found the study of orgasm, which requires two *live* bodies, far too sensitive, too delicate, too questionable socially, to cope with. Is it surprising that systematic investigation of the physiology of sexual behavior has lagged incredibly behind?

It's not that information regarding the anatomy of the sexual organs doesn't exist. Medical texts review in great detail the exact functions of such parts of the body. Diagrammatic depictions of these bodily areas have long been familiar to prepubescent boys and girls in most of America's grade schools. Yet sex research, the analysis of the actual process of intercourse and the experience of orgasm, is a study still in its infancy. Yet when one contemplates how often our teenagers are today watching explicit enact-

ments of it in the movies, the reticence of the medical profession
is all the more incredible.

Discounting discussions, from classical times to the nineteenth
century, of sexual behavior in the abstract, one of the first serious
scientific analysts in the field was an English physician and a
Victorian, Henry Havelock Ellis, whose seven volumes, compiled
between 1896 and 1928, contained in narrative form every kind
of material available on sexual behavior and practice. Case histories, correspondence, and specific information on sex and marriage
collected there was new to a whole generation of readers in
England and America and became enormously popular.[1] A German scientist named Richard Von Krafft-Ebing took a different
emphasis in 1866 with *Psychopathis Sexualis*. Systematically classified and catalogued for the first time was every kind of sexual
pathology that he had encountered clinically, including deviate
sexual behavior in extreme age, and aberrations like "geronto-
philia," the erotic obsession of youth with persons of advanced
old age.[2] Of course his work is useful primarily for its historical
interest today. So altered are current views of what may be defined
as sexually pathological that Alex Comfort, the gerontologist and
writer of the best-selling manuals, *Joy of Sex* and *More Joy*,
argues that Krafft-Ebing set "understanding back a hundred years
by pasting the label of 'perversion' on everything that didn't turn
him on."[3]

In the work of Sigmund Freud the subject was expanded and
redefined scientifically as never before. Though Freud certainly
did not approach the subject of sexual research directly, his
theories led to new insights and a new focus on the profound influence of sexual development from early childhood throughout
the entire life cycle. By suggesting first that this instinct, arising in
infancy, was basically aimed towards pleasure, and second, that it
was more highly developed in man than in animals, he virtually
revolutionized its role in civilized life. This energy, when *displaced*
or *sublimated* was the origin of enormous resources of intense and
powerful activity in our culture. Freud's views broadened the concept of the sexual in all human endeavors.

And, of course, it was in the 1930s that works such as T. H.
Van de Velde's *Ideal Marriage* first appeared.[4] This manual, like

its many successors, became the bedside companion of many couples, since it dared to detail erotic positions and recommend explicit remedies for sexual problems.

Yet despite this evolving interest during the early part of the century, contemporary clinical research was not launched until the 1950s when the pioneering work of the American Alfred Kinsey appeared and dominated the scene.[5] Kinsey, trained as an entomologist (a specialist in insect life), took up sex research in his forties, when he found himself unable to answer his students' most basic questions regarding human sexual habits. He tackled this taboo subject with a new freedom, reflecting the changing climate on sexual subjects becoming evident in postwar America. At this point, for the first time, and in the interests of science, of course, the silence regarding older participants in the sexual act was broken.

Many Americans were reluctant to tolerate investigations of this nature, and were appalled when the experiments involved the practices of people in their later years. Such research was not just considered indecent, but disgusting. Sexuality in later years had never been a proper subject for open discussion; it was a function neither necessary nor possible, and if practiced at all, not normal. What has been termed the "D.O.M.," or the "dirty old man" syndrome is the derogatory handle for any "over age" male who shows any noticeable interest in sex. And in our culture an old man accompanied by a very young woman is considered the most unforgivable combination of them all. As for his female counterpart, the lascivious old lady, she is not to be contemplated, she simply does not exist. If she is acknowledged it is as an aberrant, a deviant defying the basic values of respectability and morality upon which our American nation is founded.

There is more involved here than mere Puritanism. Obviously, in the Catholic view, sex is essentially a procreative function and little pretense can be made for continued encounter in sexual terms. To pursue the pleasures of the body may be conceivable for the exuberance of youth, but in feeble old age? Impossible! The psychologist, Eric Pfeiffer, has gone further, observing that the prohibition against sex in age might well be an extension of the incest taboo. Oedipal fears in association with parents are ever

active, and the common unwillingness of a child to accept the fact
that his parents actually make love is thus extended to include all
older persons:

> In our society children of all ages often experience a great deal
> of anxiety from observing or imagining their parents engaged in
> sexual activity. Since the elderly represent the parent generation,
> some of the discomfort may be accounted for on this basis.[6]

Considering the feelings of inadequacy, the "psychic castration,"
as Isadore Rubin terms it,[7] and, as we discussed earlier, the self-
hatred fostered by our media-controlled views of ourselves, it
is not surprising that the image of the elderly is preserved and
fostered as an *asexual* group whose desires have ceased at mid-
night, whose urge for intercourse has vanished with menopause,
and whose battle with turbulent nature is mercifully over and done
with.

Recent findings of science have emphatically challenged this
picture. Kinsey studied the sexual histories of more than sixteen
thousand people, collecting more than seven thousand of these histories himself over ten years. Within this large group the over-six-
ties were ridiculously underrepresented; however, a breakthrough
had certainly been made. Kinsey's work had invited an attack
upon the scientific community's stubborn silence concerning what
R. L. Dickinson had in the 1920s termed science's "sole timidity."
Masters and Johnson were still lamenting this timidity as late as
1966. However tentative was Kinsey's research, it did prepare the
ground for more serious efforts to come.

Of his 14,084 men, only 106 were over sixty, and only 18 over
seventy. Yet they *had* been singled out and included. And in spite
of these limitations, many of his conclusions reflected significantly
upon sexuality in age. For example, from his research he concluded that men are most sexually active in late adolescence and
young adulthood, approximately between ages sixteen and twenty-
nine; from that point on there seems to be a gradual decline. However, the "rate at which males slow up in [their] last decades does
not exceed the rate at which they have been slowing up and dropping out in the previous age group."[8] Thus the rate of decline is
highly individual, following the pattern it has taken earlier rather

than speeding up with age. But Kinsey goes on to show that impotence rapidly increases in later years, with figures that rise from 20 percent at age sixty to 75 percent at age eighty. However, impotence and its causes are far more complex phenomena than the physiological factors taken alone and are therefore not convincingly a function of age. Kinsey also concluded that married men tended to show greater frequency of sexual activity and that this often persisted into later years.

His sample for older women was even more inadequate, fifty-six over the age of sixty, and thus even less reliable. But he did conclude that "there is little evidence of any aging in the sexual capacities of the female until late in her life."⁹

It was Kinsey's overall portrait that caused the furor. He found that four out of five men over sixty were capable of normal sexual relations, and that women showed little or no sexual decline until much later in life. This was revolutionary news.

Meanwhile, at Duke University's Center for the Study of Aging and Human Development, a far more complex survey was focused upon human sexuality. Beginning in 1954, it continued over a twenty-year period in what is termed "longitudinal" research. By means of lengthy interviews with psychiatrists, information was obtained from 254 subjects, both men and women, black and white, married and single, ranging in age from sixty to ninety-four years at the outset of the study. Since numbers dwindled with the passage of time, the study was left with a panel of thirty-one couples from whom investigators drew their information, cross-validating it with individual interviews with sexual partners. Conducted at approximately three-year intervals, interviews included degree of enjoyment, intensity of sexual feelings, and frequency of intercourse over the years.

Specific statistics on older people were now available and many validated Kinsey's original findings. Eighty percent of those who indicated a lively sexual interest at the start of the study reported that it had declined little over a ten-year period. Two out of three men reported sexual activity past sixty-five, and one out of five into their eighties. Even eighty and ninety-year-olds reported a moderate interest. The studies at Duke found that older women were less enthusiastic; a far smaller number were found to be still sexually interested or coitally active. Yet the study director, Eric Pfeiffer, has suggested some explanations for this, among them the lack of available men for this group, their unwillingness to consider nonmarital sex, and their lingering acceptance of the idea that menopause marks the cessation of sexual desire. And the anxiety that most women feel regarding the loss of physical attractiveness often contributes to their reluctance concerning sexual encounters. But the question of whether there is truly a physiological difference between male and female interest in sex during later life remains unanswered. A longitudinal study currently in progress at Duke on persons ages forty-five to seventy should shed new light on the subject.[10]

Yet another dimension was explored in sex research in the work of William H. Masters and Virginia E. Johnson.[11] In addition to interrogations of large numbers of people regarding their sexual experiences, for the first time actual laboratory participation was solicited to provide a controlled environment in the performance of the sexual act. Thus their studies represented a great innovation: observation as a systematic means for research into sexual intercourse. Interestingly, this research included a special section devoted to the physiological changes due to aging, specifically focusing upon bodily changes notable during the coital act.

Masters and Johnson argued forcefully against the continued existence of what they referred to as "a massive state of ignorance of human sexual response to the detriment of millions of individuals." They asked the question:

> Can that one facet of our lives affecting more people in more ways than any other physiologic response other than those necessary to our very existence be allowed to continue without benefit of objective, scientific analysis?[12]

Kinsey had, they admitted, opened the doors through monumental compilation of statistics elicited by direct interrogation. But his were sociological data not designed to elucidate questions regarding what physiological reactions develop during intercourse and why men and women behave as they do when responding to such stimulation. Masters and Johnson were thus charting unexplored territory in order to accurately *define* and *describe* the sexual process itself in physiological stages: its course, its progress, its climax, its aftermath.

Obviously, there were a number of pitfalls inherent in this technique. Direct observation, particularly when it involved the sexual act, raised questions concerning the ability of even the most highly trained scientists to be objective. No matter how enlightened, there was always the danger that an observer might unconsciously bring his values or his prejudices forward. Masters and Johnson knew that reliability of reporting was the answer, and they devised scientific controls for their experiments. They frequently recorded subjects on color film so that the sexual response cycle could be reviewed and rejudged. To systematize their method, they developed a four-phase scheme which followed the entire cycle of intercourse: the *excitement* phase, the *plateau,* the *orgasmic,* and finally the *resolution* phase. Within this framework variations could be classified.

Their system showed that after initial excitement through embrace and stroking, the human being passes onto a plateau where sexual tensions intensified to a level which made orgasm possible. How long this stage lasts depends mostly upon the stimuli employed. Whether orgasm is achieved depends upon the individual's drive for culmination of sexual release. The orgasmic phase itself is described as involuntary and of short duration, a few minutes perhaps, during which "the vasoconcentration [a congestion of blood vessels] and myotonia [increased muscular tensions] developed from sexual stimuli are released."[13] The researchers saw that when sexual climax arrives the body is totally engaged in a specific physiological process which varies among individuals; usually, sensual focus is pelvic, and most often centers upon the areas of "the clitoral body, vagina, and uterus of the female and in the penis, prostate, and seminal vesicles of the male." Most commonly, there is greater variation noted in the "intensity and duration of female orgasmic experience, while the male tends to follow standard patterns of ejaculation reaction with less individual variation."[14] The resolution phase follows orgasm and completes the process. Tensions are reduced by the orgasmic function and the individuals return to the unstimulated state.

A problem confronting researchers was the selection of their experimental population. Masters and Johnson showed preference towards those with higher than average intelligence (many with postgraduate education) and socioeconomic backgrounds, while also considering many other factors: the willingness to participate, the physical state of the prospective participant's health, and the ability to communicate accurately the details of sexual response. As for the older sample included, a mere 61 females from ages forty-one to seventy-eight (out of a total 382 female sample), and only 39 males ranging between fifty-one and eighty-nine (out of a total sample of 312) participated. Researchers have stressed how very difficult it was to gain cooperation in that age group, particularly of women, and Masters and Johnson recommended that any evaluations must be made with caution since clinical data on the older groups are so inadequate.

Yet Masters and Johnson's findings concerning our group are some of the most significant on record. Physiological changes are indeed notable in the aging human as observed during the performance of the sexual act, according to these data. For the female such changes can include a thinning of the vaginal wall, a shortening of both vaginal length and width, or a loss of elasticity. The cervix and uterus may shrink in size during the post-menopausal years and can result in a condition known as "steroid starvation." Some women suffer discomfort during sexual intercourse that they had never experienced earlier in their lives. Though common, there is little reason to conclude that they impede sexual performance. Doctors can treat such discomforts with estrogen and estrogen-like products to restore a healthy eroticism. Masters and Johnson conclude "there is no time limit drawn by the advancing years to female sexuality."[15] Physiologically they confirm earlier findings that the frequency of sexual expression found satisfactory for the younger woman can be carried over into postmenopausal years.

Their observations on psychic disturbances so common in menopause indicate that these may be disorders resurfacing from patterns developed earlier in the patient's life, a reactivated form of psychoneurotic behavior which comes forward in this crisis time of life. Most women fortunately are of a healthier constitution, and, having had considerable regularity in their sexual lives, show a more consistent capacity for sexual performance in later years. Some, enormously relieved from the fear of pregnancy, actually develop a greater interest in erotic activities. With their families raised, they are no longer faced with the physical exhaustion they once felt. Masters and Johnson suggest that a woman who has had a well-adjusted and stimulating marriage may move through her climacteric years with little or no interruption in her sexual life. These older women often show a greater capacity for sexual activity, they tell us, than younger ones who have not had the same opportunities.

The researchers' physiological portrait of the male over fifty presents us with a man who takes longer to achieve an erection, but once erected, can maintain that erection for extended periods without ejaculation. In addition, the efficiency of the ejaculatory process may be impaired by the aging process. An older male may feel the urge to ejaculate yet may have lost control of the process. This was found to be common in later years, though often transitory in character. The situation is complex, but Masters and Johnson concluded that the sexual responses of the human male wane as he grows older. The turning point seems to be around age of fifty, when sexual inadequacy markedly increases, yet exceptions to this rule are common and often dramatic. Maintaining sexuality for the male, like the female, is a function much dependent upon consistency of active sexual expression; patterns from formative years emerge and dominate. When a man has established a pattern of continued sexual expression over thirty or forty years, he most likely will maintain it through his seventies or even eighties.

Masters and Johnson spell out the many obstacles to such continuing relations. Men may lose sexual responsiveness for a variety of reasons; monotony, or an overfamiliarity with the sexual partner, often reduces the sexual tensions. And the American male between forty and sixty is often preoccupied with a demanding daily work life, one which consumes all of his energies and strength. Tension and physical fatigue result from this absorption with work—a great deterrent to sexuality. The tendency in America towards the consumption of large quantities of alcohol not only reduces sexual tensions between partners but also makes sexual performance all the more difficult for the aging male. But most inhibiting for the older male is his fear of failure. Once he has experienced impotence for one reason or another he may secede from coital activity altogether, rather than face the "ego-shattering" experience again. Some react negatively towards their partners, while others search out younger females to prove to themselves their unimpaired prowess. There are better ways to deal with such difficulties, to be discussed later.

Masters and Johnson's findings conclude that though man's capacity for erection may be lessened, this hardly detracts from the pleasure he experiences during intercourse. His ability to hold an erection longer contributes substantially to greater satisfaction for himself and his partner. They believe that older people can and should continue their sexual functioning indefinitely.

So researchers in these three major studies have familiarized the American public with the biological facts concerning sexual behavior in age, and helped to dispel some encrusted prejudices, erroneous notions, and prejudicial fears. What was once considered abnormal and even shameful is now openly explored, and to admit to continuing sexual desire after youth is no scandal. *Time* reported in 1973 that in Sun City, Florida, a community near Tampa, old people are dancing and dating, holding hands, kissing in public, even talking about "steadies."[16] Informal liaisons have become more accepted in such communities all over the country, and if erotic relationships have to be kept clandestine, it is to avoid the censure of children and grandchildren, not that of contemporaries! Old people mostly pair off in what has been called "unmarriages of convenience," in which many live together but do not marry because of the reduced social security benefits such change in status would involve.

This is not to say that such companionships are carefree. Many suffer from guilt felings and embarrassment and keep their liaisons secret. Having grown up with the specific prohibitions against such extramarital encounters and with the clear understanding that sexual desire in age is improper and unnatural, such arrangements often cost them their self-esteem. Yet reports from France, ever advanced in sexual practices, describe brothels staffed by older prostitutes that now specially cater to aging men.[17] A clinical psychologist in Sepulveda, California, Dr. Mary Ann P. Sviland, has her elderly patients doing erotic exercises, reading sex manuals, and viewing pornographic films, on the hypothesis that such activities reduce anxieties, increase sexual fantasies, and, most important, strengthen the associations of sex with pleasure.[18]

The continuing popularity of such a book as Isadore Rubin's *Sexual Life After Sixty* brought scientific findings to the lay public and relieved that prevailing anguish and guilt. (Despite the fact that his book appeared before Masters and Johnson published the results of their experiments, Rubin knew and considered their research.) Vigorously attacking the hypocrisy surrounding the subject, he tells us:

> The fullest expression of the sexual needs and interests of men and women over sixty cannot take place in a society which denies or ignores the reality of these needs and interests or in an atmosphere which prevents full and open inquiry into them. Nor can it take place in a soil which nourishes every kind of myth and misconception about these later years.[19]

Rubin demands the recognition of such needs as natural and normal. He explodes what he calls the "self-defeating myths" which stifle the free expression of sexuality in later years. One of the most common, for example, is the folk fantasy that the emission of semen, or indeed the participation in sexual activity at all, weakens the constitution, hastens debility, and even brings on early death. According to this notion, each drop of semen ejaculated equals the loss of forty drops of blood. There is nothing new about this idea. He notes that certain Chinese handbooks and Hindu texts and the works of the ancient Greek philosopher Pythagoras and doctor Galen echo the theme that coition enervates and robs the body of its vital force. And such theories persist even today in the pseudo-scientific gobbledygook of the "rejuvenation doctor."

An even more pervasive myth persists: that the abstention from sex in early years can prolong the total sex life of the individual, that a person is "used up" through continued or excessive intercourse since it drains energy and the life fluids. There is little mystery about the eternal recurrence of this belief. Throughout history it has been a standby for moralist preachers and has been immensely useful in a world where contraception was virtually unknown.

Yet scientific research blatantly contradicts these myths. Kinsey, Masters and Johnson, and the Duke studies demonstrated that the most active sexually tend to continue so both in early and late life! All have stressed the importance of continuing activity to prolong sexual ability. As for the effects of the loss of semen upon the male organism, Rubin compares it to the loss of saliva, and there is absolutely no scientific evidence to the contrary. The body is a self-regulating organism, and, assuming that it receives a healthy diet, will act to replace any missing fluids by replenishing its own supplies.

Another commonly accepted misconception is that menopause in women brings with it the fading of desire. The menopausal period has so long been associated with "sexual death" that it has become virtually impossible to separate the two, and many women are deeply confused regarding this matter. It is quite true that in these climacteric years there can be notable physical changes. Some women find their voices may lower, and a growth of facial hairs, which they may regard as humiliating, defeminizing changes. Yet they are only a result of hormone changes involved with the disappearance of ovulation, and can be easily rectified. Menopause is nature's physiological means for ending that time of a woman's life in which she is capable of bearing children; her *reproductive* life is over. Thus, menopause is only minimally connected to her sexual gratification in later life.

We have already discussed the various physiological changes found common to postmenopausal years which can be medically treated in order to normalize sexual relations once again. However, Masters and Johnson have indicated that the psyche is at least as important to the sex drive as our physiology. The Victorian complex emerges again, which specifies that women in later years are *unsuited* for sex, that to think, fantasize, or dream of it is unnatural and improper, and to act upon it is not only sheer self-indulgence but an unwillingness to acknowledge the passing of the years! Clearly then, until the psychological shame associated with sexual desire after one's maturity is exposed as unfounded and conquered, there is little likelihood for healthy acceptance of the true function of menopause.

On the subject of masturbation Rubin is equally outspoken. Thought of as a "pernicious habit" practiced mostly by children, adolescents, and immature adults, "onanism," as it is technically called, is firmly associated with such deviations as sadomasochism and the realms of pornographic fantasy. Until very recently it was firmly discouraged and considered destructive to the body, mind, and soul. To speak of it in connection with older people was shocking. Yet scientific findings have demonstrated that autoerotic practices are common among older men and women, married and unmarried, in every social sphere. Herant Katchadourian has pointed out that, after a slump between ages thirty and forty, masturbation once again becomes a souce of orgasm for many at age fifty.[20] Masters and Johnson explain that unmarried females who have used such techniques in their youth continue it for relief of sexual tensions as they age. The numbers of this group are enlarged by widows or divorcees who find sexual tensions mounting yet whose new situation makes the possibilities of intercourse limited. Older males are often found returning to masturbation during temporary illnesses of the spouse, or during enforced separations. Many physicians find that those practicing self-stimulation over the years enjoy better health than those who have no such outlets. Given the increasing numbers of older people who find themselves without sexual partners today, it is possible that masturbation, once dissociated from the unhealthy, immoral, and illicit, will become an increasingly acceptable form of gratification.

Yet another stereotype that Rubin examines is that of the D.O.M. (Dirty Old Man). Exhibitionism, child molestation, and even rape are the common accusations made when an older male shows interest or affection for younger people. So unnatural does it seem for the old male to feel such emotions that most children today (boys and girls) are taught to avoid being touched by an aging stranger for fear that he has sexual designs for them. By enforcing this suspicion, the damage done to children's attitudes towards the aging is incalculable. Police reports indicate that most sexual assaults on children are committed by offenders between the ages of thirty-nine and fifty, not by the older group. The dangerous age is middle-age.

Perhaps the importance of Isadore Rubin's contribution is that he *dared* more than ten years ago to suggest that it is the *right* of every older person to express sexuality freely and without guilt. As he saw it, our duty was to clear away the obstacles to the creative expression of that sexuality. This is the language of liberation! His was an indictment of a culture whose negative attitudes towards sex were bestowed upon every child, setting in concrete a life-long framework that no amount of awareness or information could reverse. He calls older people today "neurotically conditioned," a group so weighed down by anxiety and guilt that there is no evaluating their true sexual potential. Only when such distorted views are exposed and uprooted, so that young children are not infected by them, will there be a possibility of our seeing a more emotionally mature, freer being, whose preferences for or disinclination from sexual activities in later life is not guilt-bound.

Whatever patterns of sexual activity eventually emerge among older people (and they may well be less than revolutionary), the repression of them can only be unhealthy. A sane atmosphere must be maintained so that old-fashioned inhibitions do not smother free sexual expression. Suggestions that continued discussion of the subject is akin to preaching the "need" for sex in old age also miss the point. Research to date has amply demonstrated that sexuality in later years is not merely the invention of journalists or gerontologists; in one form or another it expresses itself among people in every social class. Responding to a piece on the subject by Norman M. Lobenz[21] in the *New York Times Magazine* in which he discusses the sources of sexual guilt in both old and young, one letter writer reflects this confusion:

To The Editor:
Alas, something else to feel guilty about. Instead of a minority feeling guilty about having sex after sixty-five, the majority are now encouraged to feel guilty if they don't.

Leave the senior citizen alone. He's paid his dues and earned the privilege to do as he damn pleases without having some "expert" advising that he be pumped full of hormones so that he may do what he "ought."[22]

Another correspondent called Lobenz (who'd been described by the *Times* as not yet sixty-five) a "dirty young man," asking in a fury, "Don't we have problems enough with V.D. among young people? Do we need additional problems with old people?"[23]

Such readers are threatened by any frank approach to sexuality. But for the many thousands whose continuing urges oppress them with guilt and shame, the predicament of the aged today as the class of "sexually underprivileged" must be challenged in very specific, professional ways. The family physician, internist, social worker, welfare worker and psychiatrist must become better educated regarding such needs. The professional community has been as infected by dangerous stereotypes as the public at large, and has been responsible for immense resistance to change. E. M. Feigenbaum, M. F. Lowenthal, and their associates reported that most professionals are unwilling to probe the question at all. When older patients complain to doctors of ineffective sexual performance or loss of desire, for example, they are often greeted with indifference or at best a homily on the limitations on sexuality imposed by age. Yet these researchers found older people are "vitally interested, terribly confused and hunger eagerly for information about the norms of sexuality in the geriatric population."[24]

Physicians must concern themselves with their patients' sexual needs and the tremendous variations possible among older people. They must volunteer specific medical details concerning illnesses which require sexual moderation or abstention. As the practicing geriatric nurse Irene Burnside stresses:

> People are often uncomfortable talking about sexuality. Most of them have not been educated to deal with sexual difficulties. Even though there are more than 14 million Americans with heart and blood vessel disease, there is little literature about the effects of sexual activity on the heart and circulatory system.[25]

The cardiac patient, for example, who is already in a state of anxiety, refrains from asking his doctor about the effects of intercourse on his condition. This often results in extended periods of abstinence, possibly causing frustration and marital strain, and is hardly conducive to recovery. Yet there are activities doctors recommend which consume far more energy than sex to hasten recovery from heart disease, such as vigorous wallking or jogging and calisthenic routines. Domestic arguments or emotional flare-ups can tax the heart far more than sexual activity. While the effects upon the patient of these possibilities are much discussed, sexual activity goes unmentioned, as though it were a frivolity which could easily be dispensed with in times of trouble.

A wealth of information is available for such situations. New York physician Richard Stein reported to a November 1975 meeting of the American Heart Association on his experiments with middle-aged cardiac patients in which he attempted to lower their heart rates during intercourse so that they could function sexually without paralyzing fear and anxiety. Measuring their coital heart rates first by means of a complicated system of portable electrocardiographs during intercourse, he then exposed them to a training program of sixteen weeks of riding stationary bicycles. After training, the men's hearts were found to be pumping the same amounts of blood with less effort. It assisted in efficient and pain-free lovemaking and promoted a feeling of health and optimism about eventual recovery.[26] Others have described further possibilities. Particular positions for intercouse are more relaxed than others, thus requiring less effort. Or, intercourse in the morning after a night's refreshing sleep makes use of the energy level when it is at its highest.

What about the sexual problems associated with high blood pressure, diabetes, arthritis, emphysema, and Parkinson's disease? Though physical infirmities can reduce sexual performance at any age, in later years there is a dramatic incidence of such illnesses. Cannot people receive specific counsel for living normal sex lives despite such ailments? The loss of the sexual outlet can be even more debilitating both physically and psychologically than some of the diseases themselves.

Diabetes, for instance, is a disease which may result in the loss of potency in the male since it tends to interfere with nerve cell functions. Yet some physicians assert that diabetic impotence is partly psychological; a common symptom is a preliminary weakness in erection, and this is so traumatizing for many that they are unable to complete the act. Anxieties should be allayed early through counselling so that a man is not defeated immediately by his first few failures.

Many men suffer great fears concerning the need for prostate surgery, assuming that it will mean the end of their sexual lives. The prostate gland is a secondary organ of reproduction and a common source of trouble for aging males mostly because of its location near the bladder. Its major function is to provide seminal fluid which is ejaculated during an orgasm. When, with age, it slowly enlarges and can sometimes cause great difficulties in urination, surgery in indicated. Yet the surgery need not cause alarm (though it may once have justifiably done so), because today's operational techniques are very attentive to the future sexual needs of older men.

Similarly, many women who have undergone hysterectomy feel they have lost the physical ability for intercourse. This is often true of their spouses as well, who associate such operations with loss of all desire and even physical attractiveness. Actually, it is the couple's attitude alone which may have been affected.

These are vastly neglected areas crying out for help. Older people today must be able to discuss their sexuality with their peers without ridicule or contempt, and with their children and grandchildren if they choose to do so. As for the professionals who must counsel them, they must create a free atmosphere for open and honest communication. As research progresses we will all become more educated; self-awareness will grow and along with it the ability to assess the true nature of sexual needs for older people. It is clear that the sexual picture is changing radically for everyone. Projections for the year 2000 consistently include the growing legitimization of all sorts of informal liaisons, trial marriages, renewable marriage contracts, mutual polygamy, homosexual marriages, single parent families, communal living, and even polygamy for older people. (The prediction is that by the turn of the century there will be half again as many women as men over the age of sixty-five. According to Roger Revelle, Director of Population Studies at Harvard University, polygamy, usually associated with primitive peoples, may be a reasonable solution for a society which has two women for every man.)[27] And the availability of reasonably safe contraceptives to large segments of the population will mean that for the very first time in history, sex will be securely separated from reproduction and freely associated with pleasure.

But whatever patterns emerge for the future, our interest here in sexual activity arises from its representing one part of our search for the whole being. Simone de Beauvoir has aptly reminded us of Freud's point that sexuality is not confined to genitality alone —it serves several functions. In youth, she tells us, the tension relieves itself with extreme urgency, but in age there is perhaps more of a positive pleasure than a release. Desire can bring a "transformation of the world" and a unification of all the elements within it. It is through the erotic pursuit that Mme. de Beauvoir believes we assert the manly and womanly qualities so valuable for preserving our identities throughout life.[28] She is describing that much abused concept, love, of which sexuality is but a part: love being a basic human hunger which begins at birth and endures to the grave. It is this need which must be attended, in age as well as in youth, in whatever forms it may take. Free sexual choice for the old is yet another step towards love, towards the realization rather than the abandonment of self.

10.
The Money Fight

By now the patient but practical reader may be muttering under his breath that none of the foregoing amounts to a jot when it comes to the bottom line. Quite right too! All the liberation in the world won't get you past the checkout counter at the supermarket or cover your prescription at the pharmacy. Without a doubt there is no discomfort that has created more misery for older Americans than insufficient incomes and the lack of financial security. No source of aggravation has been more explicit, no humiliation more complete than the necessity of meeting a future without prospects or expectations. No rejection by American society has been more persuasive and final than this financial one.

It's not just money that is at issue here—it's *every single material thing* which sustains and supports us and makes it possible to continue life in old age with freedom of choice. Today, older people are drifting in a vast inflationary sea, desperately trying to stay afloat, scrimping, making do, getting by, but seeing no rescue in sight. Some sink into depression and despair, others become embittered and give up, demonstrated by the shocking rise in suicides by those over sixty-five. For millions what was once an eagerly awaited dream, the prospect of relief from toil, and the promise of ease and pleasure in retirement, has now become a nightmare of poor housing, poor food, insecurity, loneliness, sickness, and fear of assault and robbery. No amount of prudence and attention to providing for their old age seems to make a difference anymore. Inflation in the 1970s has eaten into buying power, eroded the value of pensions, and shrunken savings. Social security benefits, even scaled to cost of living, were never sufficient in the first place.

Department of Health, Education and Welfare figures about older Americans released for 1976 show just how bleak the picture is. Over 15 percent, (more than 3 million people of the nearly 21 million then over sixty-five) were found to be living below the poverty level; among elderly whites, one out of every seven was found below poverty standards, and for elderly blacks, it was more than one of every three. In the latter group more than 1 million households lacked plumbing facilities. One in every five couples with a husband aged sixty-five or over had an income of less than $4,000 in 1974. In fact, the median income of families headed by someone over sixty-five was less than half of those with younger heads. People living alone were in worse condition: 32 percent were in poverty, and of this group almost 75 percent were old women. Those in the cities of the nation fared a little better than people in the country, at least when it came to income; but vital services were much more costly in cities. The old pay a disproportionate share (up to 35 percent) of their incomes for rent and home ownership, and great numbers of them whose property and appliances are worn live in continuous dread of repair bills.[1]

Juanita Kreps, the Duke University economist who has served as Secretary of Commerce in the Carter administration, observes that there is "systematic deterioration in the aged's relative income position" during periods of economic growth.[2] Such growth may raise the standards of living for workers and investors but for fixed-income persons, the higher rate of industrial growth makes workers' pay outstrip them. Along with such higher pay for workers comes higher prices for consumer goods. The result: reduced buying power and poorer living standards for the old.

Brandeis University analyst James Schultz has said that old people were even poorer some decades ago and that noticeable improvement can be seen in their economic status.[3] In 1967, according to Social Security Administration figures, they received an aggregate money income of around $60 billion, and 1974 Bureau of Census data showed that the aged's share was up to $95 billion.

Yet the real gain is questionable because fixed income recipients have suffered severe losses in standards of living in recent years.

According to Kreps, inflation will continue to plague us in the coming decades. It is in food and fuel that the most rapid rises are to be felt, both of which, she observes, "loom large in the budget of the elderly." The general impact of inflation, which was calculated at the rate of 5 percent in the 1960s, is now running at an annual 12 percent. As for the specific rise in costs for a retired couple, *The Wall Street Journal* estimated in 1975 that it was 11 percent. From December 1969 through January 1974, Bureau of Labor Statistics figures show medical care costs increased 22 percent, rent 10 percent, and food skyrocketed 40 percent.

Inflation hits older people hardest precisely because of their inability to anticipate any financial relief in their future. Beyond the obvious losses associated with it, inflation affects the quality of life in many subtle ways. It tends to put debtors in an advantageous position. This is because repayment of loans is made in inflated dollars. The aging are not commonly among those who incur such debts—they are not buying furniture, washing machines, or freezers. Most hold their wealth in the form of fixed assets, thus having no access to such gains. Another example: those suffering from chronic or degenerative diseases (39 percent of those sixty-five and over as compared to 7 percent of the younger population) face the ever-rising costs of medical care.

But whatever the loss, they all amount to persistent deterioration of financial stability, and with it insecurity, anxiety, and fear of the future. Sylvia Porter, the popular syndicated columnist on consumer problems, has pointed out that to calculate one's needs for the upcoming years a conservative inflation factor would be an annual 5 percent, although rises will vary on different consumer goods. She estimates that in ten years a suit you would pay $125 for today will cost over $200, that the steak now costing $1.80 per pound will run approximately $3, and that the hospital room now $100 will cost $170. In twenty years, she forecasts, what you can buy for $3,000 will require nearly $8,000. And she recommends cold, hard thinking in terms of what she calls the "realities of retirement." Even if we are "sufficiently informed, affluent, thrifty," we will have at retirement about *half* of what other Americans are then earning. "With an income geared to to-day's living standards," she adds, "[we] will be way, way down the scale in comparison to incomes geared to tomorrow's living costs and living standards."[4]

Again we find ourselves facing all the service books and the advice of Sylvia Porter, Edmond LeBreton, Sal Nuccio, Sidney Margolius, and a hundred other financial experts. They caution us to plan ahead, to study our predicament, and to budget wisely. But can such guides for planning our retirement bring any real relief in our current situation? Money-saving schemes and figure-juggling techniques *can* prove of value in managing one's assets. And, it is a vital necessity to think out and review one's financial position in terms of future income well before retirement. But is this enough? Can such piecemeal action succeed in relieving financial anguish for the majority of upcoming old, and in maintaining their former lifestyles?

It now seems highly unlikely. The Federal Council on the Aging, a fifteen-member group nominated by the President and confirmed by the Senate for the specific purpose of reporting annually on the current state of older Americans, underscored this pessimistic view. As described in their initial report to the President, in March 1975, "the urgent humanitarian needs of older Americans require special attention in strategies by both the executive and legislative branches of government to offset the effects of recession and inflation."[5]

So we need overall reforms: we need to review the entire financial picture to bring the kind of relief which can best serve growing numbers of people. We need coordinated social service planning for the elderly on local, state, and federal levels. This means reviewing the tax structure to learn the impact of particular kinds of taxation on the elderly, reexamining the social security system for its growing inadequacies, investigating the Medicare program for its shortcomings, analyzing the private pension plans of this nation for loopholes, and reorganizing the government's various social welfare programs to overcome costly duplications and overlapping.

Our government is no newcomer to the role of provider. Like most of the governments in the advanced societies of the world, it has had to assume some responsibility for overseeing the social welfare of its elderly citizens. Since the 1920s with the continuing decline of the three-generational family, the American government has gradually taken over this task as its own. Today it is a well-accepted opinion that governments *must* accept this obligation. But as University of California political scientist Sanford Lakoff has pointed out, intervention as it now stands is "a patchwork of policies rather than a coherent and farsighted effort of social planning and foresight."[6] As this older population grows in numbers and becomes more vigilant of its own rights and privileges, it will come to expect and demand far more from government than previous generations, and aging Americans will increasingly constitute a viable interest group.

As Lakoff observes, instead of a group which is regarded as dependents or handicapped citizens, *burdens* on society, "the elderly form a significant part of the polity, and as such are in a position to compete against other interested groups for a share in the distribution of the social product."[7] Increasingly, serving the old may be not merely philanthropy, charity, or the humane way of dealing with an unhappy situation, but good politics as well.

This new attitude reflects the emergence of a different view of freedom and social justice: that without exception each individual in our nation is entitled to pursue his or her own kind of development without reference to race, sex, or age, to a full life unhampered in personal liberty, and that, above all, these human rights must not be allowed to dissipate themselves as the individual grows older. It could be called our current ideal of social justice, our twentieth century redefinition of the "pursuit of happiness" as it was laid out by our founding fathers.

Here we can only hope to touch upon these intricate and tangled issues; we can glimpse some of the stresses government programs are facing, and the dangers they present to up-coming beneficiaries. Foremost in our minds for older Americans is the demand for income levels in accordance with the American standard of living—for an adequate income *floor* under *all* older people, along with the certainty that as inflation soars upward, so will this level rise for the aging. But money is not the only mechanism for meeting financial needs. There are services and facilities which enable people to make their income go further. We need to consider such services before we can hope to devise financial strategies for the future.

We may well ask, If our government has accepted the responsibility for assuring our older people a basic floor of income, how, in practical terms, is this provided? Since its inception in the Roosevelt Administration in 1935, the partial answer to this question has been the Social Security System, the rock upon which financial stability for the retired and disabled stands. Millions have collected from the program over the years, and nine out of ten American workers are covered today. It is a current source of income for 89 percent of the public sixty-five and over.

Despite the American inhibition against federal intervention, despite the Puritan ethic of hard work, industriousness, and prudent financial investments, the Great Depression so shook the nation that the public stood ready to try some new approaches. The growing determination that such disasters must never be allowed to happen again made for a more receptive climate for new legislation. Indeed, it was considered a revolutionary step for a conservative-minded nation. Many called it creeping socialism then, and some still do today. Historian Frederick Lewis Allen remarked that if there hadn't been strong pressures on Franklin Roosevelt both from Huey Long with his "share the wealth" campaign and Dr. Francis E. Townsend, the Social Security bill might never have seen the light of day.

When the Roosevelt braintrusters proposed the Act as a "first line of defense against destitution," they were striking out against two major social problems: old age dependency and widespread unemployment. Its original design was a modest one based on compulsory contributions from employers and employees. It was not meant to provide for retirement fully, but to supplement private savings and pensions. Roosevelt called it a "cornerstone which is being built but which is by no means complete."[8]

Social Security is now an expanded scheme that ranks as our second-most expensive program ($85 billion in 1977), only after national defense—a complex, confusing, and controversial system. In the last twenty years alone, the maximum pension, for a retiring worker has jumped from $156 a month to $581. There are also vastly broadened benefits for survivors, the disabled, hospital insurance, and coverage for widowers as well as widows. Millions of aged poor, having no other source of income, are forced to live on Social Security alone. Social Security has been and is a mainstay of financial security for older citizens, and it must remain so in the future.

Somewhat disquieting then are continuing reports that the system is in trouble. Despite the many changes and improvements over the years, some critics have suggested that because its initial goals were not consistent in the first place, they are beginning to undermine the organization as a whole. They argue that it is impossible to provide benefits related to retirees' previous earnings (the insurance function) and to simultaneously lift all beneficiaries out of poverty (the welfare function). The dilemma as described by economists from the Brookings Institution is that Social Security "has attempted to solve two problems with one instrument: How to prevent destitution among the aged poor, and how to assure people (who had) adequate incomes before retirement of benefits that are related to their previous standards of living. . . ."[9]

The tension between these goals, along with pressing population problems added in recent years, has resulted in gross inequities in the program. Take the striking injustices in the cases cited by Emma Pullen and Paul Steiger:

> A sixty-five-year old man who retires this year after having worked all his life at the federal minimum wage is entitled to a Social Security benefit of $194 a month. That is just $1.25 a day more than he would get from federal welfare if he had never worked at all.
>
> A man and wife who both worked full time for forty years to earn a moderate combined income will get $462.90 a month in Social Security benefits if they retire today—$83 less than their neighbors who earned the same amount with only the husband working.
>
> A retired industrialist who clips bond coupons and collects dividends netting him $1 million a year receives an additional $6,552 in tax-free Social Security benefits annually for himself and his spouse, undiminished by his huge outside income. By contrast, a former truck driver with no portfolio of securities to fall back on has his retirement check pared by the government if he takes a part-time job paying more than $53 a week.[10]

So more and more voices are calling the entire system downright unfair, denying that it is social insurance of any sort, and questioning the system's right to compulsory payroll deductions. Milton Friedman, the Nobel Prize-winning economist, has argued that the Social Security tax is "the most regressive tax in our tax system." The growing fear of economists is that the entire system could go bankrupt within the next twenty years due to population decreases. In *Business Week's* estimate, the $44.4 billion trust funds backing Social Security will surely be exhausted by the early 1980s. With decreases in the working force because of declining birth rates, funding for the program will demand higher and higher payroll deductions from those still working.

Legislation passed in December 1977 attempted to put the system back on its feet by raising the taxable wage base gradually so that the tax rate would be 6.65 percent by 1981 on the first $29,700 earnings (as compared to 5.85 percent on the first $16,500 in 1977). Congress hoped that this would assure the financing of the program for the next couple of decades. They may have succeeded for now, yet many analysts feel that keeping it functioning makes unjust demands on the present work force.

In a book called *Social Security: The Fraud in Your Future,* Warren Shore attacks the system as a major source of the current recession, calling it full of "double taxation, hidden taxation, and destructive limitations" and maintains that it is in need of complete overhaul.[11] The Social Security system, he says, is demanding that the generation of young Americans pay from twenty to fifty times as much in payroll taxes as the one that came before it in order to provide benefits for the huge numbers now becoming disabled or approaching retirement. The young now, he says, are "a generation of victims."[12]

Whether justly argued or not, such an accusation is particularly serious for older Americans because it reflects an emerging attitude and may be revealing of forthcoming negative pressures. Brookings economist John A. Brittain has noted that Social Security is basically an "intergenerational transfer system" through which today's workers finance the pensions of yesterday's workers.[13] Of course, the latter do so in hopes that tomorrow's group will do the same for them. The big trouble is that current projections of population decreases, in combination with longer life expectancy, are playing havoc with the system's structure. If great numbers of the older population not only continue to retire on Social Security but live longer to draw greater sums from it, the drains on young workers' salaries will grow steadily, and along with them will grow a discontent and, conceivably, even a rebellion against the burdens of supporting the vast numbers of old of the nation.

Other difficulties stem from reports of many withdrawals from the Social Security system. New York City government employees have already announced their intention to do so, with Los Angeles County and hundreds of other smaller municipal employees contemplating doing the same. These local government employees are not compelled to remain in the federal system like the rest of the country's employed, who must pay into the program. Though the impact of such dropouts has not yet been estimated, it is likely to mean even higher payroll deductions to cover this deficit.

Specific complaints about the system continue to come in from working wives, divorced women, single people, minority groups, and particularly the retiring and retired. The program's "earning test" regulation, which penalizes pensioners up to seventy-two years old by reducing their Social Security checks by fifty cents for every dollar they earn over the allowable limit (in 1979, this was $4,500 for those from sixty-five to seventy-two and $3,480 for those under sixty-five) seems not merely questionable policy but age discrimination. Senator Barry Goldwater has called it an outrage, and demanded its repeal, pointing out that while income on investments in stocks and bonds is not involved in such reductions, the person who continues to work for a salary is being severely penalized.[14]

It is apparent that some very serious problems have developed within this particular support system. We simply can no longer afford to take its solidity for granted. It needs to be reexamined, redesigned, and streamlined, specifically with the future welfare of the new-olds in mind.

Another solid prop upon which retired people have relied over the years has been their private pensions. In Britain, Italy, France and particularly in West Germany (which has one of the most secure and the oldest pension systems of all, tracing its beginning back three hundred years to the Miners' Relief Associations), workers' pension plans have provided such coverage to defend people from want.

As the family began to fail in its role as the traditional provider, business and industry were compelled to take over. What was thought of as a philanthropic benevolence, or a reward for loyalty (like the ritual dinner and the gold watch), the pensioning of older workers was also a way for industry to phase out its least productive elements and put in younger and more vigorous ones. The attitude prevailed that the retiring worker had better accept gratefully whatever was offered.

Yet consider this: By the middle 1970s over 30 million men and women in America alone were enrolled in such insurance plans, and today, practically every business, large or small, and every labor union is heavily involved in pension provisions. An estimated $180 billion or more is tied up in these funds, with prospects that the sum will double by the early 1980s. Economist Peter Drucker has pointed out that through their pension funds, employees own at least one-half of the equity capital of American business today, something he calls "pension fund socialism."[15]

Until very recently, accusations have been rampant about irresponsible investments and lack of control over such programs. Senator Jacob Javits had called these assets, "the largest concentration of wealth with the least regulation in the country," and Ralph Nader's investigative group maintained in 1973 that "at least half the people covered by pensions will never collect a penny."[16] Since the passage of the 1974 Pension Reform Law, a landmark in setting standards for private plans, some of the most obvious loopholes have finally been plugged. The Employees Retirement Income Security Act (ERISA) was passed after a decade of legislative hearings and intensive lobbying by consumer groups, labor, and business, bringing to public attention the injustices and helplessness which were facing many prospective pensioners. While the new act does not actually force companies to set up pension plans, it does demand that when such systems are in operation they be fully regulated, and that they offer covered employees assurances and guarantees surpassing their past coverage.

If a company should go out of business, for example, the employees of that company, under the ERISA, are assured of at least a portion of the pension benefits coming to them. This is because the law establishes a Pension Benefit Guarantee Corporation to which all qualified plans must contribute. If a firm goes broke, this federal agency will pay up to $750 a month to those workers who are vested in it.

Correcting a far more common problem is the new law's protection against losing one's vested rights should one leave or be discharged from one company to join another. There is hardly a worker in America who does not find that changing jobs, locations, even professions is a frequent demand of his work life. So the ERISA, in making possible portability of vested pension benefits, is a liberation for those in our country's mobile labor and management force. Up until 1974, such losses were continuous and often disastrous. Now, when an employee joins a company which also has a tax-qualified plan, he can simply transfer his vested funds from the old into the new system.

More specified eligibility provisions prohibit plans from establishing requirements of more than a year's service, or an age greater than twenty-five. Minimum standards are set by the law for vesting rights in the three varying government plans, which explicitly assure employees of 100 percent vesting within ten years. Finally, the law assures these programs of more solid funding than they had in the past, and greater financial responsibility behind handling and investment of such assets. Employees are entitled to be informed in reasonably clear and simple language of all major provisions, and must periodically receive financial statements concerning the pension's investment earnings.

Greater benefits of security and mobility are noticeable under ERISA for increasing numbers of employees. It has been a long step towards correcting the many inequities which have been characteristically associated with such plans. Despite visible improvements under the reform law, the liberalized age and service requirements and extended survivors benefits, there remain some serious problems with private pensions, which in fact, the current legislation is said to have engendered. Ohio State University professor of law Merton Bernstein, an outspoken advocate of pension reform, is among ERISA's critics. He finds it "the most complicated law ever to hit the books." Other analysts see it as frustrating, confusing, even destined to end the pension system in America. Some distressing signs have appeared. Since the law's passage in 1974, thousands of small pension systems have gone out of business, maintaining that the excessive paperwork demanded by ERISA has put impossible burdens on them, that the new regulations concerning personal liability for their pension executives makes them undue targets for lawsuits, and that the government has imposed far too many new restrictions on ways in which companies may invest their pension funds. By mid-year 1975, *Newsweek* reported that four thousand pension plans were going out of business. (By the middle of 1978, the figure was twenty thousand.)[17] Planners are concerned about the estimated higher costs resulting from such strict legislation. Estimated at 5 percent to 10 percent of the annual payroll now, pension costs are expected to skyrocket to 20 or 30 percent.

Even more immediate is the criticism that not all the effects of the law are welcome to older workers. In rewriting their plans many companies adopted mandatory retirement provisions; some even *lowered* their mandatory retirement ages. This has complicated the new laws prohibiting forced retirement at sixty-five.

Another key issue is that few companies have coped with lagging benefit scales in terms of rising consumer prices. Inflation has generally cut so heavily into pension allotments that what was once adequacy is now insufficiency and want. The period between 1970 and 1974 has been estimated as having seen the sharpest inflation of any five-year period since World War II, and the pace has accelerated since. A leading financial institution in the management of pension programs, the Bankers' Trust Company of New York, in a study of 190 of the nation's largest companies with pension funds totalling above $50 billion, reported in April of 1975 its conclusion that these employers are *not* keeping their pension systems in line with inflation. Of the companies studied, 74 percent allowed at least one increase in retirement benefits during the period. But the average pension plan restored only three cents of the twenty-seven cents which had been eroded in the purchasing power of the dollar for that time. By the end of 1974, it was estimated that most pensioners were actually at least six cents per dollar poorer than they had been on the same pension in 1969. Only a few firms were basing their increases in salaries on the last five-year earnings or on terminal earnings; instead, they were using an average of a thirty-year or total career-wage base. The difference in actual benefits between the two methods of calculation means a significant loss for the worker.[18]

Obviously, the complicated 1974 legislation needs clarifying, and both its authors, Senators Jacob K. Javitz and Harrison A. Williams, have been working on such revision. As the impact of the new standards can be evaluated, Congress must continue to refine its operation if it is to protect the interests of the on-coming retirement population. More than ever, we must be vigilant on our own behalf to see to it that improvements are enacted into law!

The 1974 law has concerned itself primarily with reforms for corporate pension funds. But far too many abuses and inequities still go unchecked in union-based or public-funded pensions. There have been many reports of shady ventures connected with the Central States Teamsters pension funds, for example, scandalous mismanagement and outright swindles involving loans to Las Vegas gambling hotels, and questionable real estate speculation in marginal lands, all in open association with known mobsters. Lester Velie reported that one-third of the loans made by the Teamster fund, in the vicinity of $195 million, where delinquent as of February 1972.[19] Yet as late as the winter of 1976, Peter Drucker complained that the Department of Labor had failed to concern itself sufficiently with these continuing abuses, and that teamsters, coal miners, and construction workers were still receiving "pitiful pensions" as a consequence.[20]

As for public pension plans, federal, state, and local governments across the nation are being accused of duplication, waste, and mismanagement of their funds. Public pensions were originally set on higher scales than those in the private sector because public service workers earned generally lower salaries and most were not covered by Social Security. This situation has changed as Social Security has been extended to many in civil service. Labor unions have also been successfully gaining higher pay and other benefits for public servants. Their pension costs meanwhile have skyrocketed, and cities and state governments find themselves near bankruptcy in efforts to keep up. With virtually no control or regulation over such plans, corrective action is desperately needed.

Pension funds are far too important to older workers to be allowed to proceed much longer without a closer scrutiny. The system still hangs onto the actualities of forty and fifty years ago, which essentially aimed at reducing surplus labor by forcing people to retire at an arbitrarily set age. Today, this is impossible to defend. As Peter Drucker observes, the tensions between younger and older workers and between employed and retired people cannot be eliminated but certainly "they need not be aggravated by the pension system, as they are being aggravated today."[21]

Important peripheral areas also must be considered. Medical and hospital care programs, for instance, since their passage in 1965, have actually acted as subsidies for older citizens. In lieu of cash, such systems as Medicare and Medicaid are designed to assure everyone old and ailing of necessary medical attention. Such care has been long in coming, and to this day faces colossal problems. Three decades elapsed between the passage of the Social Security Act and the adoption of Medicare! Why? The provision of health services should hardly have been thought of as a more radical step than that of unemployment or old age insurance. Yet despite the many attempts to broaden legislation to include health benefits, it seemed in 1935 and longer after, that there was not a chance for success. The then-Secretary of Labor, Frances Perkins, observed that the opposition from the American Medical Association was so great that any inclusion of health care could have defeated the entire Social Security package. It is said that Dr. Harvey Cushing, a brain surgeon who was father-in-law to Franklin Roosevelt's son James, convinced the President that "no legislation can be effective without the good will of the American Medical Association, which has the organization to put it to work."[22]

So hopeless did its enactment seem that health insurance came to be known as the "lost reform." The notorious opposition of the AMA, which did manage to block the legislation, was based on the notion that such plans would inevitably result in the loss of individual choice of doctors and hospitals, in the subsequent decline of quality care, and in public abuse of the entire system.[23] In this effort to defeat a national health plan, the organization's tactics were political and propagandistic. Morris Fishbein, the articulate editor of the *Journal of the American Medical Association,* charged that organized medical group care was *subversive* and *alien* to American ideas. He would refer to group practice as a form of "medical soviet." In 1949, the AMA responded to President Truman's plea for new health care legislation with a statement to the effect that a system of "regimented medical care" was the

> . . . discredited system of decadent nations which are now living off the bounty of the American people—and if adopted it would not only jeopardize the health of our people but would gravely endanger our freedom. It is one of the final, irrevocable steps toward state socialism —and every American should be alerted to the danger.[24]

The Murray-Wagner-Dingel Bill (one of many) was dubbed by the AMA "Marxist medicine." It never even reached the floor of Congress.

The health care fight continued to rage through the Eisenhower, Kennedy, and Johnson administrations, with AMA opposition every step of the way. The organization attacked every single proposal, from the Forand Bill in 1957, which was specifically designed to extend health services to recipients of Social Security, to the Anderson-King Bill in 1962. One of the latter's most vociferous opponents, incidentally, was former governor of California and Republican Presidential contender in 1976 Ronald Reagan, who was then a movie actor scouting the political arena. His lecture, "Ronald Reagan Speaks Out Against Socialized Medicine," was subsequently produced as a phonograph recording, which the AMA used for its "Operation Coffeecup," a campaign designed to defeat the Anderson-King plan. The battle raged for three more years, until Medicare legislation was finally blasted through the Congress to defeat the AMA-sponsored Herlong Eldercare Bill.

The AMA finally beaten, even Dr. Morris Fishbein, its spokesman for more than two decades, conceded that "as conditions change, we must adapt to the changes. . . ."[25] It was a moving moment in 1965 when President Lyndon Johnson signed the bill into law in the presence of Harry Truman, the man who twenty years earlier hand sent the first message exclusively devoted to health care to the Congress. Yet sad too because Medicare, as it passed the Congress in 1965, was far less comprehensive than the bill Truman had originally designed.

Barely was the law a reality before Medicare was beset with its own great financial problems, spurred by the spiraling inflation of the late 1960s and early 1970s. In the years it has existed, the federal health insurance program for older citizens has paid out a progressively smaller share of the medical bills for the group. *Consumer Reports* estimated in January 1976 that of the average (1975) annual bill of $1,218 for someone over sixty-five, Medicare paid only $463. In 1974 Medicare paid 62 percent of older people's hospital bills and 52 percent of covered doctor bills. It paid nothing towards out-of-hospital prescription drugs and medical appliances like eyeglasses, hearing aids and dentures, and little for nursing home expenses.[26] It should be noted that the program as it now stands was not designed to be comprehensive. But the proportion of coverage is shrinking, and the elderly have had to rely more on private health systems to fill the gaps. Over 11 million older people now own such policies and pay over $500 million a year for private coverage. Besides the expense of these "medigap" insurance supplements (and there are many who cannot afford them at all), they present their purchasers with a big question: Which policies will best cover them where Medicare does not? Many rely on insurance agents for advice. A study conducted by the Senate Special Committee on Aging reported that commonly "preying on the fears of the elderly of being 'wiped out' financially by a costly illness, the agent will sell what appears to be extra protection."[27] In many cases, such investments do not live up to promises. Salesmen are also accused of writing new policies while canceling old ones simply to collect new commissions. The older person is cheated, not only financially, but because most new policies specify that pre-existing illnesses are not covered until months after they are in force.

As coverage declines, the real questions arise: What is Medicare actually accomplishing for older Americans today? What are its strengths and its failures? What kind of health care does our group really need, and what can we hope for in terms of government support?

Since July 1966, when the act went into effect, its two kinds of health insurance, hospital and supplemental medical insurance, have served millions in paying partly at least for their illnesses. Yet with the steady rise in the cost of medical services, so has the cost of the program continued to escalate. In 1950, the estimate was $12 billion; in fiscal 1976, it was $133 billion! Hospital costs in the last decade have risen four times faster than the Consumer Price Index. Grumbling has been growing louder from both provider and recipient; it seems that neither is served well by the program. In March 1976, President Ford sought to limit increases in Medicare payments during 1977 and 1978 to 7 percent for hospital fees and 4 percent for doctor bills. But how are patients to place similar limits on hospitals and doctors whose bills will surely reflect the much higher inflationary trends?

When government programs grow to monster proportions, there is always danger of cutbacks and freezes and talk of "reshifting the burden of health care costs back to the people." The recent exposure of widespread fraud and waste within the Medicaid program has strengthened this argument. It has been estimated that of the $15 billion spent annually, 25 percent or more has been wasted or paid out in fraudulent claims. The aged poor often are being treated by charlatans and quacks, and thousands of medical promoters are getting rich at government expense. At "storefront clinics" or "Medicaid mills," mostly found in ghetto areas, old people are treated for fictive diseases with unnecessary tests, X-rays, and injections, not only unnecessary but also harmful when administered too frequently. The huge bills for such "services" and for others which are never rendered at all are sent off for collection via Medicaid. Such cheating has been going unchecked for many years, mainly because of the complexities in pinning down the unethical practitioners. But in 1976, Senator Frank Moss, Chairman of the Special Committee on Aging, who had been frustrated by unsuccessful attempts to initiate investigations through the House Ways and Means, the House Commerce and the Senate Finance Committees, decided to do a little investigating of his own. He sent out committee people to pose as prospective Medicaid recipients, after first having them diagnosed as healthy by reputable doctors. All were diagnosed with one or more exotic and fantastic ailments, and treated with expensive cures. Allergy and glaucoma tests, electrocardiograms, and blood and urine analyses were designed to fatten the bills. Abuses were found in New York, Los Angeles, Chicago, Detroit. Most ironic is that in all the years of AMA opposition to the program, the association never once conceived of *this* particular pitfall: the potential for illicit activities on the part of entrepreneurial physicians, the skullduggery of their own sacred profession.[28] Chaucer saw it six hundred years ago, when he observed his Doctor's taffeta and silk garment and remarked, "For gold in physik is a cordial,/ Therefore loved he gold in special."

Dan Thomasson believes that Medicaid is particularly susceptible to such cheating because the Congress, the Department of Health, Education and Welfare and the states and their attorneys have shown little interest and failed to prosecute such difficult and complicated cases. They will now, after a decade of leniency, be forced to take firm action.[29]

If we are to see real progress in health care for older Americans, it will take more than the reform of one scandal-ridden aspect of the government program. Consider the key areas still left uncovered by Medicare today: prescription drugs, dental care, and vital medical appliances such as eyeglasses, hearing aids, dentures and trusses. U.S. Department of Health, Education and Welfare figures gauge the need: as of 1974, half of the older population either had not seen a dentist for five years or had *never* visited a dentist at all; older people are twice as likely to wear glasses and thirteen times as likely to use hearing aids as younger ones; about 92 percent of people sixty-five and over do or should have glasses, and 5 percent hearing aids.

We need fuller coverage and better methods of obtaining it. Fortunately, current opinion polls assure us that a sizeable majority of Americans are now ready for such "fundamental" changes in health care. So altered are American views that the Democratic Party Platform for 1976, which reflects such attitudes, called for a "comprehensive national health insurance system with universal and mandatory coverage." President Carter has put a high priority on reforming the whole health care delivery system. It is predicted that within the next several years very serious attention will be given to the creation of a new national health insurance and that it will be available to both young and old. "The program," predicts Richard Margolis, "will go about as far as it can go: all of the people insured all of the time for all of their care."[30]

Before Congress are at least half a dozen plans which incorporate major changes in the law, from the "Catastrophic Health Insurance Reform," the modest plan of Senators Russell Long and Abraham Ribicoff, to a sweeping federalized system to be managed by Health, Education and Welfare called "Health Security," sponsored by Edward Kennedy and James Corman.

Admittedly, the experts concede, there are great difficulties involved in achieving such aims; the ability to provide people with full medical, dental, and hospital protection without causing intolerable tax burdens for the public is not the least of them. There is little hope for improvement until there are solid solutions to the incredible rate of medical inflation, cost controls, and checks upon hospital and doctors fees, even if new legislation is enacted. This is where the Carter Administration must begin if any comprehensive plan is to have a ghost of a chance. The Department of Health, Education and Welfare, in conjunction with its preparation of a new, administration-sponsored health bill, proposes extensive reorganization and the establishment of new federal agencies with the authority to control just such costs.[31]

We've talked of social security, pensions, and health care; these are the most obvious sources of income or subsidy for older citizens. There are many other vital areas where the money fight must be vigorously waged.

Housing is one of these. Shelter is a basic need at all times for everyone, and housing costs have come to comprise a higher and higher percentage of retired people's income each year. Those who own their homes suffer from rising property taxes and maintenance costs; for those renting, landlords make increases in their rental fees. Many older homeowners today can neither afford to maintain their property nor move to other quarters, since these are even more expensive. Many are trapped in deteriorating neighborhoods and suffer from a great fear of crime. Proposed remedies like property tax rebates, credits, and housing allowances for the poor have not yet been sufficient to change the picture. Older citizens must not continue to be imprisoned by inadequate housing; they must have open to them arrangements designed and located to suit their needs, at costs they can afford.

The cost of transportation is also rising steadily and is annually becoming a heavier burden on the fixed income. Most older people must rely on public transport (where it exists, that is) to reach shops, recreation, friends, and doctors. Access to transportation means independence; if deprived of their mobility, old people are without their liberty. Yet transportation difficulties are intensifying all over the country, and the three-quarters of the elderly population now living in the large cities are feeling more and more isolated, lonely and anxious because of it. Those in rural areas are even worse off because of the almost exclusive dependence on private automobiles. Thus our demands must include the maintenance and improvement of public transportation, with fixed fares for fixed incomes.

Wherever we turn, we find this intense money struggle. It surrounds us and engulfs us in the sales taxes we pay, in the life insurance coverage we must buy, in the loans we finance, in the estates we plan for our children. But it is obviously not our aim to tackle tangled economic issues here, or to come up with concrete solutions. We merely set these financial agonies alongside the rest, as part of the mosaic. For real answers, it would seem wiser to defer to the experts. We urgently need a task force composed not merely of sympathetic legislators, but a panel of the very best financial brains that this nation possesses. Specialists brought together to rethink, restate, reformulate every single phase of the economic situation older Americans are facing. Only such braintrusters, knowledgeable about the needs of the future aged and working exclusively in their behalf can hope to devise innovative solutions to restore for the old: (1) their right to an income in retirement that will provide an adequate standard of living; (2) their right to suitable housing; (3) their right to proper medical, dental, and pharmaceutical services; and (4) their right to opportunity and access. This last would provide the means to participate in every possible civic, educational, and cultural activity they might wish to seek out.

Meanwhile, the money fight continues to beset the life of every aging citizen. We cannot overemphasize the importance of such deprivation. Besides the misery it involves, it hampers the development of the new kind of old person whom we seek. Not one of us has a chance for liberation while we suffer from financial insecurity.

Our search has persistently been for the autonomy of older Americans and in a democratic society such rights are intricately entwined with money matters. Financial liberation is pivotal; without it there is little hope. If we are to emerge from our current outcast state, we *must* win this battle.

11.
The Wisdom Search

This young nation is now more than two hundred years old. If you stop to think about it, many of us span over one-fourth of that history! We have seen a good deal in our own time: we've witnessed two wars and we have faced the threat of total annihilation. There has been such unprecedented growth in this country since World War II that it has already altered the very substance of our daily lives. Above all, we have had to adjust ourselves to the fact that as a people, we are a mere fraction of a complex, uncertain, developing world. Such events would surely have confounded the sober imaginations of those admirable eighteenth century gentlemen who were our founding fathers.

In 1776, the estimated lifespan was thirty-two, and far too few lived on long enough to answer to the current description of "elderly." Now, life-expectancy among us stands at around seventy-one years. The ever-mounting numbers of long-living Americans may be a comparatively new phenomenon, but under no circumstances can they go unrecognized any longer. After decades of virtually exclusive attention to the young, there are now signs that the center of political gravity is shifting towards the more mature and the aging American. The new population trends clearly augur profound changes in our economy, education system, medical care, manufacturing processes, in every aspect of American life.

Repeatedly we have heard the statistics. As the birth rate sags and the death rate slows, the median age rises: *more Americans are older people.* Yet, ominously, along with these striking population figures have come the worriers, the protestors, the doomsayers, the fearful statisticians who talk of decline, of the loss of vigor, or stagnation. French demographer Alfred Sauvy sees the coming aged society as likely to cause a "slide towards inevitable decadency, like a tree with too much foliage for there to be any young growth," and laments "a population of old people ruminating over old ideas in old houses."[1]

It is important for us to consider just how realistic such fears are. Are we seriously jeopardized as a nation, even as a world, because of this emerging population of old? This kind of forecasting is severely limited not only by unforeseen circumstances but by the fact that such determinations are almost always predicated on the theory that the *future* must be seen in terms of the *past.* People may be living longer, but whether they must continue to do so as sickly, stale, disillusioned beings is much in doubt. Dr. Bernard Strehler, a professor of biology at the University of Southern California and a key figure in research on the physiology of aging, insists that "this ugly picture is totally false, for there is no way to appreciably increase lifespan except by improving the body's physical state."[2]

Recent research on longevity definitely shows how narrow and unimaginative such thinking is. The extraordinary breakthroughs over the last twenty-five years in the study of the living human cell, and the discovery of the existence within every living organism of DNA (deoxyribonucleic acid) present us with just the opposite danger, namely that our new knowledge of the possible *immortality* of DNA may be leading to a kind of *manipulation* of human life which could shake the very foundation of natural law! No, there may be great hazards ahead, but the "world's population swollen with vast numbers of decrepit, half-senile men and women, anchored in wheel chairs and kept alive only through the administration of countless tubes and endless injections," is not the most realistic picture of them.[3]

Instead, research is daily bringing us closer to an understanding of the physiological processes of aging. Gairdner B. Moment has expressed that

> . . . there is no reason to doubt a continuing flow of beneficent discoveries. The goal of making it possible to age well will be achieved so that satisfying old age both physically and mentally will be the good fortune of people everywhere.[4]

Until recently, these scientists, though obviously aware that different species had varying lifespans and that the "biological clock" was ticking away in each of us, had little idea of what activated that clock. One explanation for mortality was that it was an intrinsic characteristic of higher organisms which made evolution possible. If any given specimen lived too long it could not possibly evolve swiftly enough to cope with the many environmental challenges in the surrounding world. A contrary view specified that the body simply ages because after the reproductive years there was no advantage to the species for its continuation.

Scientific writer Albert Rosenfelt has likened human life to the planetary "fly-bys" launched by NASA into space. These vehicles are monitored on their missions to Mars and Venus every minute by the engineers who create them, but only while they perform their functions of sending back new information to Earth. Once this is accomplished, the designers abandon them; whether they continue to travel about in space or not is then of little interest since they have served their purpose. Humans, however, are not merely programmed machines; we take a more comprehensive view of their fates, hoping to discover what makes them function and what prevents their running down. As Rosenfelt observes, "if there is a self-destruct mechanism aboard—we can find it, and abort or dismantle it."[5]

Key experiments have been speedily moving science forward in its quest for such discoveries. In 1951 Dr. George O. Gey of Johns Hopkins University Medical School removed cells from a cancer patient, Henrietta Lacks (sometimes called Helen Lane), and by placing these cells in a tissue culture has succeeded in keeping them flourishing and dividing ever since, though the patient is now long dead. The famous strain, known as HE-LA, is still growing in laboratories today, and it is a demonstration that *certain* cells, released from their bodily boundaries and supplied with needs for growth, can go on indefinitely.[6]

In 1961 while doing cancer research at the Wistar Institute in Philadelphia, Dr. Leonard Hayflick of Stanford University chanced on another important discovery. Normal cells of a particular sort, he found, were capable of dividing only a *fixed* number of times. They were actually programmed to die, their lifespan always limited by the particular species from which they came. His fibroblasts, a type of dividing cell found in human connective or skin tissues, replicated themselves regularly about fifty times before they quit, and as they reproduced, the number of cells capable of division was constantly dwindling. Cells taken from adults showed far less ability to divide and were used up much sooner than those taken from children. And when Hayflick froze such cells and then thawed them again, they retained a "memory" concerning their former doubling activity. Nothing, it seemed, could alter their program; the ticking of the biological clock was merely temporarily suspended by the freeze.

Current researchers have various views about where and how the process of aging actually originates. Some say the brain controls this progression, others consider that a cellular timekeeper exists, while still others believe that the truth lies in some combination of these theories. In Dr. Bernard Strehler's interpretation, mature cells lose their ability to decode certain instructions and as a result are "turned off" after a given point in their development. He feels this heralds the coming of age. According to the view of W. Donner Denkla of the Roche Institute of Molecular Biology in New Jersey, a brain-based clock releases certain "death hormones" at various intervals in life. As for Hayflick and others in his school, they believe that we age not because our cells no longer divide, but rather as a result of functional changes that occur in the cells as they do so. When the human cell nears the thirty-fifth doubling such changes become more visible. The body's immunal systems begin to become less effective, and such failure can result in the occurrence of various diseases like cancer, amyloidosis (an abnormal amount of proteins in the aging brain), late diabetes, emphysema, and chronic lymphatic leukemia.[7]

Particularly fascinating in the new research has been recent investigation into a very rare disease known as progeria, which causes unnatural aging in humans. A victim of progeria has a life-span of no more than twelve to eighteen years. This child may seem normal until his third or fourth year, but then suddenly ceases development, and many functions go awry. Growth stops abruptly and the body comes to resemble that of a dwarf. The skin wrinkles, the hair goes white, the features sharpen, the limbs weaken, and the joints stiffen. As early as the fifth year of life, the child develops cardiac problems, atherosclerosis, elevated cholesterol levels, or even high blood pressure. In short, the physical properties of these victims seem in every possible way to mimic old age. The biological clock is wildly off schedule, speeding up symptoms which normally might not appear until decades later. What interests scientists most about the disease is its implications, for if the clock can be so misdirected and so speeded up, it can also *conceivably* be slowed down as well.[8]

In the coming decades, such research will bring important and dramatic changes in the health and physical welfare of longer-living people. No more will older people need to proceed like the seasick voyager, who, realizing a life-long ambition to see the world, is then so engrossed in the discomforts and miseries of his malady that he is blind to the wonders of the blue Aegean and the Greek Islands spread out before him! Sustained health will make us alive to the possibilities once out of reach. It will open up experiences formerly inaccessible, for we will be a heartier, fitter people. Not just extraordinary individuals or a handful of geniuses will profit, but all of us will become the beneficiaries of this medical progress. Longer, healthier, easier living is the gift science can give us, but we must be ready to receive this bounty, and to make it worth having. The only way for us to accomplish this is to take our place once more within society.

It is time to reexamine the ways of life we value most, to reconsider the uses of work, the uses of leisure and play. To arrive at old age is to arrive at the opportunity for careful and critical consideration of *which* energies go into *which* activities and just what fulfillments are to be drawn from them. Unfortunately, while the expectations and duties of our early years are well defined and strongly overseen, the lack of guidelines for later life and leisure is notorious. In a sense, we come to this new phase of life as pioneers—a familiar and appropriate role for an American. We will have to define the potentials and extend the possibilities to add new dimensions to the contemporary American way of life.

Not only have older Americans come unprepared for such choices, having long believed that such options were closed to them, but the environment they live in today has provided them only with boredom and isolation. The narrowing circles of friends, the disappearance of business associates upon retirement, the loss of meaningful roles, and the deprivation of active family life contribute to a kind of frustration previously unknown: that of suddenly having *time,* but no energy, interest or means to venture into new situations. So our social climate must be made to stimulate, encourage, and insure the participation of older people instead of their retreat into obscurity. The growing momentum of activist aging groups everywhere can mobilize to demand a hearing for the cause of the older American!

James Michener has described the traditional act of the Japanese who dons a kimono lined in flaming scarlet when he reaches the age of sixty, as a sign that he has attained the rank of elder statesman. Until then he has worn only gray or black, worked hard and obediently, and said little. With the red kimono comes a new freedom, the right to state opinions on any subject, to be heard, and to be heeded.[9] Americans could use such a symbol, some liberating gesture to assert our continued significance within our own world. But for us such acts must take different forms—new colors, so to speak, from the blazing scarlet to the subdued pastels. All of us will be moving on diverse paths to attain the freedoms we value. Twenty-four million people are bound to include every taste and every style known to our land. Yet space must be found here for every older person's future.

Up until 1978, with the signing of legislation, thousands of men and women whose commitments have been to the work they chose for all their adult years were prevented from continuing at sixty-five. According to a 1975 Louis Harris Survey, 61 percent of those in the work force had no choice but to retire when their sixty-fifth birthday arrived. Of that group, Harris estimated 40 percent were reluctant and unhappy about it.[10] Mandatory retirement had become standard practice throughout American business. Carin Clauss, associate solicitor of the U.S. Department of Labor, pointed to "a growing trend towards compelling retirement prior to sixty-five" through agreements built into pension plans which allow the employer to retire a worker as early as fifty-five.[11]

The assumption that one automatically becomes unfit at sixty-five is about as realistic as is the notion of the 1960s that "everyone over thirty is suspect." Yet the choice of age sixty-five as a cut-off point was assigned only as a convenience. In 1935, when New Deal administrators were drafting the Social Security Act, the designation was set primarily for industrial or manual workers, for work of a physical nature rather than for office or professional jobs. At that time, 25 percent of the work force was unemployed, and it was important to keep older workers from competing for jobs.[12]

So, mandatory retirement at sixty-five was accepted as though it were a natural law. Employers found the designation a great administrative convenience. But we have demonstrated in our earlier discussions that there is simply no proof that skills automatically decline with age for most jobs people hold today. Compulsory retirement is a waste of human talent, and the psychological damage it did to those left "disengaged" was criminal. Many people whose self-esteem was strongly tied to work found that forced retirement threatened their very personalities. Ignoring the individual and enforcing a uniform standard could be seen as a violation of the Constitution, which assures us that no person will be deprived of life, liberty, or property without due process.

Bills against forced retirement had been introduced into Congress since 1974 and were steadily gaining support from both liberal and conservative groups. Many legislators took the position of Thomas R. Fortune, the chairman of the New York State Assembly committee on the aging: "A person should only be forced to leave a job if that person cannot perform the assigned tasks." To be retired on the basis of age, sex, or race is discriminatory, unjust, and economically unsound.[13]

When President Carter signed the bill extending retirement to age seventy in April of 1978, Senator Claude Pepper, himself well over seventy-five, proclaimed "a day of elation for millions of our fellow citizens."[14] No man or woman who wants to work and is able to perform his duties should be penalized because of some abstract, irrelevant calendar dates. A far more reasonable provision for aging employees would include the right to retire early if they chose as well as the right to work if they are equipped to do so; the right to a reduced schedule of working hours; the right to longer vacations; and the right to return to work after a specifed absence. Instead of the *penalties* for extension of the work life, we need *incentives* to keep people within it The possibilities present economists with a wonderful unexplored territory for a system that is now rigid and notoriously wasteful. Such liberalization is within our reach for two very immediate and practical reasons. First, the worrisome numbers of older people now in retirement and those upcoming are a devastating drain on the Social Security System, threatening the future of the program itself. Second, unlike earlier periods in our history, the 1980s will see fewer young people entering the job market as a result of an ever-lowering birth rate; it will be a time when the highly trained and experienced in our labor force will be valued as never before.

As a next step we must turn to those who would search out new careers, who find that their early work may have provided sustenance but not personal growth, and who, now freed from the constraints of rearing and caring for family, are able to give themselves the attention they have always craved. Their opportunities must be broadened to include the right to learn again, to qualify again and to practice anew. Never again must they be told categorically that they are "too old for training." For the newly retired school teacher whose love of books determines her to study for librarianship, for the business executive who would test for and qualify for law school, for the sales person with artistic skills who would become an interior decorator, for all those with curiosity, ambition and stamina, the doors must be opened, the barriers let down. The idea that chronological age automatically disqualifies must be exposed and deplored for the empty notion it really is. We must make age discrimination as obsolete as those notices once a common sight on the American frontier: "No Irish need apply" or "Chinese not allowed."

Consider the great numbers of civil servants, the firemen, policemen, postmen, military retirees, (or those in physically demanding jobs from which people are fired earlier) who at fifty-five are pensioned off to that supposed paradise of full-time leisure. Some find it a dream come true. But what of the people who find such a life undesirable, idle, and intolerable? Such individuals, with the vigor and drive to begin again in a new business or a different profession, need support and cooperation, not the raised eyebrows and skepticism that now greet them in job interviews.

There are so many people who need or wish to change careers in their middle and late years that the United States Office of Education's Community Services and Continuing Education Section in the spring of 1977 awarded several University of California professors a large grant to study and develop possible ways to ease this transition. Meanwhile, in the job market, the unspoken policy widely prevalent among employers is that "human beings become obsolete sometime between ages thirty-five and sixty-five," and further, that this idea seems to be accepted with a "strange resignation, as though it was something, like cancer, that happens to many unfortunate people but about which nothing can be done."[15] Such views by those hiring and firing are inhumane and unrealistic, and they deprive the country of one of its major sources of competent talent.

Long ago, a special development in the needs of the mature citizens was accurately described by the prophetic writer, Edward Bellamy, in a society he projected far into the future from his mid-nineteenth century vantage point. In *Looking Backwards,* old age, not youth was to be the "enviable time of life," because it was then that, having completed the more irksome tasks of serving society, an individual could and should devote himself to what are judged to be the good things of this world. These good things might include the higher exercise of his faculties in scientific, artistic, literary, or scholarly pursuits or enjoyment of tennis, golf, traveling the world, or simple cordiality and social relaxation in the company of good friends. Indeed it is widely held that the *respon-*

sibility of a humane society is to provide older citizens with such opportunities.

We in twentieth century America are now confronting such demands. Besides the many who wish to continue their employment or who seek new and diverse work areas, there are others pressing different claims, clamoring for outlets, petitioning for releases. These people require the chance to grow, to expand, to change, to continue learning. In a democratic society this is a vital necessity for all adults. Many who have only had minimal schooling now find a second chance to learn and to teach themselves. Their receptiveness has been called the "maturity attitude," one in which "energies are most fully absorbed in being [one's self] and fulfilling [one's] purpose."[16]

Older people come to education as they never have before: active, energetic, and with a new understanding which was hardly possible in childhood or young adulthood. This hunger can be as acute as any physical pain, and restrictions put on the intellectual, aesthetic, or spiritual development deprive them of the very growth that gives ultimate meaning to their lives.

We are talking about something called in contemporary parlance "continuing education," but which we prefer to think of as the search for wisdom. That search is a life-long task, and one that should never be abandoned while we draw breath. We have mentioned that the various forms of wisdom—discretion, judgment, profundity, and astuteness—were once considered synonymous with age, the province of the sage, the very essence of that "enviable time," the "afternoon of life." Our generation must track such understanding once again, to uncover wisdom, ferret it out wherever it is to be found, and then reinstate it in our lives.

For some this will mean creative encounters with the world of knowledge, with the arts, the sciences, philosophy, foreign languages, and religions, in a quest for new perspective on the humanities and on man's achievements. For others learning can be more personal and practical, starting off, for instance, with the study of aging processes, the physiology, the psychology, and the new research in gerontology and geriatrics. There are those who will seek creative outlets in drawing, sculpting, taking pictures, making pottery, playing music, and writing poetry. Others will go out for sheer contact, for group involvement, for social relationships, for the experience of learning together and of communicating to others what has been newly comprehended. Whatever strategies are devised, they must aim to produce for each aging person a life of independence, of dignity, and of personal fulfillment. This is the vital need which can be achieved only by the individuals themselves.

There are programs springing up everywhere around the country to satisfy such requirements. At universities, state and community colleges, and centers for the aging, courses are being designed uniquely for those seeking personal growth through lifetime learning. In suburban Minneapolis, at Hennepin State Junior College, tuition-free seminars are held to teach older people lip-reading, about the "Psychology of Dying," and "Sex after 65," At Mercyhurst College in Erie, Pennsylvania, old people are learning to speak French, understand painting, and "How to Live on a Fixed Income." At St. Petersburg Junior College in Florida and at the University of California's San Francisco Center for Learning in Retirement, older people are pooling their experience and talent to create for themselves a learning and social environment. Such aims are beginning to be served in communities across the nation.

One splendid example of innovative thinking in education has been the *Elderhostel*. In the summer of 1976, more than one thousand older people were part of such programs at twenty-one New England colleges. They lived in the dormitories on various campuses (the University of New Hampshire, Franklin Pierce College, and Franconia College in New Hampshire, Eastern Connecticut State College and Wesleyan University in Middletown) and socialized informally with their contemporaries and with younger students. Participants were excited by the intellectual stimulation, enjoyed sharing experiences, and were inspired by something new in their lives: groups seeking to gain greater understanding through cultural endeavors. So successful were these Elderhostel programs that they have continued to expand on campuses across the nation. The promise of a program such as this lies in its effective combination of vacationing with experimental lifestyles in a new educational atmosphere, for it takes place in the charming and secure settings of our ivied university campuses.[17]

Over the last several years, attempts have been made at TV programming for the elderly through public service broadcasting. However, little has been serious, systematic, or effectively presented, despite the statistics showing that daytime TV watchers, once almost exclusively housewives, now include more older people, particularly male.[18] There is some question as to the real value of the medium for continuing education purposes. TV tends to be far too passive, too debilitating, too isolating—it may even, in the long run, be entirely harmful for our group. But there has been little intensive thought given to it. The combined use of TV, for example, along with weekly or biweekly meetings for groups of participants is one system as yet virtually untapped. Certainly, there are many unrealized potentials which need to be studied and developed by educators with government assistance and support before we can gauge how useful the medium is for this purpose.

The notion that adults would wish to continue studying in any formal way is still quite new. Large universities with federal assistance are jumping in and expanding programs for older students. One venture of the early 1970s is the sort of thing that might well be experimented with further. The National Endowment for the Humanities designated three major centers across the country—at Princeton, at UCLA, and at Wisconsin—and funded them to produce programs to be carried into small communities. Scholars, writers, lecturers, and group discussion leaders were dispatched to the little towns dotting the nation to hold two-day seminars on literature, poetry, drama, history, and mythology. The attempt was to engage citizens in a new kind of dialogue and to encourage them to look at our cultural origins and heritage so that they might gauge how these have affected and continue to influence daily community experience. Their programs were a huge success. Most fascinating on the new "Chautauqua circuit," as it came to be known, was the number of older Americans who participated and the eagerness with which they welcomed such cultural events.

Of course, some legislators think it neither the province nor the responsibility of government or universities to educate older citizens. In California, Governor Edmund G. Brown, Jr., has steadily maintained that his state government's major task is to teach the "three Rs" properly to the young, not to sponsor older

groups in their "macrame-making" pastimes at community colleges. "What is important are the grammar schools and the
high schools. What they're teaching you can't get along without," says the governor. He then concluded:

> When we get to the adult education and the extended university
> and the eternal degree program and some of these other activities,
> we may be offering a service that's interesting but it's not what I
> would call a survival service.[19]

Perhaps it is the governor's youth that accounts for his callous line
on this issue. Whatever the case, we certainly have no intention of
waiting until he discovers the inevitable: his own susceptibility to
growing old and to the specific needs that accompany that universal process.

Our own emphasis here is to push on every front for a more
active, concentrated fight against psychic deficit, which stems from
the oldest enemy of them all: boredom. Vastly underestimated, this
is a painful malady, and it is not prevalent only among the old.
It besets a great many in our country and essentially its results
from sensory deprivations and a lack of stimulation. Scientific
experiments have demonstrated that it afflicts prisoners of war,
space pioneers, long-distance truckers, and fire-watchers in much
the same way—their nervous systems suffer from a kind of
starvation, making for irritability, discomfort, and torment in the
tedium of their existence. "Emotional and intellectual health depends on the appropriate amount of action in a varied environment," observes Dr. Estelle Ramey. It is exactly this kind of
social atmosphere that we are searching out for each older person,
so that we can use our own powers to the fullest and continue to
live with gusto.[20]

To avoid deprivation, isolation, loneliness, and to ease the pain
of separation from families or the loss of a spouse, growing
numbers of people have been taking a completely different angle.
They have changed their lifestyles altogether! These people have
banded together with strangers to pool their resources and share
in joint household arrangements in "extended family communes."
Instead of struggling alone and being overwhelmed with their
everyday problems, they form these "families" to help each other.

The idea is spreading and in some places even old and young have teamed up. In Orlando, Florida, a nonprofit organization called Share-A-Home, where 112 people live in eight residences, has communards who are voted into membership and then run their daily lives cooperatively, planning menus, and arranging entertainment, trips to doctors, and so on. It's more than basic needs that are attended here; a sense of belonging is achieved. Many feel cooperative living is the ideal solution; they find that they are no longer depressed, and have come alive again.[21]

In Evanston, Illinois, at a commune called Weinfeld Group Living Residence, supported by the Council for Jewish Elderly, the aim is to provide only as much help as people really need, so that they can remain independent and still turn to their "families" when they must. There are long waiting lists for membership to Weinfeld and places like it. But as Marie Thompson, an expert on housing for the elderly, points out, Weinfeld living "isn't everybody's glass of tea." She reminds us that, "many older people don't want to share with a stranger or live in a strange house." Still, few would question the need to develop new concepts in congregate housing, to experiment with every combination and to review all the possibilities. Unfortunately, funding has come mostly from private sources, with government backing lagging behind, mired in bureaucratic restrictions.[22]

Older people are using other strategies for activism. Tired of being cut off, imprisoned in their own apartments in the central cities, and threatened by crime, they are banding together into teams, army-style, to do battle for their own freedom and safety. In high-crime areas, the patterns are familiar: the aged living alone in deteriorating neighborhoods are followed into apartment buildings by teen-aged boys; they are beaten, gagged or stabbed, then robbed in elevators, doorways, or secluded hallways. In the slum street these operations are commonly known as "crib jobs" because the young hoods regard the process as easy as "taking candy from a baby."[23]

No matter what precautions, patrols, or security measures the police may take, old people are prime targets in these situations and cannot always be sufficiently protected. So they've decided to fight for themselves. In New York City in 1974, the Bronx Senior

Citizens Robbery Unit was formed. It launched a vigorous attack on street criminals and since has been serving as a model for New York City as well as the rest of the country.

In Far Rockaway, Queens, older residents have organized street lobby patrols. At least fifteen such patrols operate in the lobbies of large apartment buildings throughout the area. Elderly volunteers station themselves in the lobby, whose front doors are securely locked; they are equipped with citizens' band radios directly tuned into the police. Anyone entering the building must state his business through an intercom system, and if the patrollers are suspicious or unsatisfied as to the identity of such a person, they contact the police immediately.

Other protective systems are the organization of groups for shopping excursions or the high school volunteer escort services. Some old people are preparing themselves physically by studying the arts of self-defense—fists, judo, karate. The most indignant of all these are those filing regularly into the courtrooms in large groups to see justice done, to be sure that offenders are not let off lightly. Court monitoring by elderly groups has encouraged older people to speak out, to testify against their attackers with less fear of reprisals. They are aware that older citizens are preyed upon precisely because it is so easy to do, and they are determined to make it far more difficult.[24]

Which brings us in our search for alternatives, to the largest, most militant category of all: those older citizens who are eagerly turning to public life for variety, diversity, and significance in their new lives. These people are becoming activists in their own towns and cities, working full or part-time at volunteer or at paid positions to serve their communities. They bring with them to their new jobs the skills they have sharpened as high-paid executives in business, as planners, as supersalesmen, as authorities on hundreds of subjects. And they bring the responsibility, devotion, and stability that comes only with maturity. Because they have chosen their own particular mode of action, the path most meaningful to them, they make the most energetic and successful advocates!

A variety of federally sponsored and administered programs allow them to break into public affairs and make their presence felt. Through the Older Americans Act, enacted in 1965, all the states and territories were supplied with Offices of Aging, and a variety of services to older Americans followed. First came counseling and referral services as well as social and recreational programs. But this was just a tentative beginning. The Office of Aging began to expand their functions to include grants to nonprofit organizations and institutions for a nutrition program for the elderly, thus assuring that they receive at least one hot meal a day, five days a week. In 1974, observing an even greater need, the government began to assist older people with employment opportunities. Funds were released which meant meaningful jobs in community services for thousands over sixty years old.

The U.S. Department of Labor, through its Older Americans Community Service Program, has made available several kinds of meaningful paid jobs. For those eager to assist in maintaining the environment, an organization known as "Green Thumb" offers conservation, beautification, and community-improvement projects. Sponsored directly through the National Farmers Union in more than twenty-four states, and partly reimbursed through the Labor Department's Manpower Administration, this is a limited employment program for people who come from rural or farming backgrounds. Another, administered by the Forestry Service of the Department of Agriculture in twenty states, is "Operation Mainstream," through which conservation-minded citizens can work at preserving our natural resources.

There are social service projects through which older people can serve. The AARP/NRTA group, Senior Community Aides, which is operating in thirty-one cities to recruit, trains and finds work for older people in child care centers, schools, and public service offices. Add to this the National Council of Senior Citizens group, Senior Aides and the Senior Community Service Project of the National Council on the Aging, who are attempting to provide jobs in Social Security and state employment service offices, in libraries, hospitals and school food programs. Most recently, they have been funded for jobs with escort services, and with homemaker and home repair assistance for the elderly.

Through the Teacher's Corps, another government-sponsored program, retired teachers can assist as tutors or instructional assistants. Many other government programs exist for teachers.

The best source of information is the local office of the State Employment Service, whose staff is qualified to counsel and refer applicants for such jobs.

Likely to be exciting for those eagerly searching for meaningful commitment are the volunteer groups sponsored by the federal government under the program called ACTION. Created in 1973, ACTION is an independent government agency which coordinates all of the government's domestic and international volunteer activities. Among its programs is the Foster Grandparents, which offers older people the chance to give their love and attention to handicapped or deprived children in institutions or private settings. Foster Grandparents are trained carefully in tasks that vary from feeding and dressing a child, to playing games, reading stories and helping to administer speech and physical therapy. The program pays a small stipend, a transportation allowance, and some useful peripheral benefits like accident insurance and prepaid annual physical examinations. In 1974 more than 156 such projects activated over fifteen thousand older people across the country.

For those who prefer to help their contemporaries, there is the Senior Companion Program. Patterned along the lines of the Foster Grandparents, it provides people with the chance to serve the elderly in their own homes, nursing homes, and institutions.

Another group doing remarkable work is ACTION's Volunteers in Service to America (VISTA), which engages people of all ages for the period of one year to work in impoverished urban and rural areas. Some live with migrant families, others on Indian reservations, and others in institutions for the mentally handicapped. They help with every kind of problem: day care, education, health, legal difficulties, drug abuse, and so on. There are extended training periods in preparation for such assignments, as well as in-service training. VISTA also provides service benefits like food, housing and travel allowances. Some critics have attacked the program, calling it "meddling" or "patronizing" to disadvantaged groups, but its ideas and aims seem singularly fitted for engaging the older citizen in meaningful work. Many older VISTA participants like Ella Rigley of San Franscisco see this work as a turning point in their lives. In her mid-seventies when she first joined VISTA, Mrs. Rigley helped organize a play school in a black community in

South Carolina, and observed that "the need was so great for compassion and understanding that you forgot yourself. So it really wasn't hard."[25]

Older volunteers are being recruited by the Peace Corps to join in developing countries over the world. Their programs are involved with teaching agricultural techniques, methods of conservation and natural resource development, as well as training people for vocations, business, and the professions. Participants need to commit themselves for two-year periods, and are prepared through extensive training in the language, history, and culture of the country they will live in. Transportation and expenses are included in the arrangement.

There are numerous possibilities. Retired executives can use their know-how in counseling newly formed small businesses or community organizations through the two hundred offices in every state of Service Corps of Retired Executives (SCORE). People from many professions can, through Retired Senior Volunteer Program (RSVP), serve in courts, hospitals, and other community service centers. Hundreds of thousands are doing so— and these are only the federal government's programs.

In every area, combating every kind of problem facing communities today are volunteer groups. Older people are making their voices heard in politics, education, the arts, consumer affairs, environmental and pollution problems, legal matters, safety and crime, and welfare. Organizations such as the above are tackling the immediate and practical problems of living in today's America; they are eagerly searching for citizens from all economic and social strata and of every age to join them in making their townships, cities, and suburbs vital places in which to live. For older people seeking engagement, any one of these organizations can provide fertile and satisfying endeavor.

In fact, volunteers in health care today virtually carry the fundraising functions for such causes as the Muscular Dystrophy Association, the American Heart Association, the March of Dimes, and the National Red Cross. Hospitals are almost totally dependent on nonprofessional volunteers to bring sympathy and warmth into the institutional world. Since the 1960s, the rights of consumers have to a large degree been defended by dedicated volunteers. Organizations like the Consumer Federation of America, the AFL-CIO's Department of Community Relations, the Consumer Education and Protective Association, and Nader's Raiders are manned by people who are committed to fight against victimization of the consumer. And there is the Consumer Office of the AARP, which since 1970 has been highly successful in alerting older citizens to potentials in health quackery, home improvement frauds, and misrepresentation in insurance sales.

Volunteers have historically been active in combating other social problems, in protecting the environment, fighting crime, providing health care and educating the handicapped. Politics has been a rewarding area for meaningful participation by the elderly because through such activity an individual is accepting a sense of responsibility for the policies which govern our lives and devising ways to influence them. The support of citizen volunteers has elected or defeated many a candidate, and volunteer enthusiasm or lack of it has passed or defeated endless numbers of issues. Through the nonpartisan League of Women Voters with close to 200,000 members and local offices in every state of the Union, with such citizen's lobbies as Common Cause, or with the AFL-CIO's Committee on Political Education (COPE), devoted volunteers have demonstrated the powerful impact of the citizen activist in a free society.

Everywhere we look, there is important civic work of all kinds to be done in this country. Few are better qualified or more eager to be involved in it than that solid, capable, and stable force, the nation's mature citizens. Many already are responding vigorously to such challenges and newspapers are reporting their accomplishments daily, whether they are in Columbus, Ohio, where grandparents have installed themselves in the schoolrooms to buoy the confidence of fearful first-graders launching their reading program, or in San Rafael, California, where they are qualifying and serving as paralegal aides to sue for grievances of their wronged and neglected contemporaries. Older Americans are already getting back into the action.

Whatever way people choose—through their life's work, through the enhancement and recreation of body, spirit, and mind, through the excitement of public service, or through direct politicking, canvassing, or propagandizing for their own cause—such reengagement can mean the chance to stand up for their own welfare in their own way.

The new, activist, militant awareness must free us to shout about our present dissatisfaction, to speak out on specific issues, to clamor for reforms. It must now urge us to tackle our own situation, form our own groups, pressure our politicians, write to our congressmen, fight our local and state battles for better housing, more efficient transportation, safer streets, lower property taxes, better medical and dental attention, and more community services and cultural opportunities. It must alert Americans to the existence of a new, strong breed of older citizens. It must remind people that we are here to stay, and that never again will we permit ourselves to be relegated to a pitiful, second-class status.

Above all, such reentry and recommitment in every walk of life demonstrate that we, as older people, represent no selfish vested interest. We plead for everyone. We speak for all humankind—for its life and preservation.

Notes

Chapter 2
The Invisible American

1. Margaret Mead, *From the South Seas* (New York: William Morrow, 1939), pp. xvii–xviii.

2. Conrad Arensberg, *The Irish Countryman* (Garden City, N. Y.: Natural History Press, 1937).

3. Gordon F. Strieb, "Old Age in Ireland: Demographic and Sociological Aspects," in D.O. Cowgill and L.D. Holmes, eds., *Aging and Modernization* (New York: Appleton, Century, Crofts, 1972), pp. 167–81.

4. Charles Edward Fuller, "Aging among Southern African Bantu," in Cowgill and Holmes, *Aging and Modernization*, p. 57.

5. In a study completed in the mid-1970s of the Chagga tribe of Tanzania, anthropologist Sally Moore described the elaborate rite of ritual slaughter over which the eldest still preside in great honor. She also remarks on the fact that to this day Chagga men may still not know the chronological ages of their kinsmen, but everyone can recite in correct order, from the eldest to the youngest, the names of every single relative in the lineage, much as "we'd recite the alphabet." Sally Moore, "Old Age in a Life-Term Social Arena: Some Chagga of Kilimanjaro, 1974," in *Life's Career: Cross Cultural Studies in Growing Old* (Los Angeles: Sage Publications, 1978).

6. Leo Simmons delineated the various ways such prominence has been accomplished and sustained in his comprehensive work, *The Role of the Aged in Primitive Societies* (New Haven: Yale University Press, 1945). I am heavily indebted to Simmons, a sociologist, who examined data of many distinguished anthropologists on seventy-one widely dis-

tributed tribes, comparing their findings about the status and treatment of old people worldwide. I have drawn liberally from his collection to illustrate the historical importance of old age among developing peoples everywhere.

7. Simone de Beauvoir, *The Coming of Age* (New York: Warner Paperback Library, 1973), p. 147.

8. Margaret Mead, *Coming of Age in Samoa* (New York: William Morrow, 1964), p. 36.

Chapter 3
Where Has Everybody Gone?

1. "Shrinking Households," *New York Times,* July 13, 1975, p. 6.

2. Talcott Parsons, as quoted by Robert Winch, *The Modern Family* (New York: Henry Holt, 1952), p. 306.

3. Gordon F. Strieb, "Old Age and the Family: Facts and Forecasts," *American Behavioral Scientist,* 14, 1 (Sept.-Oct. 1970): 25–39.

4. Lilian E. Troll, "The Family of Later Life: A Decade Review," *Journal of Marriage and the Family,* May 1971, pp. 263–90.

5. Sheila Johnson, "The Three Generation Family," *New York Times Magazine,* Aug. 19, 1973, p. 24.

6. Matilda Riley and Anne Foner, *Aging and Society,* Vol. 1 (New York: Russell Sage Foundation, n.d.), pp. 551–52.

7. Elaine M. Cumming and William E. Henry, in *Growing Old: The Process of Disengagement* (New York: Basic Books, 1961), as quoted by Troll, "The Family of Later Life," p. 279.

8. Margaret Clark, "Cultural Values and Dependency in Later Life," in R. Kalish, ed. *The Dependency of Old People* (Ann Arbor: Institute of Gerontology, 1969), as quoted by Troll, "The Family of Later Life," p. 279.

9. Cuber and Haroff, "The More Total View, Relationships of American Men and Women of the Upper-Middle Class," *Marriage and Family Living,* 25 (1963): 140–45, as quoted by Troll, "The Family of Later Life," p. 279.

Chapter 4
The Road to Activism

1. David Hackett Fisher, "Aging: The Issue of the 1980s." *New Republic,* December 2, 1978, pp. 31–36.

2. "Gray Panther Power: An Interview with Maggie Kuhn," *The Center Magazine,* 8, 2 (March-April 1975), pp. 21–25.

3. "Life for the Elderly in 1975—Many are Hungry and Afraid," *U.S. News and World Report,* Feb. 10, 1975, pp. 48–51.

4. Bernice Neugarten, "Age Groups in American Society and the

Rise of the Young-Old," *Annals of the American Academy Bulletin,* Sept. 1974, pp. 187–98.

5. "The Courts Reinterpret Old-Age Discrimination," *Business Week,* Feb. 24, 1975, p. 91.

6. "A Blow at Agism," *Newsweek,* May 26, 1974, p. 73.

7. "Old People's Revolt: At 65 Work Becomes a Four-letter Word," *Psychology Today,* March 1974, p. 40.

8. "Life for the Elderly in 1975 . . . ," p. 51.

9. "Old People's Revolt. . . ," p. 41.

10. Ed Meagher, "Effects of Inflation on the Elderly," *Los Angeles Times,* April 22, 1974, p. 1.

11. Betty Liddick, "Easy Prey for the Criminal," *Los Angeles Times,* July 21, 1975, p. 1.

12. Abraham Holzman, *The Townsend Movement* (New York: Bookman Associates, 1963.)

13. Ibid., p. 33, as quoted by Richard Milane, *That Man Townsend* (Long Beach: Private printing, 1934), p. 2.

14. Ibid., p. 41.

15. From "Peroration," in *Modern Crusader,* October 17, 1934, as quoted by Jackson Putnam, *Old Age Politics in California* (Stanford: Stanford University Press, 1970), p. 56.

16. Holzman refers to the "promoters" and "real estate operators" whose ventures in selling security to the old involved not inconsiderable self-seeking.

17. H. L. Mencken to H. M. Hyde, as quoted by William Leuchtenberg, *Franklin Roosevelt and the New Deal* (New York: Harper Torch Books, 1963), p. 98.

18. Holzman, *The Townsend Movement,* p. 174.

19. John T. Colson and J. W. McConnell, eds., *Economic Needs of Older People* (New York: Twentieth Century Fund, 1956), p. 125.

20. From *Christmas Beacon* of National Ham 'n Eggs, Dec. 24, 1938, as quoted by Putnam, *Old Age Politics in California,* p. 104.

21. Frank Pinner, Paul Jacobs, and Philip Selznick, *Old Age and Political Behavior* (Berkeley: University of California Press, 1959), p. 25.

22. George McLain, as quoted by Putnam, *Old Age Politics in California,* p. 131.

23. As quoted by Pinner, Jacobs, and Selznick, *Old Age and Political Behavior,* p. 27.

24. From Albert Maisel, *Look,* 14, 3 (1950), as quoted by Pinner, et al., *Old Age and Political Behavior,* p. 27.

Chapter 5
The New Militancy of the Old

1. Robert H. Binstock, "Aging and the Future of American Politics," *Annals of the American Academy Bulletin,* Sept. 1974, pp. 199–212.

2. Angus Campbell, "Politics Through the Life Cycle," *Gerontologist,* 2, (Summer 1971), as quoted by Binstock, "Aging and the Future of American Politics," p. 203.

3. John Schmidhauser, "The Elderly and Politics," in Adeline M. Hoffman and William Beehill, eds., *The Daily Needs and Interests of Older People,* (Springfield, Ill.: Charles C. Thomas, 1970), pp. 70–82.

4. Clark Tibbitts, in Wilma Donahue and Clark Tibbitts, eds., *Politics of Age:* Proceedings of the University of Michigan 14th Annual Conference on Aging (Ann Arbor: University of Michigan Press, 1962), pp. 16–25.

5. Elaine M. Cumming and William E. Henry, *Growing Old: The Process of Disengagement* (New York: Basic Books, 1961).

6. Nancy Hicks, "The Organized Elderly: A New Political Power," *New York Times,* June 22, 1975, p. 1.

7. Henry J. Pratt, "Old Age Associations in National Politics," *Annals of the American Academy,* September 1974, p. 111.

8. *Washington Post,* February 13, 1972, p. 1, as quoted by Pratt, "Old Age Associations . . .," p. 111.

9. Margaret Abrams, "The Story of the AARP," *Modern Maturity,* Oct.-Nov. 1971, p. 72.

10. *Proceedings of the 86th Congress, 1st Session,* 13–17, July 1959 pp. 510–11, as quoted by Pratt, "Old Age Associations . . .," p. 110.

11. As quoted by Hicks, "The Organized Elderly," p. 37.

12. Richard Harris, "Annals of Legislation," *New Yorker,* July 16, 1966, p. 51, as quoted by Pratt, "Old Age Associations . . .," p. 110.

13. John J. Colson and John W. McConnell (New York: Twentieth Century Fund, 1956), *The Economic Needs of Old People,* pp. 128–30.

14. Pratt, "Old Age Associations . . .," p. 111.

15. Binstock, "Aging . . .," p. 206.

16. Theodore J. Lowi, *The End of Liberalism* (New York: W. W. Norton and Company, 1969).

17. Robert Binstock, "Interest-Group Liberalism and the Politics of Aging," *Gerontologist,* Autumn 1972, p. 271.

18. Binstock, *"Aging . . .,"* p. 211.

19. "How to Get Old and Do It Right," *Esquire,* April 1975, p. 73.

20. Maggie Kuhn, as reported in *California Parks and Recreation,* Aug.-Sept. 1976, pp. 14–17.

21. Eleanor Hoover, "Gray Panthers Wage War on Wrinkled Babyhood," *Los Angeles Times,* May 24, 1975, pp. 1, 3.

22. Saul Alinsky, *Reveille for Radicals* (Chicago: University of Chicago Press, 1946), p. 28.

23. "Rationale for Social Change," Gray Panther Broadside (Philadelphia: Mimeo, undated).

24. "How to Fight Age Bias: A Gray Panther on the Prowl" *MS.,* May 1975, p. 91.

25. "Gray Panther Power, An Interview with Maggie Kuhn," *The Center Magazine* (Center for the Study of Democratic Institutions, Santa Barbara, Calif.) 8, 2 (March-Apr. 1975), p. 23.

26. Maggie Kuhn, "AMA and the Elderly," *Gray Panther Network,* June 1975, p. 1.

Chapter 6
The Search for Self

1. Arnold Rose and Warren Peterson, eds., *Older People and Their Social World* (Philadelphia: F. A. Davis, 1965).

2. Claire Booth Luce, "Growing Old Beautifully," *Ladies Home Journal,* Jan. 1973, p. 75.

3. "How You Can Look and Feel Fantastic from 40 On," *Harpers Bazaar,* Aug. 1975, pp. 72–82.

4. "Frauds and Deception Affecting the Elderly: Investigations, Findings and Recommendations" (Washington: U.S. Government Printing Office, 1964), p. 1.

5. Lester David, "Worst of the Medical Swindlers: The Arthritis Quacks," *Reader's Digest,* Jan. 1970, pp. 98–102.

6. *Frauds, Quackery Affecting the Older Citizen,* Hearings of the Senate Special Committee on Aging, 81st Congress, Jan. 15, 16, 1963. (Washington: U.S. Government Printing Office, 1963.)

7. E. J. Kahn, *Fraud* (New York: Harper and Row, 1973).

8. Ellen Switzer, "How to Look Young at Any Age—Well, Younger Anyway," *Vogue,* May 1974, p. 88.

9. Patricia Peterson, "She Creates Her Own Style," *New York Times Magazine,* Mar. 2, 1975, pp. 30–37.

10. "The Old in the Country of the Young," *Time,* Aug. 3, 1970, p. 49.

11. Clark Tibbitts and Wilma Donahue, *Aging in Today's Society* (Englewood Cliffs, N.J.: Prentice Hall, 1960).

12. Shura Saul, *Aging: An Album of People Growing Old* (New York: John Wiley and Sons, 1974), pp. 20–27.

13. As quoted by Ursula Vils, "Distilling 50 Years of Family Needs," *Los Angeles Times,* May 4, 1974, p. 24.

14. Carl G. Jung, *Modern Man in Search of a Soul* (New York: Harcourt, Brace, 1933), p. 109.

15. Charlotte Buhler, "Meaningful Living in the Mature Years," in *Aging and Leisure,* Robert Kleemier, ed. (New York: Oxford University Press, 1961), pp. 345–87.

Chapter 7
Body Worship: What's Fit, What's Fad

1. Irene Gore, *Add Years to Your Life and Life to Your Years* (New York: Stein and Day, 1974), p. 17.

2. As quoted in Herbert DeVries, *Vigor Regained* (Englewood Cliffs, N.J.: Prentice Hall, 1974), pp. 17–18.

3. DeVries, *Vigor Regained*, p. 20.

4. Alice Hornbaker and Lawrence Frankel, *Preventive Care* (New York: Drake Publishers, 1974), p. 24.

5. George Leonard, "Running for Your Life: How the Masters Are Redefining Human Potential," *New West*, Aug. 16, 1976, pp. 34–44.

6. Beth Ann Krier, "Fitness Boom: No Energy Crisis," *Los Angeles Times*, April 13, 1975, p. 22.

7. Leonard Morehouse and Leonard Gross, *Total Fitness in 30 Minutes a Week* (New York: Simon and Schuster, 1975), p. 83.

8. DeVries, *Vigor Regained*, p. 50.

9. Lawrence Galton, *How Long Will I Live* (New York: Macmillan, 1976), p. 132.

10. M. F. Graham, *Prescription for Life* (New York: David McKay, 1966), p. 73.

11. Jean Mayer, *Overweight; Causes, Cost and Controls* (Englewood Cliffs, N. J.: Prentice Hall, 1968), p. 131.

12. David Reuben, *The Save-Your-Life Diet* (New York: Random House, 1975), p. 18.

13. Henry G. Bieler, *Food Is Your Best Medicine* (New York: Random House, 1965).

14. David K. Leslie and John W. McLure, *Exercises for the Elderly* (Iowa City: University of Iowa Press, 1975).

15. Moshe Feldenkrais, as quoted by Mary Lou McKenna in *Bodypower* (New York: Simon and Schuster, 1976), p. 174.

16. Indra Devi, *Yoga for Americans* (Englewood Cliffs, N. J.: Prentice Hall, 1959).

17. Edward Maisel, *Tai Chi for Health* (New York: Holt, Rinehart and Winston, 1972).

18. *Shiatzu: Japanese Finger Pressure for Energy, Sexual Vitality and Relief from Tension and Pain* (New York: J. B. Lippincott, 1976).

Chapter 8
Body and Mind: A Holistic View

1. "Abraham Maslow, Father of Humanistic Psychology," *Los Angeles Times*, April 6, 1975, p. 3.

2. B. F. Skinner, as quoted in *A Guide to Psychologists and Their Concepts* (San Francisco: W. H. Freeman, 1974), p. 155.

3. Sigmund Freud, as quoted by Eleanor Hoover, "New Psychology: New Image of Man," *Los Angeles Times*, April 6, 1975, p. 3.

4. Charlotte Buhler and Melanie Allen, *Introduction to Humanistic Psychology* (Monterey, Calif.: Brooks, Cole, 1972), p. 16.

5. Abraham Maslow, as quoted by Calvin Tompkins, "New Paradigms," *New Yorker*, Jan. 5, 1976, p. 42.

6. Abraham Maslow, *Towards a Psychology of Being* (New York: Van Nostrand, 1962). p. 4.

7. Ibid.

8. Cecil Sheps, "Health in Middle Years," in *The New Frontiers of Aging*, Wilma Donahue and Clark Tibbitts, eds. (Ann Arbor: University of Michigan Press, 1957), p. 130.

9. Paul Baltes and K. Warner Shaie, "The Myth of the Twilight Years," *Psychology Today*, March 1974, pp. 35–40.

10. Lissy Jarvik, "Research Debunks Old Myth about Mind's Decline," *UCLA Alumni Review*, 5, 1 (Oct. 1974), p. 2.

11. Maslow, *Towards a Psychology of Being*, p. 97.

12. Roberto Assagioli, *Psychosynthesis*, (New York: Viking, 1965).

13. Ibid., pp. 215–16.

14. Bruno Geba, *Vitality Training for Older Adults* (New York: Random House, 1974).

15. Moshe Feldenkrais, *Awareness Through Movement*, (New York: Harper and Row, 1972).

16. Gae Luce, "The Sage Pilot Study" (Berkeley: Mimeo, no date), p. 89.

17. C. C. Ewell, "The Sage Spirit," *Human Behavior*, March, 1976, p. 41.

18. Ragni I. Griffin, "Life After 65, Relax and Enjoy It," *Los Angeles Times*, Jan. 25, 1976, p. 8.

19. Barbara Brown, *New Mind, New Body* (New York: Harper and Row, 1974) p. 16.

20. "Sage, by Laughingbird" (Berkeley: Sage Publications, undated).

Chapter 9
The Sexual Revolution

1. Henry Havelock Ellis, *Studies in the Psychology of Sex* (New York: Random House, 1942).

2. Richard von Krafft-Ebing, *Aberrations of Sexual Life* (after *Psychopathis Sexualis*), Alexander Hartwich, ed. (New York: Capricorn Books, 1951).

3. Hugh Kenner, "The Comfort Behind the Joy of Sex," *New York Times Magazine*, Oct. 27, 1974, p. 69.

4. T. H. Van de Velde, *Ideal Marriage* (New York: Random House, 1930).

5. Alfred C. Kinsey, W. B. Pomeroy, and C. J. Martin, *Sexual Behavior in the Human Male;* Alfred C. Kinsey, W. B. Pomeroy, C. J. Martin, and P. H. Gebbard *Sexual Behavior in the Human Female* (Philadelphia: W. B. Saunders, 1948, 1953.)

6. Eric Pfeiffer, "Sexual Behavior in Old Age," in *Behavior and Adaptation in Later Life,* Ewald W. Busse and Eric Pfeiffer, eds., (Boston: Little, Brown, 1969), p. 153.

7. Isador Rubin, *Sexual Life after 60* (New York: Basic Books, 1965), p. 111.

8. Kinsey et al., *Sexual Behavior in the Human Male,* p. 235.

9. Kinsey et al., *Sexual Behavior in the Human Female,* p. 353.

10. Pfeiffer, "Sexual Behavior in Old Age," pp. 157–61.

11. William H. Masters and Virginia E. Johnson, *Human Sexual Response* (Boston: Little, Brown, 1966).

12. Ibid., Preface VII.

13. Ibid., p. 6.

14. Ibid., p. 6.

15. Ibid., p. 247.

16. "Romance and the Aged," *Time,* June 4, 1973, p. 48.

17. "Police Raid Senior Citizen's Brothel," *Los Angeles Times,* Feb. 9, 1975, p. 15.

18. Patrick Young, "Rx: Sex Over 60," *National Observer,* Feb. 1975, p. 1.

19. Rubin, *Sexual Life after 60,* p. 231.

20. Herant Katchadourian, *Human Sexuality, Sense and Nonsense* (San Francisco: W. H. Freeman, 1972) pp. 50–51.

21. Norman Lobenz, "Sex and the Senior Citizen," *New York Times Magazine,* Jan. 20, 1974, p. 8.

22. *Letters,* from Mrs. Emily Gollin of Claremont, Calif., *New York Times Magazine,* Feb. 10, 1974, p. 35.

23. *Letters,* from Fanny B. Sanders of Hollandale, Fla. *New York Times Magazine,* Feb. 10, 1974, p. 4.

24. E. M. Feigenbaum, M. F. Lowenthal, and M. L. Trier, "A Report on a Study," *Geriatric Focus,* 1967, 5 (20):2., as quoted by I. Burnside in *Sexuality and Aging* (Los Angeles: Ethel Perry Andrus Gerontology Center, 1975), p. 44.

25. Burnside, Ibid., p. 28.

26. Richard Saltus, "Heart Patients Exercise for Sex Life," *Los Angeles Times,* Nov. 20, 1975, I, 3.

27. Tom Littlewood, "Expert Sees Aged Taking Up Polygamy," *Los Angeles Times,* Feb. 10, 1974, I, 4.

28. Simone de Beauvoir, *The Coming of Age,* (New York: Warner Paperback Library, 1973), pp. 472–73.

Chapter 10
The Money Fight

1. *Facts about Older Americans, 1976,* U.S. Department of Health, Education and Welfare, Government Publ. No. 77-20006.

2. Juanita Kreps, "The Economy and the Aged," in *Handbook of Aging and the Social Sciences,* R. Binstock and E. Shanas, eds. (New York: Van Nostrand, 1976), p. 277.

3. James Schultz, "Income Distribution and the Aging," ibid., pp. 560–90.

4. Sylvia Porter, *Sylvia Porter's Money Book,* (New York: Doubleday, 1975), p. 762.

5. *Developments in Aging, 1974-75* (Washington: U.S. Govt. Printing Office, 1975), p. 3.

6. Sanford Lakoff, "The Future of Social Intervention," *Handbook of Aging and the Social Sciences,* R. Binstock and E. Shanas, eds. (New York: Van Nostrand, 1976), p. 643.

7. Ibid., p. 645.

8. "Propping Up Social Security," *Business Week,* July 19, 1976, p. 35.

9. Ibid., p. 43.

10. Emma Pullen and Paul Steiger, "Social Security Inequities Under Attack," *Los Angeles Times,* Feb. 23, 1976, I, p. 1.

11. Warren Shore, *Social Security: The Fraud in Your Future* (New York: Macmillan, 1976), p. 4.

12. Ibid., p. 92.

13. "Propping Up Social Security," p. 35.

14. Barry Goldwater, "This Law Robs Our Senior Citizens," *Reader's Digest,* Aug. 1974, p. 55.

15. Peter Drucker, "Pension Fund Socialism," *The Public Interest,* Winter 1976, p. 3.

16. Ralph Nader and Kate Blackwell, *You and Your Pension* (New York: Grossman Publishers, 1973), p. 3.

17. "Pensions: Unexpected Problem," *Newsweek,* Jun. 23, 1975, p. 80.

18. Ronald Soble, "Pensioners All Lose, but Less in California," *Los Angeles Times,* Apr. 6, 1975, VI, p. 1.

19. Lester Velie, "How the Teamsters Bankroll the Underworld," *Reader's Digest,* Sept. 1974, pp. 105–7.

20. Drucker, "Pension Fund Socialism," p. 16.

21. Ibid., p. 35.

22. Richard Margolis, "National Health Insurance: The Dream Whose Time Has Come," *New York Times Magazine,* Jan. 9, 1977, p. 12.

23. Max Skidmore, *Medicare and the American Rhetoric of Reconciliation* (University: University of Alabama, 1970), p. 107.

24. As quoted by Skidmore, Ibid., p. 71.

25. As quoted by Skidmore, Ibid., p. 146.

26. "Health Insurance for Older People: Filling the Gaps in Medicare," *Consumer Reports,* Jan. 1976, pp. 27–30.

27. Ibid., p. 29.
28. Stuart Auerbach, "Medicaid Examiners Cite Fraud Findings," *Los Angeles Times,* Aug. 3, 1975, p. 1.
29. Dan Thomasson, "Medicaid Abuse Is About as Old as the Program," *New York Times,* Sept. 5, 1976, News of the Week in Review, p. 4.
30. Margolis, "National Health Insurance," p. 12.
31. "Controlling Hospital Costs," *New York Times,* Feb. 20, 1977, News of the Week in Review, p. 2.

Chapter 11
The Wisdom Search

1. Robert Reinhold, "New Population Trends Transforming U.S.," *New York Times,* Jan. 6, 1977, p. 1.
2. Rona and Laurence Cherry, "Slowing the clock of Age," *New York Times Magazine,* May 12, 1974, p. 92.
3. Ibid., p. 92.
4. Gairdner B. Moment, "The Ponce de Leon Trail Today," *Bioscience,* Oct. 1975, p. 627.
5. Alfred Rosenfelt, "In Only 50 Years We May Add Centuries to Our Lives—If We Choose To Do So," *Smithsonian,* Oct. 1977, p. 41.
6. Alfred Rosenfelt, *Prolongevity,* (New York: Knopf, 1976), p. 50.
7. George Alexander, "Science Fights to Stretch Out the Good Years," *Los Angeles Times,* March 24, 1973, I, p. 1.
8. Rosenfelt, "In Only 50 Years . . . ," p. 44.
9. James Michener, "The Red Kimono," *New York Times Magazine,* May 26, 1972, p. 35.
10. Beth Ann Krier, "Alternative to Retirement at 65," *Los Angeles Times,* Dec. 23, 1976, IV, p. 2.
11. Harvey D. Shapiro, "Do Not Go Gently . . . ," *New York Times Magazine,* Feb. 6, 1977, p. 40.
12. Paul Woodring, "Retirement At 65 Cuts Many Workers Short," *Los Angeles Times,* Aug. 15, 1976, IV, p. 3.
13. As quoted by Shapiro, "Do Not Go Gently . . . ," p. 40.
14. "Bill Extending Retirement Age to 70 Signed by Carter," *Los Angeles Times,* April 7, 1978, p. 11.
15. Pat Watters, "Middle-Aged, Jobless, Despairing," *New York Times,* March 27, 1977, News of the Week in Review, p. 1.
16. Edgar Z. Friedenberg, as quoted in Clark Tibbitts and Wilma Donahue, *Aging in Today's Society* (Englewood Cliffs, N.J.: Prentice Hall, 1960) p. 335.
17. "Elderhostel: An Intellectual Summer Tonic for Both Young and Old," *New York Times,* Aug. 13, 1976, II, p. 1.
18. Richard Zoglin, "TV's Futurists: Seers in a Shortsighted Industry," *New York Times,* Jun. 29, 1975, II, p. 27.

19. "Brown School Plans Emphasis on Basics," *Los Angeles Times,* July 20, 1975, I, p. 3.

20. Estelle Ramey, "Boredom: The Most Prevalent American Disease," *Harper's Magazine,* Nov. 1974, pp. 12–22.

21. "Old Folks Commune," *Newsweek,* April 19, 1976, p. 98.

22. Judith Wax, "It's Like Your Own Home Here," *New York Times Magazine,* Nov. 21, 1976, p. 38.

23. William Claiborne, "Young Hoodlums Prey on the Elderly," *Los Angeles Times,* Dec. 10, 1976, VII, p. 1.

24. Victoria Graham, "Elderly Fight Back Against Urban Crime," *The Berkeley Independent and Gazette,* March 25, 1977, p. 10.

25. "Crusading Life Begins in Earnest at Age 84 for a VISTA Graduate," *New York Times,* March 19, 1977, p. 37.

Bibliography

Aging and Culture

Arensberg, Conrad M., *The Irish Countryman* (Garden City, N.Y.: Natural History Press, 1937).

Beauvoir, Simone de, *The Coming of Age,* (New York: Warner Paperback Library, 1973).

Cowgill, D. O., and L. D. Holmes, *Aging and Modernization* (New York: Appleton, Century, Crofts, 1972).

Diamond, Stanley, ed., *Primitive Views of the World* (New York: Columbia University Press, 1960).

Hartland, Edwin S., *Primitive Society* (New York: Dutton, 1953).

Mead, Margaret, *From the South Seas* (New York: William Morrow, 1939).

Simmons, Leo, *The Role of the Aged in Primitive Societies* (New Haven: Yale University Press, 1945).

Aging and the Family

Anshen, Ruth Nanda, *The Family, Its Function and Destiny* (New York: Harper and Brothers, 1959).

Boyd, Rosamonde R., "The Valued Grandparent: A Changing Social Role," in *Living in the Mulitgenerational Family* (Ann Arbor: Institute of Gerontology, University of Michigan, and Wayne State University, 1969), pp. 90–102.

Burgess, Ernest, "The Older Generation and the Family," in Wilma Donahue and Clark Tibbitts, eds., *The New Frontiers Of Aging* (Ann Arbor: University of Michigan Press, 1957), pp. 158–71.

Field, Minna, *The Aged, the Family and the Community* (New York: Columbia University Press, 1972).

Fritz, Dorothy B., *Growing Old Is a Family Affair* (Richmond, Va.: John Knox Press, 1972).

Moore, Wilbert, "Changing Family Patterns, Why?" in Clark Tibbitts, ed., *Aging in the Modern World*, (Ann Arbor: University of Michigan Press, 1956), pp. 74–78.

Shanas, Ethel, *Family Relationships of Older People* (New York: Health Information Foundation, 1961).

Shanas, Ethel, and G. F. Streib, eds., *Social Structure and the Family: Generational Relations* (Englewood Cliffs, N. J.: Prentice Hall, 1965).

Streib, Gordon F., and Wayne Thompson, "The Older Person in a Family Context," in *The Handbook of Social Gerontology* (Chicago: University of Chicago Press, 1960) pp. 447–75.

Sussman, Marvin B., "Family Relations and the Aged," in Adeline M. Hoffman, ed., *The Daily Needs and Interests Of Older People* (Springfield, Ill.: C. Thomas, 1970), pp. 300–324.

Thompson, Wayne E., and Gordon F. Streib, "Meaningful Activity in a Family Context," in Robert W. Kleemier, ed., *Aging and Leisure* (New York: Oxford University Press, 1961), pp. 177–211.

Tibbitts, Clark, and Wilma Donahue, *Social and Psychological Aspects of Aging* (New York: Columbia University Press, 1962).

Townsend, Peter, "The Household and Family Relations of Old People," in Ethel Shanas, Peter Townsend, et al., eds., *Old People in Three Industrial Societies* (London: Routledge and Kegan Paul, 1968) pp. 177–225.

Troll, Lillian E., "The Family of Later Life: A Decade Review," in *Journal of Man and the Family,* May 1971, pp. 263–90.

Winch, Robert F., *Modern Family* (New York: Henry Holt, 1952).

Aging and Politics

Abrams, Margaret, "The Story of the AARP," *Modern Maturity,* Oct.-Nov. 1971, pp. 71–78.

Binstock, Robert, "Interest Group Liberalism and the Politics of Aging," *The Gerontologist,* Autumn 1972, pp. 265–80.

"A Blow at Agism," *Newsweek,* May 26, 1974, p. 73.

Colson, John T., and J. W. McConnell, eds., *Economic Needs Of Older People* (New York: Twentieth Century Fund, 1956.)

Developments in Aging, published annually (Washington: Government Printing Office).

Donahue, Wilma, and Clark Tibbitts, eds., *Politics of Age,* Proceedings of the 14th Annual Conference of Aging (Ann Arbor: University of Michigan Press, 1962).

Gray Panther Network, Age and Youth in Action, a quarterly publication of The Gray Panthers. (Philadelphia, Pa.: 3700 Chestnut Street).

Gray Panther Organizational Manual, 1973–74 (The Gray Panthers, 3700 Chestnut Street, Philadelphia, Pa. 19104.

"Gray Panther Power," an interview with Maggie Kuhn, *The Center Magazine* (Santa Barbara: The Center For Democratic Institutions), VIII, 2, March-April 1975).

Harris, Fred, "Old People Power," *New Republic,* March, 1974.

Holzman, Abraham, *The Townsend Movement* (New York: Bookman Associates, 1963).

Neugarten, Bernice, "The Young Old," *The University of Chicago Magazine,* Autumn 1975, pp. 22–23.

"Old People's Revolt: At 65 Work Becomes a Four-letter Word," *Psychology Today,* March 1974, p. 40.

Pinner, Frank, Paul Jacobs, and Philip Selznick, *Old Age and Political Behavior* (Berkeley: University of California Press, 1959).

"Political Consequences of Aging," Special Issue, *Annals of the American Academy,* September 1974. See articles by Robert Binstock, Henry Pratt, and John Schmidhauser.

Putnam, Jackson, *Old Age Politics in California* (Stanford: Stanford University Press, 1970).

Riley, Matilda, and Anne Foner, *Aging and Society,* Vols. 1 and 2 (New York: Russell Sage Foundation, n. d.).

Aging and the Individual

Birren, James E., ed., *Handbook of Aging and the Individual* (Chicago: University of Chicago Press, 1959).

Buhler, Charlotte, "Meaningful Living in the Mature Years," in Robert Kleemier, ed., *Aging and Leisure* (New York: Oxford University Press, 1961).

Butler, Robert N., *Why Survive? Being Old in America* (New York: Harper and Row, 1975).

Cant, Gilbert, "How to Stay Younger Longer," *McCall's,* Oct. 1974, p. 87.

Donahue Wilma, and Clark Tibbitts, *The New Frontiers of Aging* (Ann Arbor: University of Michigan Press, 1957).

Dreifus, Claudia, "The Fear of Growing Older," *McCall's,* July 1973.

Ellison, Jerome, *The Last Third of Life* (Philadelphia, Pa.: Pilgrim Press Books, 1973).

"Fraud and Quackery Affecting the Older Citizen," Hearings before the Special Committee on Aging, U.S. Senate, Jan. 16, 1963 (Washington: U.S. Government Printing Office, 1964).

Jung, Carl G., *Modern Man in Search of a Soul* (New York: Harcourt Brace, 1933).

Hunt, Bernice, and Morton Hunt, *Prime Time* (New York: Stein and Day, 1975).

Kahn, E. J. *Fraud* (New York: Harper and Row, 1973).

Knopf, Olga, *Successful Aging* (New York: Viking, 1975).

Loether, H. J., *Problems of Aging* (Belmont, Ca.: Dickenson Publishing Company, 1967).

Mead, Margaret, "Dealing with the Aged: A New Style of Aging," *Current*, Jan. 1972.

"The Old in the Country of the Young," *Time*, Aug. 3, 1970.

Rose, Arnold, and Warren Peterson, *Older People and Their Social World* (Philadelphia, Pa.: F. A. Davis, 1968).

Rosow, Irving, *Socialization to Old Age*, (Berkeley: University of California Press, 1974).

Saul, Shura, *Aging: An Album of People Growing Old* (New York: John Wiley, 1974).

Aging and the Body

Devi, Indra, *Yoga for Americans* (Englewood Cliffs N.J.: Prentice Hall, 1959)

deVries, Herbert, *Vigor Regained* (Englewood Cliffs, N.J.: Prentice Hall, 1974).

Galton, Laurence, *How Long Will I Live?* (New York: Macmillan, 1976).

Gore, Irene, *Add Years to Your Life and Life to Your Years* (New York: Stein and Day, 1973).

Guild, Warren R., *How to Keep Fit and Enjoy It* (New York: Harper and Row, 1962).

Hornbaker, Alice, and Lawrence Frankel, *Preventive Care* (New York: Drake Publishers, 1974).

King, Frances, and Wm. F. Herzia, *Golden Age Exercises* (New York: Crown and Company, 1968).

Kopell, Harvey P., and Nancy C. Kester, *Help for Your Aching Back* (New York: Grosset and Dunlap, 1969).

Li Po and Ananda, *Wave Hands Like Clouds* (New York: Harper Magazine Press, 1975).

Mayer, Jean, *Overweight: Causes, Cost and Control* (Englewood Cliffs, N. J.: Prentice Hall, 1968).

McKenna, Marylou, *Bodypower!* (New York: Simon and Schuster, 1976).

Miller, Benjamin, and Laurence Galton, *Freedom from Heart Attacks* (New York: Simon and Schuster, 1972).

Morehouse, Lawrence E., and Leonard Gross, *Total Fitness* (New York: Simon and Schuster, 1975).

Reuben, David, *The Save-Your-Life Diet* (New York: Random House, 1975).

Ross, Karen, *The New Manual of Yoga* (New York: Arco, 1974).

Shiatzu, Japanese Finger Pressure for Energy, Sexual Vitality and Relief from Tension and Pain (Philadelphia and New York: J. B. Lippincott, 1976).

Steincrohn, Peter J., *Don't Die Before Your Time* (Los Angeles: Nash, 1971).

Steincrohn, Peter J., *How to Get a Good Night's Sleep* (Chicago: Henry Regnery, 1968).

Aging and the Mind

Assagioli, Roberto, *Psychosynthesis* (New York: Viking, 1965).

Britton, Joseph, and Jean O. Britton, *Personality Changes in Aging* (New York: Springer, 1972).

Brown, Barbara, *New Mind, New Body* (New York: Harper and Row, 1974).

Buhler, Charlotte, *Introduction to Humanistic Psychology* (Monterey, Calif.: Brooks, Cole Publishers, 1972).

Chaudhuri, Haridas, "Psychology: Humanistic and Transpersonal," *Journal of Humanistic Psychology*, 15, 1 (Winter 1975): 7–15.

Donahue, Wilma, ed., *Education for Later Maturity* (New York: Morrow, 1955).

Erikson, Eric H., *Childhood and Society* (New York: W. W. Norton, 1950).

Erikson, Eric H., *Identity and the Life Cycle* (New York: International University Press, 1959).

Freeman, G. L., *Self-Fulfillment and Aging* (Watkins Glen: American Life, Family Study Institute, 1973).

Geba, Bruno, *Vitality Training for Older Adults* (New York: Random House, 1974).

Geist, Harold, *The Psychological Aspects of the Aging Process* (St. Louis, Mo.: Warren H. Green, Inc., 1968).

Inside Yourself (based on the Alexander Method) (London: Hutchinson and Company, 1954).

Lasch, Christopher, "Sacrificing Freud," *New York Times Magazine*, Feb. 22, 1976.

Luce, Gae, *Body Time* (New York: Bantam, 1973).

Maslow, Abraham, *Towards a Psychology of Being* (New York: Van Nostrand, 1962).

May, Rollo, *Love and Will* (New York: W. W. Norton, 1969).

Nordby, Vernon, and Calvin Share, *A Guide to Psychologists and Their Concepts* (San Francisco: W. H. Freeman, 1974).

Parloff, Morris, "Shopping for the Right Therapy," *Saturday Review*, Feb. 21, 1976, pp. 14–16.

Perls, Frederich, Ralph H. Hefferline, and Paul Goodman, *Gestalt Therapy* (New York: Dell, 1951).

Progoff, Ira, *The Symbolic and the Real* (New York: Julian Press, 1963).

Rogers, Carl R., *On Becoming a Person* (New York: Houghton Mifflin, 1961).

Scarf, Maggie, "Turning Down with TM," *New York Times Magazine*, Feb. 9, 1975, p. 12.

Seligman, Martin E. P., *Helplessness* (San Francisco: W. H. Freeman, 1975).

Smith, Adam, "The Meditation Game," *Atlantic Monthly*, Oct. 1975, pp. 33–45.

Soddy, Kenneth, *"Men in Middle Life* (London: Tavistock Publishers, Ltd., 1967).

Tompkins, Calvin, "Profile: Michael Murphy," *New Yorker*, Jan. 5, 1976, pp. 30–51.

Welfore A. T. *Aging and Human Skill* (New York: Oxford University Press, 1958).

Williams, Richard H., and Claudine G. Wirths, *Lives Through the Years* (New York: Atherton Press, 1965).

Aging and Sex

Burnside, Irene M., ed., *Sexuality and Aging* (Los Angeles: University of Southern California Press, 1975).

Butler, Robert N., and Myra Lewis, *Sex after Sixty* (New York: Harper and Row, 1976).

Ellis, Henry Havelock, *Studies in the Psychology of Sex* (New York: Random House, 1942).

Freud, Sigmund, *Sexuality and the Psychology of Love* (New York: Crown, Collier, 1963).

Katchadourian, Herant, *Human Sexuality, Sense and Nonsense* (San Francisco: W. H. Freeman, 1972).

Kenner, Hugh, "The Comfort Behind *The Joy of Sex*," *New York Times Magazine*, Oct. 27, 1974, p. 18.

Kinsey, Alfred C., W. B. Pomeroy, C. J. Martin, and P. H. Gebbard, *Sexual Behavior in the Human Female* (Philadelphia, Pa.: W. B. Saunders, 1953).

Kinsey, Alfred C., W. B. Pomeroy, and C. J. Martin, *Sexual Behavior in the Human Male* (Philadelphia, Pa.: W. B. Saunders, 1948).

Krafft-Ebing, Richard von, *Aberrations of Sexual Life* (after Psychopathia Sexualis, brought up to date by Alexander Hartwich) (New York: Capricorn Books, 1951).

Lewin, S. A., and John Gilmore, *Sex after Forty* (New York: Grosset and Dunlop, 1952).

Lobenz, Norman M., "Sex and the Senior Citizen," *New York Times Magazine*, Jan. 20, 1974, p. 8.

de Martino, Manfred F., ed., *Sexual Behavior and Personality Characteristics* (New York: Citadel Press, 1963).

Masters, Wm H., and Virginia E. Johnson, *Human Sexual Response* (Boston: Little, Brown, 1966).

Pfeiffer, Eric, "Sexual Behavior in Old Age," in Ewald W. Busse and Eric Pfeiffer, *Behavior and Adapatation in Later Life* (Boston: Little, Brown 1969).

"Romance and the Aged," *Time,* June 4, 1973, p. 48.

Rubin, Isadore, *Sexual Life after Sixty* (New York: Basic Books, 1965).

Young, Patrick, "Rx: Sex Over Sixty," *National Observer,* Feb. 1975, p. 1.

Aging and Inflation

Binstock, Robert, and Ethel Shanas, eds., *Handbook of Aging and the Social Sciences* (New York: Van Nostrand, 1976). See articles by Juanita M. Kreps, "The Economy and the Aged," Sanfard A. Lakoff, "The Future of Social Intervention," and James H. Schultz, "Income Distribution and the Aging."

Chen, Yung-Ping, *Income Background,* 1971 White House Conference on Aging, (Washington: U.S. Government Printing Office, 1971).

Developments in Aging (Washington U.S. Government Printing Office, published annually).

Facts about Older Americans, 1976, U.S. Department of Health Education and Welfare, Office of Human Development, DHEW Publication No 77-20006.

"Federal Action for Aging Began in the 1930's: What's Happened Since," *Aging,* May 1975, pp. 13–25.

Guardianship and Protective Services for Older People (Washington: National Committee on Aging Press, 1963).

Le Breton, Edmond, *Plan Your Retirement Now, So You Won't Be Sorry Later* (Washington: U.S. News and World Report, Inc., 1974).

"Life for the Elderly in 1975—Many Are Hungry and Afraid," *U.S. News and World Report,* Feb. 10, 1975, pp. 48–51.

Loebl, Eugen, *Humanomics* (New York: Random House, 1976).

Margolius, Sidney, *How to Make the Most of Your Money* (New York: Appleton, Century, Crofts, 1966).

Neal, Charles, *Sense with Dollars* (New York: Doubleday, 1968).

"New Outlook for the Aged," *Time,* June 2, 1975, pp. 44–48.

Nuccio, Sal, *The New York Times Guide to Personal Finance* (New York: Harper and Row, 1967).

Porter, Sylvia, *Sylvia Porter's Money Book* (New York: Doubleday, 1975).

Schneider, Robert L., "A Discount Program for Older Persons," *Gerontologist,* 16, 3 (1976), pp. 257–63.

Schumach, Murray, "Lessons of Depression Fail to Help Elderly Residents of Miami Beach," *New York Times,* Apr. 13, 1975, p. 48.

Shulman, Richard, *The Billion Dollar Bookies* (New York: Harper's Magazine Press, 1976).

Aging and Pensions

Armbrister, Trevor, "Public Pension Plans—A Nationwide Scandal," *Reader's Digest,* March 1976, pp. 49–53.

Benzer, Shirley L., "Pension Funds Edge into Real Estate," *New York Times,* July 20, 1975, IV, p. 3.

Carlson, Donald G., "Responding to the Pension Reform Law," *Harvard Business Review,* Nov.-Dec. 1974, pp. 133–44.

Crawford, Bill, "Why Nation's Pension Funds Are on Rocks," *AARP News Bulletin,* April 1976, p. 1.

Davis, Harry E., "Pension Provisions Affecting the Employment of Older Workers," *Monthly Labor Review,* April 1973, pp. 41–45.

Drucker, Peter F., "Pension Fund 'Socialism' " *The Public Interest,* Winter 1976, pp. 3–46.

"Federal Pensions Provide a Bonus," *New York Times,* Feb. 16, 1975, IV, p. 1.

Hodger, Evan L., "Key Change in the Pension Plans," *Monthy Labor Review,* July 1975, pp. 22–27.

Lamson, Newton W., "The New Personal Pension Plans," *New York Times,* Dec. 7, 1975, IV, p. 1.

Nader, Ralph, and Kate Blackwell, *You and Your Pension,* (New York: Grossman, 1973).

"Pension Reform's Expensive," *Business Week,* March 24, 1975, pp. 144–55.

"Pensions: Unexpected Problem," *Newsweek,* June 23, 1975, p. 80.

Soble, Ronald L., "Pensioners All Lose, but Less in California," *Los Angeles Times,* April 6, 1975, p. 44.

Stetson, Damon, "Pensions by City Rated Generous," *New York Times,* July 6, 1975. p. 1.

Velie, Lester, "How the Teamsters Bankroll the Underworld," *Reader's Digest,* Sept. 1974, pp. 105–7.

Ward, Frances, "Teamsters' Troubles: The Pensions That Aren't There," *Los Angeles Times,* Jan. 17, 1977, p. 1.

"With Pension Shaky, Retirees Look to Family," *New York Times,* Jan. 26, 1975, IV, p. 80.

Aging and Medicare

Auerbach, Stuart, "Medicaid Examiners Cite Fraud Findings," *Los Angeles Times,* Aug. 3, 1975, p. 1.

"Controlling Hospital Costs," *New York Times*, Feb. 20, 1977, IV, p. 6.

deWolf, Rose, "Medicare: The Easy Swindle," *The Nation*, Nov. 6, 1972, pp. 429–31.

"Eldercare," *Time*, Feb. 11, 1974, p. 60.

Greenfield, Margaret, *Medicare and Medicaid* (Berkeley: Institute of Governmental Studies, 1968).

"Health Insurance for Older People: Filling the Gaps in Medicare," *Consumer Reports*, Jan. 1976, pp. 27–34.

Hess, John L., "Medicaid Help Called Lost on Wrong Care for the Aged," *New York Times*, Apr. 13, 1975, p. 55.

Hess, John L., "Regulating Medicaid" *New York Times*, Apr. 19, 1975, I, p. 1.

Hicks, Nancy, "Medicaid and Private Programs Are Similar in Cost, Data Suggest," *New York Times*, Jan. 2, 1977, p. 1.

Kennedy, Edward, "We Already Have a National Health Insurance Program," *Human Behavior*, Sept. 1976, p. 13.

Main, Jeremy, "A Word to the Wise about Old Age Groups," *Money*, March 1975, pp. 44–48.

Margolis, Richard J., "National Health Insurance—The Dream Whose Time Has Come?" *New York Times Magazine*, Jan. 9, 1977, p. 12.

"Medicaid's Sad Record," *New York Times*, Sept. 5, 1976, News of the Week in Review, p. 2.

Medicare for the Aged: Your Social Security (Madison, Wis.: Cuna International, 1976).

Skidmore, Max, *Medicare and the American Rhetoric of Reconciliation* (University, Ala.: University of Alabama Press, 1970).

Thomasson, Dan, "Medicaid Abuse Is about as Old as the Program," *New York Times*, Aug. 3, 1975, IV p. 4.

Aging and Social Security

"AARP Opposes Plans to Withdraw from Social Security, Cites Costs," *AARP News Bulletin*, May 1976, p. 1.

"Are You Planning on Living the Rest of Your Life?" U.S. Department of Health, Education and Welfare, OHD/AOA, DHEW 73–20803.

Auerbach, Alexander, "Social Security System Faces New Strains," *Los Angeles Times*, May 25, 1976, p. 1.

"The Bitter with the Sweet," *Ebony*, March 1974, p. 144.

Booth, Philip, *Social Security in America*, (Ann Arbor: University of Michigan Press, 1973).

Dale, Jr., Edwin L., "Social Security: One System That Seems to Be Working," *New York Times*, May 25, 1975, IV, p. 3.

"A Defense of Social Security," *U.S. News and World Report,* Feb. 24, 1975, p. 74.

Dietch, Robert, "Social Security's Time Bomb," *Progressive* Sept. 1974, pp. 28–29.

Goldwater, Barry, "This Law Robs Our Senior Citizens," *Reader's Digest,* Aug. 1974, p. 155.

"The Holes in Social Security," *The Nation,* May 11, 1974, p. 581.

Miller, Roger LeRoy, "Social Security: The Cruellest Tax," *Harpers,* June 1974, pp. 22–27.

"Propping Up Social Security," *Business Week,* July 19, 1976, pp. 34–43.

Pullen, Emma E., and Paul E. Steiger, "Social Security Inequities Under Attack," *Los Angeles Times,* Feb. 23, 1976, p. 1.

Samuelson, Paul A., "Social Security, A-OK," *Newsweek,* April, 14, 1975, p. 74.

Schnepper, Jeffrey A., "Social Security: Financing the Quagmire," *Intellect,* Nov. 1975, pp. 175–76.

Shore, Warren, *Social Security: The Fraud in Your Future,* (New York: Macmillan, 1976).

"Social Security Examined," *Newsletter of the New Jersey State Office on Aging,* Jan. 1975, Vol. 16, No. 7.

"Social Security: Trouble Ahead," *Newsweek,* March 24, 1975, p. 75.

Spivak, Jonathan, "Social Security System Is on Its Way to Going Broke, Analysts Warn," *Wall Street Journal,* Feb. 27, 1975, p. 1.

Spivak, Jonathan, "The Social Security Grab Bag," *Wall Street Journal,* Dec. 11, 1973, p. 1.

Steiger, Paul E., "Congress Scored on 8 Percent Hike in Social Security," *Los Angeles Times,* May 16, 1975, p. 1.

Aging and Wisdom

Alberts, Robert C., "Report from the Twilight Years," *New York Times Magazine,* Nov. 17, 1974, p. 31.

Alexander, George, "Science Fights to Stretch Out the Good Years," *Los Angeles Times,* Mar. 24, 1973, p. 1.

"America at 200" *New York Times Magazine,* July 4, 1976.

AOA Fact Sheet (Washington: Administration on Aging, DHEW Publication, 1974.)

Askwith, Herbert, *Your Retirement* (New York: Hart Publishing Company, 1974).

Baker, Russell, "The Old Rush," *New York Times,* March 9, 1975, p. 7.

Barrett, James, "Portrait of the Older American," in *Gerontological Psychology,* J. Barrett, ed., (Springfield, Ill.: C. C. Thomas, 1972).

Bernstein, Harry, "Bias Cases Flooding Court, Judge Warns," *Los Angeles Times,* Nov. 6, 1976, II, p. 1.

"Bicentennial Charter for Older Americans," *Aging,* May-June 1976, p. 5.

"A Blow at Age-ism," *Newsweek,* May 27, 1974, p. 13.

Boglietti, G., "Discrimination Against Older Workers and the Promotion of Equality of Opportunity," *International Labor Review,* Oct. 1974, pp. 351–65.

Brim, Jr., Orvill G., and Ronald P. Abeles, "Work and Personality in the Middle Years," *Items* (Social Science Research Council), 29, 3 (Sept. 1975).

Buckley, Joseph C., *The Retirement Handbook* (New York: Harper and Row, 1971).

Casey, Mara, "You Never Outgrow Your Need for Knowledge," *MS,* Nov. 1974, p. 17.

Cavalieri, Liebe F., "New Strains of Life or Death," *New York Times Magazine,* Aug. 22, 1976, p. 9.

"Changing Careers, Lifelong Learning," *University of California Bulletin,* 25, 18 (March 14, 1977).

"The Changing Patterns of Life," *New York Times,* Feb. 29, 1976, I, p. 6.

Cherry, Rona, and Laurence Cherry, "Slowly the Clock of Age," *New York Times Magazine,* May 1, 1974, p. 20.

"A Child's View of Old Age," *New York Times,* Oct. 10, 1976, IV, p. 6.

Clark, Margaret, and Barbara G. Anderson, *Culture and Aging* (Springfield, Ill.: C. C. Thomas, 1967).

Cole, K. C. "Golden Oldies: Senior Citizens Go Back to School," *Saturday Review* Feb. 1973, pp. 41–44.

Cooley, Leland Frederick, and Lee Marrison Cooley, *How to Avoid the Retirement Trap* (Los Angeles: Nash, 1972).

"Courts Reinterpret Old-Age Discrimination," *Business Week,* Feb. 24, 1975, p. 91.

"Crusading Life Begins in Earnest at Age 84 for a Vista Graduate," *New York Times,* March 18, 1977, p. 39.

Donahue, Wilma, and Clark Tibbitts, eds., *Growing in the Older Years* (Ann Arbor: University of Michigan Press, 1951).

"Elderhostel: An Intellectual Summer Tonic for Both Young and Old," *New York Times,* Aug. 13, 1976, II, p. 1.

"The Elderly Get Some Legal Clout," *Business Week,* Mar. 24, 1975, pp. 95–96.

"Fired for Being Too Old? Government Is on Your Side," *U.S. News and World Report,* June 3, 1974, pp. 75–76.

Galston, Arthur W., "In Search of the Anti-aging Cocktail," *Natural History,* March 1975, pp. 14–19.

Grant, Lee, "Old Folks at Home in the Schoolroom," *Los Angeles Times,* March 2, 1975, V, p. 1.

"Growing Older Female," *Interaction,* 4, 5 (Feb. 1976).

Halsell, Grace, "The Viejos," *Human Behavior,* Oct. 1975, pp. 25–29.

Harris, Mark Jonathan, "How to Make It to 100," *New West,* Jan. 3, 1977, pp. 16–28.

Horn, Stephen, "He Who Learns Longest, Lives Best," *Vital Speeches of the Day,* Aug. 1974, pp. 622–26.

Irwin, Theodore, "After 65: Resource for Self-Reliance," *Public Affairs Pamphlets,* Dec. 1973.

Kellog, Mary A., and Andrew Jaffe, "Old Folks Communes," *Newsweek,* April 19, 1976, pp. 97–98.

Krier, Beth Ann, "Alternative to Retirement at 65," *Los Angeles Times,* Dec. 23, 1976, IV. p. 1.

Kuhn, Margaret E., "New Life for the Elderly," *California Parks and Recreation Magazine,* Aug.-Sept. 1976, pp. 14–17.

Lakoff, Sanford A., "The Future of Social Intervention," in *Handbook of Aging and the Social Sciences,* Robt. Binstock and Ethel Shanas, eds., (New York: Van Nostrand, 1976), pp. 643–63.

"Learning for the Aged," *Time,* July 17, 1972, p. 4.

Maeroff, Gene I., "Older Americans Flocking to the Campus," *International Herald Tribune,* July 2, 1976, p. 3.

May, Edgar, *The Wasted Americans* (New York: Harper and Row, 1964).

Michener, James A., "The Red Kimono," *New York Times Magazine,* Nov. 26, 1972, p. 35.

Moment, Gairdner B., "The Ponce de Leon Trail Today," *BioScience,* Oct. 1975, pp. 623–28.

"No Methuselahs," *Time,* Aug. 12, 1974, p. 78.

"Ohio Experiment Working: Grandparents Aid Children in Classes," *Los Angeles Times,* April 30, 1975, II, p. 1.

"Older Workers Hired, Easily Placed in Contract Jobs by Mature Temps," *Aging,* June-July 1970, pp. 10–11.

Oelsner, Lesley, "High Court to Rule in Test Suit Against Retirement at Age 50," *New York Times,* May 16, 1976, p. 26.

Peterson, David, Chuck Powell, and Laurie Robertson, "Aging in America, Toward the Year 2000," *The Gerontologist,* 16, 3 (1976): pp. 264–69.

Ramey, Estell, "Boredom: The Most Prevalent American Disease," *Harper's,* Nov. 1974, pp. 12–22.

"Rent-a-Granny is a Huge Success," *New York Times,* June 29, 1975, I, p. 34.

Rosenfeld, Albert, "In Only 50 Years We May Add Centuries to

Our Lives—If We Choose to Do So," *Smithsonian,* Oct. 1976, pp. 40–44.

Rosenfeld, Albert, *Prolongevity* (New York: Knopf, 1976).

"Satisfactions of Retirement Are Dizzying, Don't Settle for Half a Life," *Harper's Weekly,* June 6, 1975, p. 14.

Score Counselor's Guidebook, (Washington: U.S. Government Printing Office, 1975).

"Seventeen Percent in U.S. to Be 65 or Older by 2030," *Los Angeles Times,* June 2, 1976, I, p. 19.

Shapiro, Harvey D., "Do Not Go Gently . . . ," *New York Times Magazine,* Feb. 6, 1977, pp. 36–41.

"A Shot of Youth for the Ills of Age," *Business Week,* Nov. 20, 1971, p. 60.

Silverstone, Barbara, and Helen Kandel Hyman, *You and Your Aging Parent* (New York: Pantheon Books, 1976).

Spiegel, Irving, "101 Is Age of the Student, Not the Number of the Course," *New York Times,* May 10, 1975, p. 23.

Stix, Harriet, "Senior Citizens as Paralegal Aides," *Los Angeles Times,* Apr. 22, 1975, IV., p. 1.

Streib, Gordon F., and Clement J. Schneider, *Retirement in American Society* (Ithaca: Cornell University Press, 1971).

Sullivan, Walter, "Scientists Seek Key to Longevity," *New York Times,* Feb. 11, 1973, p. 1.

"Supreme Court Rules on Mandatory Retirement Case," *Aging,* Sept.-Oct. 1976, p. 3.

Tibbitts, Clark, and Wilma Donahue, eds., *Aging in Today's Society* (Englewood Cliffs, N. J.: Prentice Hall, 1960).

Toth, Robert C., "Russia Takes Pride in Its Centenarians," *Los Angeles Times,* Mar. 11, 1975, p. 1.

Tuohy, William, "People All Around World Reported Living Longer," *Los Angeles Times,* Feb. 27, 1975, I, p. 4.

U.S. Volunteers in Action, *People Helping People* (Washington: U.S. News and World Report Books, 1971).

Watters, Pat, "Middle-Aged, Jobless, Despairing," *New York Times,* Mar. 27, 1977, II, p. 19.

Wax, Judith, "It's Like Your Own Home Here," *New York Times Magazine,* Nov. 21, 1976, p. 38.

Williams, Richard H., Clark Tibbitts, and Wilma Donahue, *Processes of Aging* (New York: Atherton, 1963).

Woodring, Paul, "Retirement at 65 Cuts Many Workers Short," *Los Angeles Times,* Aug. 15, 1976, IV, p. 3.

Zoglin, Richard, "TV Futurists-Seers in a Shortsighted Industry," *New York Times,* June 29, 1975, II, p. 27.

Index